D1091710

# HUBERT  WALTER

*Duke Historical Publications*

"Ad haec, archiepiscopus regis amicus adeo factus est, ut in oculis omnium dominus Angliae videretur."

Gervase of Canterbury,
*Actus pontificum
Cantuariensis ecclesiae.*

CHARLES R. YOUNG

# HUBERT WALTER, LORD OF CANTERBURY AND LORD OF ENGLAND

DUKE UNIVERSITY PRESS
DURHAM, N. C.   1968

TO MY MOTHER
AND THE MEMORY
OF MY FATHER

# PREFACE

To contemporaries like the chronicler Gervase of Canterbury the power of Hubert Walter was so great that he seemed to be "Lord of England." Historians have, of course, not ignored his career; some even consider him to have been one of the great medieval administrators. Relatively less attention has been given to his ecclesiastical career. However, in spite of the importance of the subject, no book has been written previously about Hubert Walter. In this study I have tried to view his career as a whole—his tenure in offices of both church and state—in a way that does not do violence to the easy interchange between those offices in the twelfth century. As a bishop and archbishop, his administrative ability stands out, but he does not seem to have been totally without religious dedication as has sometimes been asserted. His work as a royal administrator, though better known, is of special interest because his career extended from the governmental experiments of King Henry II and his justiciar Ranulf Glanvill to the more fully developed government of King John. The study of Hubert's administrative career confirms my belief that administrative development in the later twelfth century can best be understood in terms of the men who shaped that development. Among the English administrators Hubert Walter was pre-eminent.

Several books have appeared since this book was first drafted in the autumn of 1965, and I have tried to incorporate references to them at appropriate points. Although their conclusions do not seem to differ significantly from mine, in some cases my task would have been lighter if they had been available to me earlier.

I want to thank Dr. William Urry, Keeper of Manuscripts at the Canterbury Cathedral Library, who assisted my early ventures into the intricacies of medieval manuscripts; Professor Arthur B. Ferguson of the Duke History Department, who read an earlier draft; and Professor Patrick Vincent of the Romance Languages Department at Duke, who corrected my translation from Anglo-Norman. My wife has served as typist, critic, and general assistant throughout. For the errors that remain, I take full responsibility.

I am grateful to the owners and custodians of the following institutions for permission to use the manuscripts in their care: the British Museum, Corpus Christi College and the University Library at Cambridge, Lambeth

Palace Library, the Bodleian Library at Oxford; the Deans and Chapters of Canterbury, Ely, Exeter, Norwich, Peterborough, Rochester, Salisbury, and Wells; the Dean and Canons of St. George's Chapel at Windsor; the Kent County Archives; and the Public Record Office.

My work has been assisted by research grants and a publication subsidy from the Duke University Council on Research.

CHARLES R. YOUNG

# CONTENTS

# HUBERT WALTER

# 1
## GLANVILL'S CLERK

A few twelfth-century writers like Gerald of Wales complained that the English bishops in the time of King Henry II were more at home at the Exchequer engaged in royal business than in their cathedrals going about God's business. Most men, however, if they thought about it at all, simply accepted such duality of service. In fact, no example could be found of a career more successful than that of Hubert Walter, who rose to the highest office in both church and state, ruling England for four and one-half years as justiciar for King Richard I from 1193 to 1198 while at the same time serving as archbishop of Canterbury, and whose active career from 1184 to 1215 provided a personal link between the reigns of three kings—Henry II, Richard I, and John.

The pattern for Hubert Walter's career began when he left his paternal home to join the household of his uncle, Ranulf Glanvill, for he received his training as administrator in the household of the great justiciar and later entered royal service under Henry II as "Glanvill's clerk." Nevertheless, to him there must have been something routine, even almost inevitable, about the move. After all, his father, Hervey Walter, who held a small fief, was totally lacking in either wealth or influence sufficient to give substance to the ambitions of a younger son. What could be more natural than to join the household of an uncle, who already enjoyed some prominence by 1178, the earliest date at which Hubert can be proved definitely to have been with Glanvill?[1] Of course, it is always possible that

1. *The Cartae Antiquae Rolls,* ed. L. Landon and J. C. Davies (Pipe Roll Society [hereinafter cited as P.R.S.], 55, 71, London, 1939-1960), II (rolls 11-20), 55-57. This copy of a charter of Michael de Wanci has no dating clause and the editor gives no specific reason for his date of 1178; however, he seems to have felt no difficulty about it, for his plan is to comment only when there is any problem in dating. Another copy of the charter in B.M., Harl. MS. 391, fos. 77-78 (Register of Waltham Abbey) gives no further indication of date. If "Rannulfus de Glanvill' qui tunc fuit Justiciarius Regis" means "chief justiciar" and not simply "justice," then the char-

ter would have to be dated after Glanvill's appointment as justiciar. This date, usually given as 1180, would seem to raise a question about the assigned date of the charter. However, Francis J. West, *The Justiciarship in England 1066-1232* (Cambridge, 1966), pp. 53, 55-56, has pointed out that 1180 is the date Glanvill became regent. Richard de Lucy retired as justiciar in 1178 and King Henry II was in England from July 1178 to April 1180. Glanvill is named by chroniclers as justiciar in 1180 only because he became regent then with the departure of the king. West's argument would thus allow for the appointment to have been made

Hubert and his elder brother Theobald were in Glanvill's household even earlier than this first surviving record of their presence there, but, even so, the facts of Glanvill's career for some years before 1178 would still support the view that his household offered a greater opportunity for a boy or young man than most.[2]

In his new surroundings Hubert must have been quickly caught up in the excitement of a new life, for Glanvill was active in royal service and was in contact with many of the famous men who served King Henry II. Later, in 1188, when Hubert had become dean of York and decided to found a house for Premonstratensian canons at West Dereham, he remembered his earlier days with gratitude, specifying in his charter that the canons were to pray "for the souls of Ranulf Glanvill and Bertha his wife, who nourished us," using the plural in deference to his ecclesiastical position.[3] The relationship to Glanvill was through Hubert's mother Matilda, who was a sister to Glanvill's wife Bertha and a daughter of Theobald de Valoines, lord of Parham in Suffolk. The paternal side of Hubert's family was not distinguished. During the reign of King Henry I, Hervey Walter, the grandfather, held a small fief in the honor of Lancaster comprising the manor of Weeton in Amounderness, Lancashire (held by the service of one-half knight), Boxstede (one-half knight's service) and Newton (one-seventh knight's service) in Suffolk, and Belaugh and "Hulmested"

between 1178 and 1180; he suggests early in 1179. If the dating of this charter in 1178 is correct (and the possible dates for Glanvill's appointment do not invalidate it), the appointment had already been made in 1178. Hubert's association with Glanvill began, therefore, at least four years before they both witnessed a royal charter in 1182. See C. R. Cheney, *From Becket to Langton: English Church Government 1170-1213* (Manchester, 1956), p. 31, n. 1.

2. Theobald is listed in place of his father in a royal survey of fiefs made in 1166. See *The Red Book of the Exchequer*, ed. Hubert Hall (R.S., London, 1896), I, 445. On the basis of this record, some scholars have suggested that Hervey Walter had died by 1166 and that his death would explain why his son went into Glanvill's household. However, Hervey was still alive after 1171 when Butley Priory was founded,

for his charter conferring land to that house has been preserved and is printed in William Dugdale, *Monasticon Anglicanum* (London, 1830), VI, Pt. I, 380. A charter of John, count of Mortain, which dates about 1189 and refers to a grant of land in Amounderness made by Hervey Walter and his son Theobald, proves little other than that Theobald was the heir among the several sons. For this charter, see William Farrer, *The Lancashire Pipe Rolls* (Liverpool, 1902), p. 437.

3. B.M., Add. MS. 46,353 (Abbey Leger of Dereham), fos. 8 v-9 r. This charter is printed in H. M. Colvin, *The White Canons in England* (Oxford, 1951), pp. 348-349, and Dugdale, VI, Pt. II, 899. In making a gift to the hospital at Reading, Hubert referred to the Glanvills with the similar phrase, "qui nos educat'." See B.M., Add. Charter 19,611.

in Norfolk. His son, also named Hervey, had five sons: Theobald, Hubert, Walter, Roger, and Hamon.[4] Theobald inherited his grandfather's holdings and remained closely associated with Hubert throughout his life, but only one of the other brothers is mentioned later. Hubert was born in the Norfolk lands, probably at West Dereham, where his mother is known to have died and where he located the only monastery he ever founded.[5] Judging from the dates at which he later undertook various responsibilities it is doubtful that he was born before the middle of the century, but probably before 1160.[6]

Ranulf Glanvill had first become prominent when appointed sheriff of Yorkshire in 1163, a post he held until 1170, when he was dismissed along with all other sheriffs pending a general investigation into their activities over the preceding four years during the king's absence from

4. *The Victoria History of the County of Lancaster* (London, 1906-1914), I, 350-351. Other information about the family (not always consistent) is found in Kate Norgate's article on Hubert Walter and J. H. Round's article on Theobald Walter in the *DNB*; Colvin, pp. 130, 133; and William Farrer, *The Chartulary of Cockersand Abbey of the Premonstratensian Order* (Chetham Society, n.s., 38-40, 43, 56-57, 64, Manchester, 1898-1909), II, Pt. I, 375. Hervey named all his sons except Theobald in his charter to Butley Priory (see Dugdale, VI, Pt. I, 380). The Hubert Walter named in *P.R. 4 Hen. II*, p. 130, is thought to have been a relative; it is unlikely that our Hubert was old enough to have been this man.

5. Jocelin of Brakelond, *Chronicle*, trans. H. E. Butler (London, 1949), p. 82, mentions his mother's death, which occurred while Hubert was papal legate (1195-1198), and Abbot Samson is said to have reminded Hubert of his native land "quia quasi natiuus Sancti Aedmundi et eius nutritus fuit" (p. 85).

6. The canons of the Third Lateran Council, as given by Benedict of Peterborough, *Gesta regis Henrici Secundi*, ed. William Stubbs (R.S., London, 1867), I, 227, provided that a man must be at least twenty-five years of age on becoming a dean and at least thirty when elected bishop. Assuming that Hubert's ecclesiastical offices were conferred ac-cording to these canons and that he was at the minimum age when he attained each position, his date of birth would be 1161 or 1159. Hubert's name was presented for the archbishopric of York in 1186, which on the same system would give a birth date of 1156. Because of the influence of Glanvill with King Henry II, it is likely that Hubert was made dean of York not long after he became eligible, and the other dates coincide reasonably well. In 1196 after he had changed his mind about resigning the justiciarship, Hubert agreed to continue in office and not to plead increasing age as a reason to be relieved. See Roger of Hoveden, *Chronica,* ed. William Stubbs (R.S., London, 1868-1871), IV, 13. Such an assertion would be more understandable if he were about forty-five instead of thirty-five and would point to a date of birth near 1150 instead of 1160. Two years later when King Richard announced that Hubert was being relieved as justicar, he gave Hubert's infirmities and the burden of the office as reasons for the decision, but the only reference to age is that Hubert had used that excuse in 1196. See Thomas Rymer, *Foedera* (Record Commission, London, 1816), I, Pt. I, 71. However, it must be emphasized that a considerably earlier date of birth, although not likely, is by no means impossible and is not ruled out by the date of his death in 1205.

England. Although his name is not among the few sheriffs reinstated after the investigation, Glanvill evidently continued to enjoy the royal favor, accompanying King Henry II on his expedition to Ireland in 1171 where he is found among witnesses to a royal charter. Two years later he was named sheriff of Lancashire and custodian of the honor of Richmond, then in the king's hand.[7] Promising as these early offices were, the circumstance that really made Glanvill's career was the invasion of northern England by King William the Lion of Scotland in 1174.

Rebellion by the king's sons, led by Henry the Young King, had encouraged many royal vassals to rise against Henry II's harsh treatment. King Louis VII of France, who had instigated the rebellion by his plots with the young king, also took the field, but the military efforts of those forces opposing Henry II were not co-ordinated and thus not very effective. Nevertheless, in the spring of 1174 the situation in England looked ominous, with the king occupied in Poitou, an invasion from Flanders in the offing, and unrest among the barons of East Anglia.

In these circumstances the invasion of William the Lion posed a grave threat to Henry's English lands beyond the capabilities of the justiciar, Richard de Lucy, who ruled England in the king's absence. In practice, the defense of the north rested in the hands of loyal officials on the spot, especially William de Stuteville, then sheriff of Yorkshire, and his friend Glanvill. As it happened, the decision in the north came quickly with the defeat of William the Lion on July 13, 1174, near Alnwick. Glanvill took a prominent part in the battle. It was he who had prudently suggested scouting expeditions that enabled the English forces to catch the Scots off guard and who urged the correct moment for the attack. His men—shouting the battle cry of "Glanvill, chevaliers!"—overwhelmed the Scottish king, even killing his horse and capturing the king while he lay trapped beneath it. When the king surrendered, he insisted on surrendering to Glanvill himself.

Glanvill took William to Richmond to await King Henry's orders for dealing with the royal prisoner, but not before he had sent one of his men

7. Biographical information on Glanvill is to be found in F. W. Maitland's article in the *DNB* and S. B. Chrimes, *An Introduction to the Administrative History of Mediaeval England* (Oxford, 1952), p. 40. While on occasion helpful, W. U. S. Glanvill-Richards, *Records of the Anglo-Norman House of Glanville* (London, 1882) is not reliable. The Irish charter is given in J. T. Gilbert, *Historic and Municipal Documents of Ireland. A.D. 1172-1320* (R.S., London, 1870), p. 1, and is discussed by G. H. Orpen, *Ireland under the Normans 1169-1216* (Oxford, 1911), I, 256.

at breakneck speed to take the welcome news to King Henry II. Having hastened back to England in the face of the threat, Henry was resting at London when Glanvill's messenger reached him. Something of the relief with which the king greeted this news can be seen in his giving land to Glanvill's man as a reward for bringing first word of the victory over the Scottish king.[8] Glanvill's subsequent rise in royal esteem is reflected in his reappointment as sheriff of Yorkshire and his selection as a justice in eyre in 1176 and as justiciar by 1180, a position he held until King Henry II's death in 1189. Anyone consciously aspiring to a career in royal service could hardly have done better than attach himself to the rising fortunes of Ranulf Glanvill.

In spite of the usual assertion that Hubert Walter studied law at Bologna as a preliminary to his administrative career, it seems more likely that his education was in fact confined to the practical experience in Glanvill's household. The evidence for his education at Bologna rests upon the occurrence of his name in an obituary of the church of S. Maria di Reno at Bologna where many English scholars, probably including Thomas Becket, lived among the canons regular while they were students. Since the obituary explicitly lists "benefactors" among those honored, the presence of Hubert's name by no means proves that he was a student, even if the "frater" before his name is taken to mean that he had become a member of the confraternity of canons.[9] The statement by Gerald of Wales that Hubert made blunders in his Latin when speaking before Pope Alexander III is not very helpful in proving that he must have been educated at Bologna, involving as it does the assumption that he must have been speaking as a lawyer and, if he were a canon lawyer, then he must have studied at Bologna. On the contrary, several men who knew him in later life remarked upon his lack of formal education, especially

8. The fullest description of the battle by an eyewitness is in the poem by Jordan Fantosme and the report of a messenger, both in Richard Howlett, *Chronicles of the Reigns of Stephen, Henry II., and Richard I.* (R.S., London, 1884-1886), III, 348-354, 366-374. For a full reconstruction based on all the chronicles, see Kate Norgate, *England under the Angevin Kings* (London, 1887), II, 140 ff.

9. G. G. Trombelli, *Memorie istoriche concernenti le due canoniche di S. Maria di Reno, e di S. Salvatore insieme unite* (Bologna, 1752), p. 343 (see also pp. 329, 341). Attention was first drawn to this entry by A. Allaria, "English Scholars at Bologna during the Middle Ages," *The Dublin Review*, CXII (1893), 74-80. H. G. Richardson, *The Memoranda Roll for . . . the First Year of the Reign of King John (1199-1200)* (P.R.S., n.s. XXI, London, 1943), p. lxij, n. 7, argues for an education at Bologna, but I agree with Cheney, *From Becket to Langton*, p. 39, who rejects this argument.

his poor command of Latin, and upon his own realization that he was no scholar. Their statements make the inference that Hubert studied at Bologna—based, as it is, on such ambiguous evidence—seem quite unlikely.[10] It is more in keeping with the total evidence bearing upon his education to conclude that his preparation was confined to Glanvill's household. Useful as it must have been for training in administrative procedures, Glanvill's circle did not provide training in the finer elements of speaking or writing Latin; the normal means of communication must have been in French, which was comprehensible to both laymen and clergy of the household.[11]

Much more important for Hubert's future career was the fact that membership in Glanvill's household brought him into contact with the men who governed England. Under King Henry II the royal service was unspecialized and the personnel of the *curia regis* named in final concords were basically the same whether the fines were made at the Exchequer or at the king's court at Westminster.[12] Not only a common administrative background in Glanvill's circle but also personal friendships formed there help to explain Hubert's later success as an administrator working with many of the same men with whom he associated as Glanvill's clerk before he had himself become a member of the *curia regis*.

Even a single charter granted by Ranulf Glanvill will show something of the men with whom Hubert associated as a member of his uncle's household during his early years.[13] In 1171 Glanvill had founded a house of Augustinian canons at Butley in Suffolk, and in a charter dating after January 1185/6, he changed some of his benefactions to the Premon-

10. Giraldus Cambrensis, *The Autobiography of Giraldus Cambrensis,* ed. and trans. H. E. Butler (London, 1937), pp. 281-284; *Opera,* ed. J. S. Brewer (R.S., London, 1861-1891), II, 341, 345, 349; William Thorne, *Chronicle of St. Augustine's Abbey Canterbury,* trans. A. H. Davis (Oxford, 1934), p. 132; Gervase of Canterbury, *Historical Works,* ed. William Stubbs (R.S., London, 1879-1880), II, 406; and André Wilmart, "Maitre Adam chanoine Prémontré devenu Chartreux à Witham," *Analecta Praemonstratensia,* IX (1933), 227.

11. See Walter Map's comment on Henry II in his *De nugis curialium,* ed. Thomas Wright (Camden Society, L, London, 1850), p. 227, or the trans-lation by M. R. James (Cymmrodorion Record Series, IX, London, 1923), p. 261; and James W. Thompson, *The Literacy of the Laity in the Middle Ages* (University of California Publications in Education, 9, Berkeley, 1939), pp. 176, 182.

12. Francis J. West, "The *Curia Regis* in the Late Twelfth and Early Thirteenth Centuries," *Historical Studies: Australia and New Zealand,* VI (1954), 174.

13. B.M., Cotton MS., Vespasian E XIV (Register of the Priory of Leiston), fol. 34. The transcript printed in Dugdale, VI, Pt. II, 880-881, gives the names accurately. For the date, see Colvin, pp. 121-122.

stratensian order. Earlier, he had given his manor of Leiston to endow a religious house, and then, with the approval of the canons of Butley, he arranged for the transfer of the income of two churches from Butley to his new foundation. The list of those in whose presence the charter was made is impressive, by its very length serving as testimony to the solemnity of the occasion: Bishop John of Norwich, Glanvill himself, archdeacon Walkelin, chaplain Geoffrey, Hubert Walter, Master Renerius de Hecham, Master Robert de Waxton, Jordan de Ros, Master Lambert, Simon de Scales, Master Walter de Calna, Roger de Glanvill and Osbert and Gerard, Geoffrey fitz Peter, Alan de Valeines, and "many others." Witnesses whose names are entered at the foot of the document to some extent are duplications, but the entire list in the order given in the charter is worth citing: John, son of the Lord King; William de Aubervill; Radulfus de Ardene; Roger de Glamvill; Osbert de Glamvill; William de Valeines; Radulfus Murdac; Ranulf de Gedinge; Alard fitz William; Theobald Walter; Richard Malebisse; William de Basingeham; Roger Walter; William, son of William de Aubervill; and Thomas de Ardene.

The clergy would of course be represented on such an occasion; they include those with the title of master as well as those with obvious ecclesiastical titles. Master Lambert, Master Robert de Waxton, and Master Walter de Calna all studied at Oxford, but Master Renerius de Hecham is otherwise not known. Jordan de Ros also was a master from Oxford and rector of Hopton in Suffolk from 1182 to 1200.[14] Others in the list are members of the founder's immediate family, and some of them—like the three Walter brothers, Theobald, Hubert, and Roger—were also members of his household. Roger Glanvill and Gerard were brothers of Ranulf; Osbert was probably a son. William de Aubervill married Ranulf's daughter Matilda and later in 1189 showed his own interest in the Premonstratensian order by founding West Langdon in Kent; presumably their son comes at the end of the list. Ralph de Ardene married Amabella, another of Ranulf's daughters.[15] Prince John had been placed under the care of the justiciar by King Henry II.[16] Also significant in revealing the type of

14. Alfred B. Emden, *A Biographical Register of the University of Oxford to A.D. 1500* (Oxford, 1957-1959).

15. William Farrer, *Honors and Knights' Fees* (London, 1923-1925), III, 28, and books cited above in n. 7.

16. Benedict of Peterborough, I, 305. A charter from this period has as its witnesses Lord John, son of the Lord King; Ranulf Glanvill, justiciar; Roger fitz Reinfrid; Hubert Walter; and a number of others, mostly royal officials

men who surrounded Glanvill are the names of those actively engaged in royal administrative work at the time: Ralph de Ardene was sheriff of Hereford, Roger Glanvill sheriff of Northumberland, Geoffrey fitz Peter sheriff of Northampton, Alan de Valeines sheriff of Kent and director of work on the tower at Dover Castle, and Alard fitz William accounted for the farm of Penberga under Windsor.[17] Thomas de Ardene had been constable of Arundel. Along with the justiciar at the Exchequer were Hubert Walter, Roger Glanvill, Ranulf de Gedinge, and Ralph Murdac.[18] William de Valeines was the recipient of some land grants from the farm of Lancaster County.

Although the names which would appear in such a witness list are to a great extent a variable, even one such list provides a sample of the kind of personal influences upon Hubert Walter as a member of Glanvill's household. The occurrence of certain names often found grouped together points to the personal element that needs to be recognized among the men who filled the posts of government for King Henry II and his sons. As an example of such relationships with men who continued to be associated with Hubert Walter later in his career, Hubert and Osbert Glanvill served together as royal justices in 1189 and Osbert witnessed Hubert's own charter when he, like his uncle, favored the Premonstratensians with his foundation at West Dereham. Simon of Scales, who later held the title of master, is found in the *familia* of Hubert as bishop of Salisbury and archbishop of Canterbury. Both Hubert Walter and Geoffrey fitz Peter later served John when he became king, Hubert as John's chancellor and Geoffrey as Hubert's successor when he resigned the justiciarship.

As a result of such personal relations with men in royal service, it can be assumed that Hubert's own entry into royal service came about easily and naturally, probably without anyone actively promoting it. This move is reflected in the records. Hubert's name, which earlier is found associated with men of the royal household on such occasions as when they witnessed the private acts of Glanvill, begins to occur after about 1182

(P.R.O., Duchy of Lancaster, Ancient Deeds, 52). The author of the chronicle attributed to Benedict of Peterborough by Stubbs in his Rolls Series edition has been shown to have been Roger of Howden (incorrectly called Hoveden in older references) by Doris M. Stenton, "Roger of Howden and 'Benedict,'" *The*

*English Historical Review*, LXVIII (1953), 574-582. For ease in locating the printed volume, I continue to use the library citation, Benedict of Peterborough.

17. *P.R. 32 Hen. II.*

18. Thomas Madox, *The History and Antiquities of the Exchequer* (London, 1711), p. 744.

along with the names of the same royal servants in witness lists to royal charters and in the private charters issued by these men.[19]

Hubert also benefited from a new policy instituted by the king. In the 1170's Henry began to enrich the composition of his court by drawing in men of experience in clerical administration and in law. Geoffrey Ridel as chancellor was archdeacon of Canterbury; Walter Map and Walter of Coutances, both archdeacons of Oxford, came into prominence at this time. Glanvill's rise illustrates the growing importance of lawmen whose careers were made in law and administration.[20] With the assistance of the powerful justiciar, Hubert's future seemed assured.

Only rarely is it possible to glimpse the activities of Hubert during these years of apprenticeship when his part was not important enough for notice in the chronicles and rarely of the kind that would occasion entries under his own name in official records. However, one instance in which Hubert is mentioned—in connection with Glanvill's suppression of border trouble in Wales in 1182 and subsequent efforts to keep English authority in the area during the next two years—is perhaps significant in Hubert's training; for later, as justiciar, he himself had to deal with Welsh problems of a similar nature growing out of the guerrilla warfare that had become endemic along the border. In the summer of 1165, Henry II had failed in his all-out attempt at the conquest of Wales, and no further attempt on this scale was made by him or his sons during their reigns. The trouble in 1182 was typical. In revenge for a massacre seven years earlier, the men of Gwent managed to capture the castle of Abergavenny from the English. Their luck continued to hold when shortly after taking the castle they surprised Ranulf Poer, sheriff of Hereford and a leader in the massacre of 1175, while he was assisting William de Briouze in building a fortress at Dingestow on the river Trothy. At first, victory went to the Welsh, who killed Ranulf Poer. William escaped with great difficulty, but the arrival of reinforcements led by Ranulf Glanvill saved the situa-

19. Cheney, *From Becket to Langton*, p. 32, n. 1. A royal charter dated 1174-1181 by Joseph McNulty, ed., *The Chartulary of the Cistercian Abbey of St. Mary of Sallay in Craven* (Yorkshire Archaeological Society, Record Ser., 87, 90, n.p., 1933-1934), II, 103, is found in an *inspeximus* in *Calendar of the Charter Rolls* (London, 1903-1927), II, 163, and another charter dating prior to 1186 in III, 199. Examples of private charters are Agnes M. Leys, *The Sandford Cartulary* (Oxfordshire Record Society, 19, 22, Oxford, 1938-1941), I, 281-282 and Wells, D. and C. Mun., Liber Albus, II, fol. 160, which must date from 1182 because of the dates in office of two witnesses: Peter, archdeacon of Bath, and Jocelin, archdeacon of Chichester.

20. J. E. A. Jolliffe, *Angevin Kingship* (New York, 1955), pp. 144-145.

tion for the English and restored the balance in their favor.[21] Whether Hubert Walter accompanied Glanvill on this expedition is unknown, but he does appear to have been of assistance in Glanvill's later efforts to protect the English position by strengthening several castles and sending reinforcements to their garrisons. His name occurs as an incidental reference in the account at the Exchequer listing royal funds spent by the justiciar in the affair and naming Hubert as one of two men who delivered money to Hamo de Valognes to sustain the position in Wales.[22]

Two years later, in 1184, Hubert's apprenticeship for royal service was over, and his name appears as a baron of the Exchequer in his own right. Nevertheless, he continued to be closely associated with Glanvill in this work, and the other justices were men with whom he had been associated in an unofficial way for several years. Throughout the remainder of Henry II's reign, Hubert continued to serve both at the Exchequer and elsewhere as a royal justice. His name occurs as a member of a panel of justices before whom fines were made and as a witness to royal charters.[23]

During Hubert's early years in royal service, two incidents at Canterbury are recorded that take on added interest in light of his later promotion to the archbishopric. In 1184 the king was attempting to exercise control over the election of a new archbishop—or, as Gervase of Canterbury puts it, the king, desiring to reform Canterbury into its pristine state, sent notable envoys to observe the election by the monks of Christ Church. These included Ranulf Glanvill the justiciar, the bishops of Norwich and of Rochester, the archdeacons of Canterbury and of Derby, and Hubert Walter. The process of election became bogged down in a dispute between the bishops of the province and the monks of Christ Church over which group had the right to elect an archbishop. Glanvill, pointing out the bad effect that the dispute over the election was having on the English church, proposed a compromise formula that vested the election in the bishops, the monks of Christ Church, and the king. However, the compromise failed and it finally took direct intervention by the king to get agreement on the election of Baldwin to the vacant see.[24] Hubert, who had as yet no ex-

---

21. John E. Lloyd, *A History of Wales* (3rd ed.; London, 1954), II, 515, 568.
22. *P. R. 31 Hen. II*, pp. 5, 6, 7, 87.
23. Cheney, *From Becket to Langton*, p. 32; B.M., Cotton MS., Galba E II, f. 71 v; Liber Albus, I, f. 23, which is printed in Historical Manuscripts Commission, *Calendar of the Manuscripts of the Dean and Chapter of Wells* (London, 1907-1914), I, 23-24; J. R. West, *The Register of the Abbey of St. Benet of Holme* (Norfolk Record Society, II, n.p., 1932), I, 156, 158; *Calendar of the Charter Rolls*, II, 163, 439-440.
24. Gervase of Canterbury, I, 309, 317, 324.

perience in ecclesiastical affairs, was included in this group only because he was Glanvill's clerk. This patronage must have been sufficient to open many other doors for the younger man.

Three years later Hubert was a member of the royal party when King Henry attempted to mediate at Canterbury in a bitter dispute between Archbishop Baldwin and the monks of Christ Church. When one considers how little is recorded of Hubert's early career, it is a fortunate coincidence that this particular dispute, which Hubert was later to inherit when he became archbishop, should be among the few incidents in this part of his life that is described in some detail by a chronicler. Any detailed discussion of this complicated affair can be postponed until later, but the essential point in dispute was Archbishop Baldwin's plan to build a new church dedicated to St. Thomas Becket on the outskirts of Canterbury and to staff it with secular canons. The monks of Christ Church suspected a plot to deprive them of their right to elect the archbishop or at least a threat to that right, and the vindictiveness with which the dispute was pursued, within ecclesiastical courts and without, completely alienated the chapter of monks from Archbishop Baldwin, their titular abbot, and disturbed ecclesiastical politics to the extent that the king himself was forced to intervene.

From the moment of the king's arrival at the chapter house on February 11, 1187, both Glanvill and Hubert Walter were directly involved in his attempts to mediate the dispute. First, the king ordered the entrance to the chapter house guarded, so that only those persons specifically called by name could enter, and then he proceeded to call the bishop of Norwich, the bishop of Durham, Hubert Walter, and Peter of Blois to his side. After much discussion, the meeting broke up with nothing being settled, and the king, impatient to be off, sailed to the Continent to deal with other problems, leaving behind a quarrel that became increasingly bitter during the next two years.

After the king departed, the archbishop ordered the monks to be shut up in their monastery. By April 1188 they were complaining of their miserable situation, which forced them to rely for their survival on alms given by the citizens and even by the Jews of Canterbury. Meanwhile, sometime during 1188 Hubert Walter followed the king to the Continent, where he is mentioned in a letter sent to the monks in September by one of their number on the Continent who evaluated the attitudes of various men surrounding the king. He reported that in addition to the bishop of

Chester, who was well known for his opposition to the monastic orders, both the bishop of Ely and the bishop of Rochester were opposed to the stand taken by the monks in this controversy. As for Ranulf Glanvill, it sufficed to say that he did not love the monks and had spoken against them. Of the dean of York, Hubert Walter, the letter noted that he was certain to become a canon of the proposed chapel and therefore implies that he would be expected to favor the archbishop against the monks.[25]

Hubert's direct connection with this phase of the famous "Christ Church case" resumes when his name appears as a witness to a royal letter of February 3, 1189, announcing a second direct intervention by royal authority; he also figured in the background maneuvering that took place in connection with this letter. This background is explained by Brother Roger, the almoner, in a report to the convent about his delivery of a letter from them to the king at Le Mans. Three days after delivery the king called together the dean of York, representing the archbishop, and Roger so that they might reply to the convent. The dean dictated the letter in Roger's presence and then had it sealed. When the archbishop heard about the letter, he wished to inspect it and sent the dean of York and Peter of Blois to the chancellor and they broke the royal seal. When Roger refused to add anything to the letter, the archbishop personally came to the room and added three clauses to it.[26] How these additions favored the archbishop is not clear, although the committee named certainly included several men opposed to the monks. The letter announced the appointment of Ranulf Glanvill, the bishops of Ely and Rochester, and the deans of York and Lincoln (Hubert Walter and Richard fitz Nigel, both royal clerks) to go to Canterbury and choose representative monks, who would then come to the king himself to work out a reconciliation with their archbishop. This committee, except for the bishop of Ely, arrived at Canterbury on March 24 and tried without success to make a settlement. The subprior refused to allow the dispute to be transferred to the royal court, contending that only the pope could settle such a case. He even refused the compromise suggestion of Glanvill that at least two monks be sent to the king.

The convent later complained that after Glanvill's visit they had been unable to obtain letters of safe conduct in a satisfactory form from the

25. William Stubbs, ed., *Epistolae Cantuarienses*, in *Chronicles and Memorials of the Reign of Richard I* (R.S., London, 1864-1865), II, 159, 259.

26. *Ibid.*, II, 282-283.

dean of York. Not wanting to offend the king, however, they had sent monks to him with letters from the convent and had written the friends of the convent asking their aid in the business.[27] Still the quarrel remained unsettled, nor was Glanvill more successful later when he stopped by Canterbury on June 11 in the midst of a hurried trip to England to collect more troops for the king. Completely indignant at the repeated rebuffs to his efforts as mediator, Glanvill left with a warning for the monks: "You ask for Rome alone; Rome alone will destroy you."[28] Perhaps Hubert Walter would have felt an even greater frustration than Glanvill had he known that he would later become involved again in a royal attempt at settlement, this time by Richard I, and still later become one of the principals in this interminable quarrel when he himself became archbishop of Canterbury.

Even such incidental glimpses as these into Hubert's early career show that he had begun to take some part in royal administration. Yet the incompleteness of the evidence makes it difficult to assess Hubert's influence as a royal official during the 1180's when he was progressing from the household of Glanvill to a place in the royal court. That his position had advanced more than one might suspect from official records is indicated by an episode that took place probably in May 1189. King Henry II had called all his chief barons to council in Normandy, and Hubert Walter came in place of "his lord" the justiciar, who was ill. One decision taken at the council explains why the biographer of William Marshal included a short notice of this particular council meeting in his poem, for the king promised William that he should have the heiress of Striguil. It was obviously as the agent of the justiciar that Hubert Walter was ordered to give William possession of the girl and her land upon his return to England, but the reference is most interesting in showing that the king was willing to accept Hubert as acting in place of the justiciar.[29]

Gervase of Canterbury's statement about Hubert's position under Henry II—that Hubert in a certain way ruled England because Glanvill sought his counsel, that he was absorbed more with human business than divine, and that he knew all the laws of the kingdom[30]—might be con-

---

27. *Ibid.*, II, 284-285.

28. *Ibid.*, I, 354-356, 439, 447-448. Payments for passage across the channel on royal business for both Hubert and Glanvill are found in *P.R. 33 Hen.*

II, p. 210.

29. *L'Histoire de Guillaume le Maréchal*, ed. Paul Meyer (Paris, 1891-1901), I, 299-300; III, 100 n.

30. Gervase of Canterbury, II, 406.

sidered as overrating his importance, a natural anachronism in view of the power Hubert had attained later when Gervase was writing. However, the main points of this statement are interesting and need not be interpreted as inaccurate when one remembers that the subordinate relationship to Glanvill is stressed. Gervase's last two points also serve as a reminder of Hubert's entry into the ecclesiastical side of his career and of his relation to the famous legal treatise usually known by Glanvill's name.

About the only agreement among the experts concerning the authorship of the treatise *De legibus* is that Glanvill could not have been the author. The attribution gained currency from a statement of the chronicler Roger of Howden and from the title by which the treatise was cited, but the known facts about Glanvill as royal administrator and justice do not fit the picture given by the treatise of an author having a high degree of scholarly training and ability.[31] F. W. Maitland suggested the possibility that Hubert Walter as a close member of Glanvill's household may have been the author. More recently, R. W. Southern and Lady Stenton have shown that this suggestion is untenable.[32] Nor does the study of Hubert Walter's career, pointing up as it does his own scholarly deficiencies and his dependence upon learned men around him in his later ecclesiastical career, give support to the suggestion that he could have been the author of a treatise that shows considerable familiarity with Roman law. Thus, the question of the authorship remains unsolved. Nevertheless, the suggestion of Hubert Walter's name was not completely groundless. Clearly he had already become an authority in the interpretation of English common law. In the Balliol College manuscript of the *De legibus*, when differing views on cases of dowry are under discussion, the names of judicial authorities holding contrary opinions are given: one view is that of Hubert Walter, the second that of Osbert fitz Hervey and Hugh Bardolf. Later in the same manuscript, Hubert Walter is again cited as authority for a point of legal interpretation.[33] Less surprising in view of his years of experience as royal justice and as justiciar is a case in his later life. In the year 1200

---

31. Chrimes, p. 40 n.
32. See Maitland's article on Hubert Walter in the *DNB*; R. W. Southern, "A Note on the Text of 'Glanville,'" *The English Historical Review*, LXV (1950), 81-89; Doris M. Stenton, *Pleas before the King or His Justices 1198-1202* (Selden Society, 67, London, 1952-1953), pp. 9-10. G. D. G. Hall, the latest editor of the treatise, concludes that the author was perhaps a royal clerk and a lesser figure than any of the men usually suggested. See Ranulf Glanvill, *Tractatus de legibus et consuetudinibus regni Anglie qui Glanvilla vocatur* (London, 1965), pp. xxx-xxxiii.
33. Southern, p. 87.

he advised King John as to the correct procedure in a question of whether a minor could plead in a case concerning wardship.[34]

The fact is that Hubert was a legal authority because (like Glanvill and other royal justices) he helped to make the decisions which shaped and interpreted the law. Even as late as the reign of John, justices were usually chosen from men of proven administrative ability and loyalty to the king rather than of academic training.[35] This does not mean that the academic study of Roman civil and canon law was not having some influence upon the development of the common law at this time. Many of the royal justices were themselves presidents of ecclesiastical courts. They were closely associated with men of academic training in the royal courts and often with educated clerks in their own households.[36] The close connection and easy relationship between secular and ecclesiastical justices is shown by an anecdote told by Walter Map, himself both a royal official and archdeacon of Oxford. When he heard a judgment given at the Exchequer against the rich and in favor of the poor, Map remarked to Glanvill:

"When justice for the poor could be prolonged with many diversions, you have obtained it with a happy and heavenly judgment." He replied, "Certainly for a long time we decided cases here more quickly than your bishops in the church courts." I rejoined, "That is true, but if our king was as remote from you as the pope is from the bishops, I would believe you equally slow." He only smiled and did not deny it.[37]

Certainly more and more Englishmen were studying both civil and canon law either in Bologna or in England, where teachers were available at York in the 1170's and at Oxford during the later days of Henry's reign. H. G. Richardson has pointed out that both the *Dialogue of the Exchequer* and the *De legibus* "rather ostentatiously display the authors' acquaintance with the Institutes."[38] Even when men like Glanvill and Hubert Walter did

34. *Curia Regis Rolls of the Reigns of Richard I. and John* (London, 1922—), I, 284, pointed out by F. M. Powicke, "England: Richard I and John," *The Cambridge Medieval History* (Cambridge, 1929), VI, 218.

35. *Feet of Fines for the County of Lincoln for the Reign of King John 1199-1216*, ed. Margaret S. Walker (P.R.S., n.s., 29, London, 1954), pp. xxvij, xxxiij.

36. F. M. Stenton, "Acta Episcopo-

rum," *Cambridge Historical Journal*, III (1929), 9; Cheney, *From Becket to Langton*, p. 16. A thorough discussion of the influence of Roman and canon law on Glanvill is found in R. C. Van Caenegem, *Royal writs in England from the Conquest to Glanvill* (Selden Society, 77, London, 1959), pp. 373-390.

37. Mapes, p. 241.

38. Kathleen Edwards, *The English Secular Cathedrals in the Middle Ages* (Manchester, 1949), p. 190; Vacarius,

not themselves have academic training in law, they were in constant association with men both within and without their households who did have such training. The close connection between the administration of the common law and canon law is particularly clear in the case of men like Hubert Walter, who held both royal and ecclesiastical positions.

King Henry II often maintained the clerks of his household by obtaining ecclesiastical benefices for them, and Hubert Walter provides a good illustration of this practice. In July 1186 he was appointed dean of York by gift of the king, as we are explicitly told by the chronicler Howden, whose testimony on York affairs is usually precise.[39] Here and there a bishop, like St. Hugh of Lincoln, might object to the practice. Opposing a royal appointment of a canon to Lincoln Cathedral, Hugh stated his position:

Ecclesiastical benefices should not be conferred on royal officials, but on ecclesiastics, since their holders should not serve at court, at the treasury or the exchequer, but as the Scripture enjoins, at the altar. The lord king has the wherewithal to pay his own servants, he has possessions with which to reward those who transact secular business for him. It is only right for him to let those who are serving the king of Heaven enjoy the provision made for their needs, and not allow them to be deprived of the salary due to them.[40]

Hugh's protest had little effect, however. His biographer, describing the situation at Lincoln in May 1186 when Hugh was elected bishop, noted that "Many of the dignitaries of that church [Lincoln] were also members of the king's council and household, and were distinguished politicians [*in secularibus famosi*] and scholars and also men of considerable fortune."[41] Among the canons when Hugh was bishop was the dean, Richard fitz Nigel, one of the men already mentioned as an associate of Hubert Walter in the service of King Henry II.[42] Later he became royal treasurer and bishop of London, though he is perhaps best known today as author of the *Dialogue of the Exchequer*. When King Richard once threatened the

---

*The Liber Pauperum of Vacarius*, ed. F. de Zulueta (Selden Society, 44, London, 1927), pp. xv, xix; H. G. Richardson, "The Oxford Law School under John," *The Law Quarterly Review*, LVII (1941), 322-324.

39. Roger of Hoveden, II, 310. See also Doris M. Stenton, "Roger of Howden and 'Benedict.'" Geoffrey, the king's illegitimate son, had already been trea-

surer in the same chapter since 1182, according to Charles T. Clay, *York Minster Fasti* (Yorkshire Archaeological Society, Record Ser., 123, n.p., 1958), I, 90-91.

40. *Magna vita Sancti Hugonis*, ed. Decima L. Douie and Dom Hugh Farmer (London, 1961-1962), I, 115.

41. *Ibid.*, I, 92-93.

42. *Ibid.*, I, xxxiii.

confiscation of properties of the Lincoln diocese, Bishop Hugh journeyed to London to present his case at the Exchequer, since the king himself was absent from England; having persuaded the good bishop to sit with them, Richard fitz Nigel and the other royal clerks present joked with him that they had seen the day when the bishop of Lincoln sat with the barons of the Exchequer. Bishop Hugh was not particularly amused but managed to turn the tables on the barons before departing.[43]

The appointment of Hubert Walter as dean of York proved more than a sinecure, for it gave him his first independent experience as an administrator. The dean was one of the four principal officers of a secular cathedral, along with the precentor, chancellor, and treasurer. All four, at least in the next century, were required to be priests. From the surviving cathedral statutes of a later period, we learn that the dean presided over the cathedral chapter and had the care of souls of all the cathedral clergy. In the absence of the bishop it fell to him to conduct special services in the cathedral. At all the cathedrals the dean had a special responsibility to administer the common lands of the canons.[44] In Hubert's case the primary administrative responsibility for the spiritualities of the diocese immediately fell to his care, for the archbishop had died in 1181 and the vacancy long remained unfilled.

Soon after his appointment as dean an attempt was made to elect him to the vacancy at York. On September 14, 1186, the canons of York presented the king's council at Marlborough with a list of five names in the hope that the king might approve one of those named for archbishop. These were Hubert Walter, dean of York; Hamund, precentor of York; Master Lawrence, archdeacon of Bedford; Bernard, prior of New Borough; and Master Roger of Arundel.[45] In presenting the name of Hubert Walter, a royal clerk recently attached to their church by the king, the canons may have been attempting to insinuate themselves into the good graces of the king. If this were the motive, it failed, for the king rejected all five names. Such rejection does not necessarily mean that the king had developed a personal antipathy toward Hubert. Henry II's over-all record on ecclesiastical vacancies is suspect. Because of the income he derived from the temporalities which fell into his hands during a vacancy, Henry

43. *Ibid.*, II, 129.
44. K. Edwards, pp. 136, 137, 141, 144, 148.
45. Benedict of Peterborough, I, 352;

Raymonde Foreville, *L'Église et la royauté en Angleterre sous Henri II Plantagenet* (Paris, 1943), p. 483.

had prolonged vacancies rather notoriously in his quest for money to support his throne. Although in 1176 the king had promised the pope that in the future he would not keep a see vacant for more than a year, he inserted the phrase "unless by urgent necessity" into his promise. The truth of the matter is indicated by Margaret Howell's comment: "No doubt it was 'urgente necessitate' that the king was obliged to keep the wealthy see of York vacant for the last eight years of his reign with a regular intake of over £1,000 a year into the exchequer."[46]

Charters that have by chance survived show that as dean Hubert Walter was busy with the details of his job. When Bernard de Balliol granted the advowsons of three churches and some land to the church and monks of St. Mary's in York, Hubert's name leads the witness list, followed by that of Master Bartholomew his clerk, and there is every likelihood that his part in this gift was greater than the record indicates.[47] In a case arising over the right to present to the chapel of Lyverton at a later date, one of the parties alleged the right of Alan fitz Hervey to this presentation through Hubert Walter, then dean of York and *officialis* of the archbishop. In this case, Hubert's efforts did not end the contention, for both the next archbishop of York and papal judges delegate acting on the basis of an appeal to Rome were still trying to settle the issue some years later.[48] Hubert Walter as dean, Bartholomew his official, and the sheriff of Yorkshire led the witnesses to the charter by which Peter fitz Guimund set up a corrody for himself at Fountains Abbey.[49] When Walter de Hornington claimed damages against a prebendary of York, Hubert represented the chapter in making a final concord in the king's court which met at York on April 12, 1188.[50]

These examples of Hubert's duties as dean are all local in character, but it should be remembered that his position also meant that he might act as a small cog in the vast machinery of the Roman church. Particularly interesting in this respect is a document made at Westminster the first week of December 1187 which opens, "Hubert, by the grace of God, dean of York, and Ralph, dean of London, to all the faithful in Christ to

46. *Regalian Right in Medieval England* (London, 1962), pp. 34-35.
47. B.M., Cotton Charter, V, 75. An *inspeximus* of this charter is B.M., Stowe Charter, 509.
48. W. Brown, ed., *Cartularium prioratus de Gyseburne* (Surtees Society, 86, 89, Durham, 1889-1894), II, 186.
49. William T. Lancaster, *Abstracts of the Charters and Other Documents Contained in the Chartulary of the Cistercian Abbey of Fountains* (Leeds, 1915), I, 352.
50. Clay, I, 90-91.

whom this present letters may come."[51] The two deans, commissioned as papal judges delegate by Pope Urban III, announced that they had resolved a dispute between Walter, the abbot of Waltham, and William Cumin, parson of the church of West Waltham, over the tithes of West Waltham, in favor of the canons but with some safeguards for the rights of the church. In many ecclesiastical cases the appointment of a judge delegate became necessary when appeals were made from the courts of the English archbishops to the pope at Rome and the accompanying records and oral presentation by lawyers for the parties were too contradictory or incomplete to allow an immediate papal decision. The popes might then proceed (as Urban III apparently did in this case) by referring it to a specially appointed court of English clergy who were empowered to conduct further investigation and then make a final decision in the name of the pope, sometimes acting along general lines laid down by the terms of appointment as judge delegate. Later, as archbishop of Canterbury, Hubert was frequently brought into such cases at some stage in the process. Without this practice of using judges delegate, the machinery of ecclesiastical courts would have been even more unworkable than it was in an age when travel from London to Rome took about two months under normal conditions and half that time under the most favorable circumstances.[52]

The connection between the church hierarchy and the royal government involved more than ecclesiastical appointments for royal clerks—Hubert Walter, for example, continued to serve the king after he had become dean of York. Whether Hubert witnessed King Henry II's gift of Buckland to nuns of the Hospitallers as a church official or as a royal official is a matter of conjecture because the other witnesses to the charter represent both types of officials.[53] On February 27, 1187, Hubert was the sole witness to a royal letter given at York just before Henry sailed for the Continent.[54] Even more interesting for the combination of lay and clerical functions entailed in being at one and the same time dean of York and a royal justice are references to cases decided in the king's court before

51. B.M., Harl. MS., 391 (Register of Waltham Abbey), f. 88 v. Hubert's colleague was the chronicler Ralph de Diceto, who became dean of London in 1181 (John Le Neve, *Fasti Ecclesiae Anglicanae* [London, 1716], p. 182).

52. Cheney, *From Becket to Langton,* p. 62.

53. F. W. Reaver, *A Cartulary of Buckland Priory in the County of Somerset* (Somerset Record Society, 25, n.p., 1909), pp. 5-6.

54. Canterbury, D. and C. Mun., Chartae Antiquae, C 71 (v).

Hubert, dean of York, and other royal justices, such as Richard the treasurer, Hugh Bardolf and William Ruffus the stewards, Osbert de Glanvill, Osbert fitz Hervey, and Master Godfrey de Insula.[55] In the years 1185 and 1186 Hubert collected some £30, and the sheriffs of Warwickshire and Leicestershire another £15, from Richard le Kenteis, part of which constituted a fine for default and waste of the wood.[56]

In addition to service as judicial colleagues, personal bonds continued to unite Ranulf Glanvill and Hubert Walter after he became dean of York. Probably in 1188 Hubert—at no little expense according to Gervase of Canterbury—built a church at West Dereham in Norfolk.[57] Hubert himself in his foundation charter gave as his reasons for the foundation "the health of our soul, the souls of our father and mother, the souls of Rannulf de Glanvill and lady Bertha his wife who nourished us, and . . . the health of our brothers, sisters, relations, and of all our friends."[58] Not only was Glanvill among the witnesses, but also a foundation for Premonstratensian canons was completely in the tradition of the Glanvill family, whose members and in-laws favored this particular order with their monastic foundations.[59]

Throughout his lifetime Hubert continued to take an active interest in his foundation at West Dereham, and when his plan for a Cistercian monastery was left unfinished at his death, it remained the only monastery to have him as founder. The location at West Dereham was in the area where his family had lands and probably near where Hubert himself was born, but he had to purchase the lands with which the monastery was initially endowed from Geoffrey fitz Geoffrey. Later, as archbishop of Canterbury, he purchased other lands and conferred these on the monastery. He also seems to have used his official position later in life on behalf of his foundation. When two parties in a dispute over a knight's fee in East Walton could reach no agreement in a case heard before Hubert as royal justiciar and other royal justices, the disputants were persuaded to settle their case by selling their claims to the canons.[60] His brother Theobald joined him in giving some land in Ickleton, Cambridgeshire, to

55. Doris M. Stenton, *The Earliest Lincolnshire Assize Rolls A.D. 1202-1209* (Lincoln Record Society, 22, Lincoln, 1926), p. xxii; *Feet of Fines of the Reign of Henry II. and of the First Seven Years of the Reign of Richard I.* (P.R.S., 17, London, 1894), p. 3.

56. *P.R. 32 Hen. II*, p. 131.
57. Gervase of Canterbury, I, 534.
58. See n. 3, above.
59. Colvin, p. 33.
60. B.M., Add. MS. 46,353, fos. 8 r, 100 v, 112 v, 113 r.

the canons of West Dereham. Other donors included Theobald de Valoines; Henry de Pomerai; and Hamelin, Earl Warenne, Isabella his wife, and their son William, a family perhaps influenced by Hubert who as archbishop witnessed their charter.[61] Other names of interest in the copies of documents relating to West Dereham in the cartulary of that monastery are those of Geoffrey fitz Peter, whose presence implies a personal friendship with Hubert continuing from their early days in Glanvill's household, and Elias of Dereham and William of Yarmouth, both members of Hubert's archiepiscopal *familia*.[62] Upon Hubert's death the patronage of this foundation was left to the archbishopric of Canterbury.[63]

These early years when Hubert was best known as Glanvill's clerk and enjoyed the benefits of his uncle's influence at court came to an abrupt end with the death of King Henry II. Under the new king, Richard I, Glanvill left the justiciarship; Hubert, who was hardly important enough in his own right to expect to achieve an independent career in the royal service, was thus faced with an uncertain future. The circumstances surrounding Glanvill's departure from the justiciarship are clouded by disagreement among the most reliable chroniclers. One view is that he resigned because he was tired of the job and felt useless when the new king failed to consult him. Under these circumstances his unfulfilled vow to take the cross, a vow which he had made years earlier in company with King Henry II, seemed more pressing as he approached his last years.[64] On the other hand, Richard of Devizes tells the much harsher tale that King Richard deposed the justiciar and placed him in custody until he was redeemed by payment of £15,000 of silver and that the king at the same time placed cruel exactions upon the sheriffs. Moreover, even though the pope had given the king power to reserve anyone he wished from fulfilling the vow of a crusader and although the old royal servant easily merited any consideration, Richard made no effort to stop Glanvill from what even at that time must have seemed likely to be a fatal pil-

61. *Ibid.*, fos. 278 r, 293 v, 299 v, and confirmation of charter in *Rotuli chartarum*, ed. Thomas D. Hardy (Record Commission, London, 1837), I, Pt. I, 21.

62. *Ibid.*, fos. 290 v, 293 v; Francis Blomefield, *An Essay Towards a Topographical History of the County of Norfolk* (London, 1805-1810), VII, 331-332.

63. Colvin, p. 134. Today only a few walls standing in the middle of a field mark the site of this monastery, and these fragments of buildings are rapidly deteriorating.

64. Benedict of Peterborough, II, 87, 90; William of Newburgh in Howlett, I, 302-303. Two other men, Robert Belet and William Turpin, who were diseized by King Richard, are found making fines for the recovery of their holdings at the accession of King John ten years later. See Jolliffe, p. 70.

grimage.[65] There is no corroboration of Richard of Devizes' statement, however, and a resignation at the beginning of a new reign seems to require no special explanation. It is impossible to know for certain which explanation is more correct. In any event, Ranulf Glanvill does not seem to have been a reluctant crusader. In the company of Baldwin, the archbishop of Canterbury, he hastened to the Holy Land before King Richard even left France, and his death before the walls of Acre found him still at the center of important events, rather than forgotten in England where several men shared the responsibilities he once had borne.

65. Richard of Devizes, in Howlett, III, 385-386.

# 2 A FIGHTING BISHOP

On September 16, 1189, the day that Ranulf Glanvill left the justiciarship, the main business before the royal council meeting at Pipewell was to fill a number of vacant bishoprics. Among those promoted to the episcopal dignity was Hubert Walter. The immediate cause for this act of royal generosity is to be found in conditions in the see of York, not in any last sentimental gesture toward the old departing justiciar—in King Richard's desire to rid himself of Hubert, who as dean of York represented an obstacle to his plans there, as much as in recognition of the man's worthiness for promotion. The practice of royal nomination of candidates for bishoprics and of having the various ecclesiastical electors present to act on the king's choices had been customary since the time of Henry I and often resulted in the election of men who had records of royal service. Such was the case in 1189: Richard fitz Nigel, the treasurer, was elected to London; William Longchamp, the chancellor, to Ely; Godfrey de Lucy, son of a former justiciar, to Winchester; and Hubert Walter to Salisbury.[1] The election of King Richard's illegitimate half-brother Geoffrey as archbishop of York was also confirmed at the council. This seemingly coincidental action is more directly related to the promo-

1. Ralph of Coggeshall, *Chronicon Anglicanum*, ed. Joseph Stevenson (R.S., London, 1875), 28; Ralph de Diceto, *Historical Works*, ed. William Stubbs (R.S., London, 1876), II, 69; Benedict of Peterborough, II, 85; Foreville, *L'Église et la royauté*, p. 485. Hubert's oath of canonical obedience to Canterbury is recorded in Canterbury, D. and C. Mun., Register A, f. 227 v.

tion of Hubert Walter than years of royal service, though these undoubtedly helped, too.

During the last years of his reign, King Henry II had worked to get a bishopric for his illegitimate son and had succeeded in having him elected to Lincoln, but the consecration was never carried out. The old king died before making good a later promise to secure for his son the archbishopric of York, and it remained for Richard—after making a settlement with his brothers on July 20, 1189, a few days after their father's death—to nominate Geoffrey to York as part of the agreement. With this authorization, Geoffrey sent to England clerks armed with letters from Richard as duke of Normandy and instructed to take over the estates of York and to expel the custodians placed there both by Henry II, into whose hands the temporalities of the see had fallen during the vacancy, and by Hubert Walter, who was responsible for the spiritualities of the see by virtue of his office as dean.

On August 10 the canons obedient to Richard's command assembled to go through the formality of electing Geoffrey in complete disregard of the action taken earlier by some of their number, who had met and chosen the dean as archbishop. At this point in the proceedings, the first obstacle to Richard's plans was raised by Master Bartholomew, clerk and *officialis* for Hubert Walter, who objected to the election of Geoffrey and appealed to Rome for a ruling as to its legality in the absence of the dean; Hugh, bishop of Durham; and many other canons. When Hubert, who was at Winchester, received the news of what had happened, he immediately threw himself into the dispute by directing an appeal to the pope on his own behalf. Furthermore, drawing upon his political experience in the royal court, he obtained the help of Queen Eleanor, who hated Geoffrey as her husband's bastard and who was in a position to assist Hubert by means of the considerable influence she exercised over her son Richard and her position as regent until the new king could be crowned. With this assistance, Hubert was able to obtain letters from Duke Richard countering those he had given Geoffrey and requiring that the situation at York be returned to the status it had on the day King Henry II died.[2]

Temporarily, Hubert's maneuvers stood in the way of Richard's plan, which was not only part of his bargain with Geoffrey but also an ideal solution for removing Geoffrey as a potential threat to his crown or as a

2. Benedict of Peterborough, II, 73, 77-78; Giraldus Cambrensis, "De vita Galfridi archiepiscopi Eboracensis," in Opera, IV, 373.

rallying point for opposition to the king.[3] In the light of this controversy at York, several of King Richard's nominations at the council of Pipewell can be seen as clearly meant to conciliate the two principal opponents of his policy at York: Hubert Walter, dean of York, and Hugh du Puiset, bishop of Durham. One of the chroniclers writing at this time recognized this connection when he ended his notice of Hubert's election to Salisbury with the statement, "And thus all controversy between him and Geoffrey the elect of the church of York was put at rest."[4] The nephew of Hugh, bishop of Durham, was made treasurer at York, the bishop himself was appointed one of the justiciars, and a royal manor was granted him next day. Not surprisingly, when the election of Archbishop Geoffrey was confirmed, no dissent was heard from either Hubert or Hugh.

The sequel to the dispute at York confirms the view that both men had been won over to support of royal policy for York by arrangements made during the council at Pipewell. Further trouble arose at York when the clergy there refused to instal Henry Marshal—the brother of William Marshal, that stalwart royal supporter—whom King Richard had named to succeed Hubert Walter as dean of York and when the precentor raised difficulties about installing Bishop Hugh's nephew, Burchard, as treasurer. When he arrived at York in October, Geoffrey as archbishop-elect attempted to avoid the rising controversy by refusing to install the two officials on his own authority until his election had been confirmed by the pope and he had received the pallium from Rome. Such a refusal only served to bring down upon the hapless Geoffrey the wrath of his brother the king, who brooked no delay in the execution of his wishes and showed his anger in a practical way by seizing all Geoffrey's lands in England and on the Continent and by preventing the canons sent to obtain the pallium from leaving England.

In December, Bishops Hubert and Hugh entered the dispute. Their subsequent actions reveal that they were willing to support the king throughout his varying policies toward Geoffrey. First, they joined in an appeal against the election of Geoffrey before John of Anagni, who had just arrived at Canterbury as papal legate, raising again the issue on which they had conveniently been silent at Pipewell—that the election held in

---

3. John T. Appleby, *England without Richard 1189-1199* (Ithaca, N.Y., 1965), p. 9, comments on Geoffrey's ambitions for the throne.

4. Benedict of Peterborough, II, 85.

their absence had not been canonical. Burchard, the new treasurer at York, and Henry, the new dean, also appealed, charging that Geoffrey was disqualified on the grounds that he was a homicide and a bastard. At this time Bishop Hugh also followed the command of the king, ignored the prohibition by the archbishop, and gave his benediction to Roger, chosen abbot of Selby at the council of Pipewell. With troubles multiplying about him at the instigation of the king, Geoffrey realized he would get nothing without royal support and offered £3,000 sterling for the king's good will. No doubt Geoffrey was well aware that large gifts of money always had a remarkably soothing effect upon King Richard, who now graciously returned the see of York to his brother and confirmed the fiefs of the church to him by a royal charter. Almost at once all four of those making appeals against Geoffrey on the most serious of grounds withdrew them, thus practically admitting the frivolous nature of their opposition. However, it should be noted that Geoffrey showed himself equally able to bend on matters of principle by yielding to the king's petition and confirming the dean and treasurer at York, which he had earlier refused to do.[5] Yet this was not the end of the story, for the disputes between Bishop Hugh, the all-too-powerful suffragan of York, and his archbishop continued from time to time until as late as 1192 with the dean and the treasurer both clearly identified as belonging to the party of the bishop of Durham within the clergy at York.[6] These later disputes no longer involved Hubert Walter, however, who hardly had time to set his own bishopric at Salisbury in order before leaving England for the Third Crusade.

During most of the time prior to his leaving for the crusade, Hubert was with the king, and part of this time he was engaged in special business as a member of a royal commission attempting a settlement between the archbishop of Canterbury and the monks of Christ Church. For about three weeks after his election to Salisbury there is no evidence of his whereabouts, but on October 12, 1189, he was journeying with the king from Guildford via Arundel to Winchester. Then Hubert left Winchester to hasten to Westminster, where he was consecrated in St. Catherine's Chapel on October 22 by Baldwin, archbishop of Canterbury, to whom he swore the usual oath of canonical obedience. At least by November 7, King Richard had arrived at Westminster, and Hubert remained

5. *Ibid.*, pp. 85, 87-88, 91-92, 99-100.     6. *Ibid.*, II, 146, 237-238, 246-248.

constantly with him until Richard sailed for Calais on December 12. Summoned to the Continent along with the magnates of the realm in February, Hubert and others arrived in Normandy on March 12, 1190, and remained with the king until April 12. After a short interval in England, he was again with the king on the Continent from July 3 until August 5, when he sailed from Marseilles directly to the Holy Land with Archbishop Baldwin and Ranulf Glanvill. It was not until April 20, 1193, that Hubert again reached England on his return from the crusade and shortly thereafter, on May 29, he was elected archbishop of Canterbury.[7] When the movements of Hubert are thus traced, it is obvious that with only about two months free at the beginning of the year 1190, a similar period from April to the beginning of July, and a final month after his return from the crusade, he could give almost no time or energy to the problems of the see of Salisbury. Preparation for the crusade undoubtedly dominated those four months in 1190, and the responsibility for raising the ransom of a captive king would have been overwhelming in 1193. If Richard went down in history as an absentee king, Hubert most certainly was an absentee bishop of Salisbury, although almost all his contemporaries would have agreed that a crusade provided the best of all possible reasons.

The surviving *acta* of Hubert as bishop of Salisbury either in originals or copies in monastic cartularies are nevertheless of some interest, though more often for the information they give about the men who administered the see during Hubert's long absence than about Hubert himself. The business transacted in these *acta* is fairly routine: an *inspeximus* and confirmation of the charters by which Gilbert Basset had granted two churches to Bicester Priory, a confirmation of Bishop Jocelin's charter approving King Henry II's gift of a church at Windsor to the canons of Waltham, a decision that the churches of Figheldean and Alderbury were subject to the treasurer of Salisbury, approval of the appropriation of churches by the canons of Bradenstoke and those of Llanthony, a confirmation that the Abbey of Bec might hold the prebend of Okeburne (Ogborne, Wiltshire), and an *inspeximus* of the grant of churches at Bishop's Cannings and Britford to the chapter of Salisbury.[8] Before leaving

---

7. My notes on Hubert's itinerary were compared with Lionel Landon, *The Itinerary of King Richard I* (P.R.S., 51, London, 1935).

8. P.R.O., Exchequer, Augmentation Office, Ancient Deeds, 11830; B.M., Harl.

MS. 391; Salisbury, D. and C. Mun., Liber Evidentiarum C (ii. 3), p. 82, printed in W. H. Rich Jones, *The Register of S. Osmund* (R.S., London, 1883-1884), I, 241; P.R.O., Chancery, Masters' Exhibits, Lanthony Cartulary A 1,

for the Holy Land, Hubert obtained a license from King Richard to enclose and impark a wood for a deer run, and this license remained in effect to be renewed for his successor at Salisbury.[9] In 1191, while Hubert was on the crusade, the abbot of Sherborne granted the churches of Lyme Regis and Halstock to him for making a prebend at Salisbury, and after his return he confirmed the declaration made by the archdeacon of Dorset that these churches were exempt from the jurisdiction of the archdeacon.[10]

A few entries in the Pipe Rolls point to Hubert's handling of financial affairs as bishop of Salisbury. He paid the king two hundred marks in order to obtain his grain from Yorkshire, an action which may have been taken to protect some income as dean of York that he did not wish to forfeit by transferring to Salisbury before the harvest had been completed in the north. He also made a payment of more than £500 for the custody of three heirs and their lands until they should come of age. In this trading on the feudal right of wardship in the expectation of profits, there is a further hint that Hubert was already demonstrating a keen sense for business and financial affairs that was to mark his later career. In the same account on the Pipe Roll he made no payment toward an aid for marrying the king's daughter nor for a scutage for Ireland, but in the usual form for ecclesiastical tenants after Henry II's survey of 1166 he is recorded as disputing that Salisbury really owed the knight service to the king on which the assessment was based.[11] The bishopric possessed extensive lands in Wiltshire which in both 1166 and 1212 were assessed as owing the service of forty-three knights, thus placing the number of fees above the average for episcopal tenants.[12] The value of the temporalities can be estimated roughly from the amount collected by the king during the vacancy from December 12, 1193, to April 30, 1194, after Bishop Hubert had been elected to Canterbury. If collections during that period were typical, the annual income from temporalities would have been approximately £420.[13] Of course, income from the spiritualities

---

f. 157; B.M., Cott. MS., Vit. A. XI; Windsor, D. & C. Mun., Arundel White Book, f. 106 v.; MS. XI. G. 11, Nos. 3, 4, 6, 7, 8; and Jones, I, 222.

9. W. Rich Jones and W. D. Macray, *Charters and Documents . . . of Salisbury* (R.S., London, 1891), p. 47.

10. Liber Evidentiarum C (ii. 3), p. 82, printed in Jones, I, 247, and orig-inal charter in Box E.5 printed in Jones and Macray, p. 48.

11. *P.R. 2 Ric. I*, pp. 118, 121, 122, 131.

12. Helena M. Chew, *The English Ecclesiastical Tenants-in-Chief and Knight Service* (London, 1932), p. 19; *Red Book of the Exchequer*, II, 481.

13. *P.R. 6 Ric. I*, p. 256.

would have added to this figure when the see was being administered by the bishop, but there are no records on this portion of the income in 1194.

In witness lists on the various charters issued by Hubert as bishop of Salisbury, there are at least four names worthy of comment, for these men continued to serve Hubert when he later became archbishop of Canterbury: Master Bartholomew, Master Simon of Scales, Roger of Basingham, and Ranulf, the treasurer of Salisbury. Hubert had known the first two for a long time; their names are found on charters in association with Glanvill's household, although such association does not necessarily prove they were regular members of that household.[14] Simon was not yet a master when he witnessed Glanvill's charter for Leiston Abbey at an earlier stage in his and Hubert's career. Bartholomew has already been mentioned as *officialis* for Hubert when he was dean of York and must have come with him when he was elected to Salisbury. The background of these two men would indicate that the nucleus of the bishop's household, later to be carried over into the archiepiscopal household, was being formed from men with whom Hubert had personal ties from his early days as Glanvill's clerk. Perhaps Hubert first met the other two at Salisbury, as the title by which Ranulf was always known would imply, and there formed the association that would continue when Hubert was raised to Canterbury.

Because of the bishop's absence, the affairs of Salisbury had to be administered by his subordinates, and Hubert made definite provision for such administration. He left the see in the hands of a committee of four men, consisting of Master Bartholomew and Master Simon of Scales; Jordan, who must have been appointed by virtue of his office as dean of Salisbury; and Hugh, abbot of Reading, who may have been a personal friend. These men were authorized to act in place of the bishop by his letters patent naming them as his *procuratores* or *officiales,* as the documents variously put it. These officials also had custody of the seal of the bishop to authenticate documents issued while he was abroad.[15]

Of the royal business that competed for Hubert's attention during the fall of 1189 after his consecration as bishop, the most important was a renewed outbreak of the quarrel between the archbishop of Canterbury and his monks, in which Hubert had earlier been involved as Glanvill's

---

14. Master Bartholomew's name along with those of Glanvill and Hubert Walter is found on P.R.O., Records of the Duchy of Lancaster (Deeds) 27/51.

15. Jones and Macray, pp. 49, 50. The standard work on the *officialis* is Paul Fournier, *Les officialités au Moyen Age* (Paris, 1880).

clerk and which again threatened scandal to the English church. Archbishop Baldwin had by no means given up his intention of building a
church dedicated to St. Thomas Becket and staffed with secular canons,
and the actions of other bishops against the interests of monks on a wider
scale undoubtedly contributed to the uneasiness of the monks of Christ
Church over these plans. For example, when Hugh of Nonant, the bishop
of Coventry, bought the priory of Coventry from the king and on October
9 expelled the monks, the chronicler Gervase of Canterbury included this
information in the course of his narrative dealing with the quarrel between
his own monastery and the archbishop. This may indicate that he understood the local events at Canterbury as part of a broader struggle being
waged by bishops to replace monastic chapters with secular canons.[16]
Because of its close relation to the crown, Canterbury had more political
significance than other sees, and King Richard decided upon direct intervention in the quarrel that his father's justiciar had failed to solve. He
refused to let the archbishop or the monks choose their own arbiters, and
on November 9, 1189, he himself appointed a committee to attempt a
settlement. It consisted of the archbishop of Rouen; bishops Hugh du
Puiset of Durham, Godfrey de Lucy of Winchester, Hubert Walter of
Salisbury, and Peter de Leia of St. David's in Wales; bishops-elect Richard
fitz Nigel of London and William Longchamp of Ely; and several abbots,
among whom was the famous Abbot Samson of St. Edmund's. Some of
the ecclesiastics at the royal court already had fairly definite ideas about
this quarrel. The most outspoken was the bishop of Coventry, who not
only had acted against the monks at his own cathedral but at least since
1187 had also opposed the monks of Canterbury. "See," he is reported
to have said, "didn't I tell you about monks? If you agree with me, in no
time at all not one of them will be left in England. Monks can go to the
devil!"[17] Probably because of such known feelings among royal associates,
some of Archbishop Baldwin's clerks went so far as to boast that in a
few days the monks of Canterbury would be driven out to be replaced
by clerks.

Meanwhile the committee of arbiters headed by the archbishop of
Rouen arrived at Canterbury on November 28. As a basis for a settlement, the monks agreed to accept the relationship between themselves and
the archbishop defined in their charters, but even then they differed with

16. David Knowles, *The Monastic Order in England* (Cambridge, 1940), pp.
322 ff. discusses the broader trend.
17. Gervase of Canterbury, I, 470.

the representatives of Archbishop Baldwin on whether the charters of Archbishop Richard, who himself had been a monk, should properly be considered in such a definition. Unofficially, ecclesiastics close to the king who had shown themselves especially friendly to the monks during their long ordeal now urged them to accept a royal suggestion that in return for the removal of the prior appointed by the archbishop and the abandonment of the new building, the monks would submit to the authority of the archbishop. Other bishops and abbots, including Bishop Hubert, urged the monks to accept a peaceful solution rather than risk the wrath of the king. Under this kind of pressure the monks were prepared to submit, and the next day in the presence of the king a formal reconciliation took place, even though the monks were shocked and disturbed when the formal report of the arbiters found the archbishop within his rights in appointing a prior and building a chapel. On his side, Archbishop Baldwin, without giving up his ultimate objective, showed a conciliatory attitude. In January he entered into an exchange of land with the monks of Rochester by which he obtained the manor of Lambeth as a site for a future building, thus removing any threat to the privileges of Christ Church monastery in the immediate vicinity of Canterbury. A month later, at peace with his monks, he took the staff of a pilgrim and left England on March 6, 1190, for the crusade. The issue thus lay dormant until the plan was revived by Hubert Walter, Baldwin's successor.[18]

Shortly after forcing a settlement at Canterbury by the weight of his presence, which had overawed any objections the monks might otherwise have dared to make, King Richard turned his thoughts toward the crusade and sailed to Calais and his continental possessions, where he planned to make final preparations. Among those summoned to join him from England for a council in the middle of March were his mother, his brother John, and a number of bishops, including Hubert Walter. At this council the government of England during the king's absence was provided for by the appointment of William Longchamp, bishop of Ely, and Hugh du Puiset, bishop of Durham, as justiciars. Both the king's brothers, John and Archbishop Geoffrey, at the same time took oaths not to return to England during the next three years.[19] After the council, Hubert Walter had one more short interval in England before returning to the Continent, where

18. *Ibid.*, I, 461, 469-470, 473-474, 477-480, 483-485; Benedict of Peterborough, II, 97-98.

19. Benedict of Peterborough, II, 105-106; Roger of Hoveden, III, 32. Dating correlated with Landon.

he was with the king on July 3. Without waiting for King Richard to complete his affairs, the first contingent of crusaders, led by Archbishop Baldwin, Ranulf Glanvill, and Bishop Hubert, sailed directly for the Holy Land from Marseilles on August 5, 1190, arriving at Tyre on September 16 after an uneventful voyage that was in complete contrast to the much-delayed expedition of the king.

The English contingent in the Third Crusade departed long after news had reached Europe that the holy places in Palestine had once again fallen into the hands of the Saracens. Indeed, Richard, then count of Poitou, had taken the cross in 1187 and King Henry II had followed in January 1188, joined by various leaders including Archbishop Baldwin, Ranulf Glanvill, and Hubert Walter, but many months passed before any English leader managed to fulfil those vows.[20] Perhaps the old king never seriously intended to fulfil his vow and viewed the crusade solely in connection with the political advantage it might bring; but whatever may have been his thoughts on the matter, fighting between himself and King Philip Augustus of France, joined toward the end by Henry's own rebellious sons, would have prevented any practical fulfilment of his vow. Meanwhile, the crusade was preached by Archbishop Baldwin and others and a Saladin tithe consisting of one-tenth of income and movable goods was collected. Military action, however, had to await the accession of King Richard.

As far as the clergy was concerned, one critic argued against participation in a crusade by clerics like Archbishop Baldwin and Bishop Hubert, reasoning that they could better do penance in their own churches, that it was unlawful for them to shed blood and advocate violence, and that they would be of no practical value in the fighting anyhow. He concluded in a more spiritual vein that they would be neglecting their duty to the many at home by giving special care to the few going on the crusade while contributing nothing toward the success of the crusade.[21] Undeterred by this minority point of view, Archbishop Baldwin and Bishop Hubert showed more zeal than the dilatory King Richard, whose voyage was interrupted by long delays in Sicily and Cyprus. They arrived to take their

20. William of Newburgh, *Historia*, in Howlett, I, 272; Ralph of Coggeshall, p. 23, with the obvious error of calling Hubert Walter by his later dignity of "episcopus Saresberiae."

21. G. B. Flahiff, "*Deus Non Vult.* A Critic of the Third Crusade," *Mediaeval Studies*, IX (Toronto, 1947), pp. 174-176.

part in the crusade some nine months before the king landed at Tyre on June 6, 1191.

Tyre had become the beachhead for any reinforcements coming from the West. After the defeat at the hands of Saladin in the battle of Hattin on July 4, 1187, the survivors had straggled into the city, where the defense was organized by an able and vigorous soldier, Conrad of Montferrat. By the time the first English contingent arrived, an offensive had been launched against the city of Acre, but this effort had so far not only failed to take the city from the Saracens but had resulted in the besiegers themselves becoming besieged upon the arrival of new forces sent by Saladin to relieve Acre. Neither side had been able to dislodge the other, and for a year the situation had been stalemated with considerable degeneration in the morale of both sides.

The first direct word of the English crusaders appears in a letter from Archbishop Baldwin to the monks at Canterbury. He reports that his group has been delayed in moving from Tyre to Acre from September 16 to October 12, 1190, because some of his companions have fallen ill. All are now well, however, and they have arrived at the siege. A letter from his chaplain a few days later is more informative but less optimistic in tone. He reports that the army before Acre is in poor condition, the princes and leaders are quarreling among themselves, and the lesser people are doing nothing. "There is no chastity, sobriety, faith, love, nor charity, so that with God as my witness I could hardly believe it if I had not seen it." He continues with the comment that Saladin's army increases while the Christian army diminishes and that many are dead, including Ranulf Glanvill. Finally, he laments that still the kings do not come nor is the city of Acre captured.[22]

A month later, on November 19, Archbishop Baldwin also died, leaving Hubert Walter as the only survivor among the three original leaders of the English forces then present at Acre. However, Hubert had been taking an active leadership even prior to the archbishop's death. In a list of the various contingents in the order in which they were ranged round Acre, one chronicler places "the bishop of Salisbury and the English" between the Florentines and the Flemings.[23] On November 12

22. William Stubbs, ed., *Epistolae Cantuarienses*, pp. 328-329. Used for general background on the Third Crusade were Steven Runciman, *A History of the Crusades* (Cambridge, 1951-54), vol. III, and Kenneth M. Setton, ed., *A History of the Crusades* (Philadelphia, 1955-), vol. II.

23. Ralph de Diceto, II, 79.

Hubert demonstrated his military leadership when the crusaders launched a general attack on Saladin's camp in an attempt to remove the pressure upon their own position. The author of the *Itinerarium* gives emphasis to the prominent part taken by various clergy in this attack. Abbots and bishops led their men into battle, and even the venerable Archbishop Baldwin performed notable deeds. Of Hubert, the writer comments: "In truth the courageous bishop of Salisbury does not refrain from being present in the attack, but directs a major part of the battle, a man whose excellence is fulfilled as a knight in arms, as a leader in the camp, and as a pastor among the clergy."[24] The results of this attack were not decisive even though Saladin was forced to abandon his position during the night and move a little further from the city. In fact, his new position was in some ways stronger than the one abandoned, and the defection of Conrad of Montferrat, who returned to Tyre after this skirmish and refused to give further aid to the cause, weakened the crusaders. Following Baldwin's death a week later, Hubert, as executor of the archbishop's will, for a time busied himself in paying Baldwin's followers and making distribution of alms to the poor as directed by the deceased and "in all things carrying out the office of a good bishop."[25]

During the next three months, from December to March, the situation of the crusaders rapidly became critical because of a severe shortage of food. In a letter to an old friend, Richard fitz Nigel, bishop of London, written early in 1191, Hubert's own estimate of the situation is gloomy. He reports that the crusading forces have been unable to take Acre because it has sufficient defenders, strong walls, and enough engines of war to resist any attack they can make. Moreover, Saladin has surrounded the crusaders themselves with his army and holds them as in a siege, so that

24. *Itinerarium peregrinorum et gesta Regis Ricardi*, ed. William Stubbs, in *Chronicles and Memorials*, I, 115-116. The relation of this work with Ambroise, *L'Estoire de la Guerre Sainte*, has been discussed by Gaston Paris in his edition of Ambroise (Paris, 1897) for the "Collection des documents inédits sur l'histoire de France"; John L. LaMonte in his introduction to the English translation by M. J. Hubert, *The Crusade of Richard Lion-Heart* (New York, 1941); Dorothy Bovee, *A Comparison of the Original Sources of the Third Crusade* (Unpublished Master's thesis,

University of Minnesota, 1930), pp. 86, 93-94; J. G. Edwards, "The *Itinerarium Regis Ricardi* and the *Estoire de la Guerre Sainte*" in *Historical Essays in Honour of James Tait* (Manchester, 1933), pp. 59-77; and most recently Hans E. Mayer as ed., *Itinerarium peregrinorum* (Schriften der Monumenta Germaniae Historica, vol. 18, Stuttgart, 1962). For the purposes of this study both have to be used because sometimes one, sometimes the other, attaches the name of Hubert Walter to an incident.

25. Ralph de Diceto, II, 88.

some have become disheartened. With some of the faint-hearted leaving the army and other crusaders having died during the siege, their forces are much diminished, but those remaining are still hoping for the arrival of King Richard to bring them relief. Hubert's final comment is that help must come with adequate resources before Easter or it will be in vain.[26]

In spite of his own doubts, Hubert was not inactive. He joined the bishops of Verona and Fano in attempting to alleviate the sufferings of the poor, who were hardest hit by the famine in the army, and they organized a collection among those who still had food. We are told that he not only preached charity but also taught by his own example. By giving without a trace of stinginess, he persuaded some of the nobles to give also, and the morale of the army was somewhat improved.[27] At the same time, the long siege was beginning to tell among the Saracen leaders, too, and some left Saladin's camp without leave to return to their homes. On the other hand, some crusaders deserted to the enemy during these months of horror; a few became Moslems and others were employed as domestics.[28] Fortunately, the arrival of a ship loaded with food early in March and of other ships thereafter brought an end to the worst famine even though the military situation remained perilous.

Hubert seems also to have assumed the spiritual leadership of the English forces after the death of Archbishop Baldwin. With the arrival of food during Lent, which began that year on February 27, the problem of spiritual discipline was raised. Hubert took a commonsense view of violations of the Lenten fast and absolved the men who had eaten meat, on the grounds that they had been driven to it by necessity, administering penance by three light strokes with a rod on the shoulders of each man "like a father, kind and grave."[29] By the time King Richard arrived at Acre the position of Bishop Hubert in the army was thus completely altered. Overshadowed by Archbishop Baldwin and Ranulf Glanvill when the group left the king behind in France, he had now become the principal military and spiritual leader of the English forces in the absence of the king.

Philip Augustus, king of France, was to join the crusaders at Acre on April 20, 1191, well before King Richard I, who first became involved in the conquest of Cyprus and only reached Acre on June 8. The French

26. *Ibid.*, II, 88-89.

27. Stubbs, *Itinerarium*, p. 134; Benedict of Peterborough, II, 144-145; and Ambroise (English translation), pp. 187-189.

nâdeddîn in *Récueil des histor-...s es croisades. Historiens orientaux* (Paris, 1872-1906), IV, 488-490.

29. Stubbs, *Itinerarium*, p. 137; Ambroise (English translation), p. 191.

king spent the interval between these two dates in building siege engines and strengthening the position of the crusading army, but he was apparently waiting for Richard before making any real attempt to take the city. Unfortunately, both kings became ill soon after Richard's arrival, causing yet another delay before any full-scale attack could be launched. Philip Augustus, who recovered first, finally decided to take the initiative. Although the French attack failed to take Acre, there was an increased tempo in the siege from that moment, aided by the fact that one of the towers in the walls of Acre had been brought down by undermining. Some of the English forces decided to try to force this breach under the banner of the earl of Leicester and were joined by many, including the bishop of Salisbury, but their assault over the fallen tower and a similar attempt by the Pisans a day later were driven back by the defenders, who employed Greek fire against them.[30]

When the final assault was made against the walls of Acre on July 6, King Richard, who had not yet recovered from his illness, had himself carried on a litter to a place where he could observe both the conflict and the victory that came six days later with the surrender of Acre to the Christian forces and their entry into the city that had so long been denied them. While the soldiers repaired the walls in preparation for a possible attack by Saladin's forces and rehabilitated houses damaged in the siege for their own occupancy, the clergy with the victorious crusaders turned to a task more congenial to their vocation than some of the bloody scenes in which they had so recently taken part and prepared to reopen the churches of Acre for C      worship. The purification was done by the papal legate assisted       archbishops and six bishops (including Bishop Hubert),       t e altars so that once again the rhythmic chant of the L       d with the cl    r of European voices in the streets of the

Little more than a week after the     l of  cre, King Philip, in virtue of their agreement made at the begin        the  xpedition, asked King Richard's approval of his d        home and retire from the crusade, leaving his share of the captured city to Conrad of Montferrat and the command of the Fre     army to the duke of Burgundy. When he returned to Tyre,  Philip took       m his share of the hostages that

30. Stubbs, *Itinerarium*, p. 372; Ambroise (English translation), pp. 209-210.

31. Benedict of Peterborough, II, 180-181.

Saladin had given the two kings as guarantees that he would fulfil the surrender terms made at Acre. But differences between King Richard and Saladin regarding the carrying out of the surrender agreement arose, and the English king found himself handicapped in negotiations with the Moslems by not having all the hostages under his control. Determined to remedy this situation and to strengthen his position against Saladin, Richard gladly accepted the advice of his companions and on August 5 sent Bishop Hubert to Tyre to obtain the hostages being held prisoner there. Two days later Hubert returned only to report that the king of France had sailed, leaving his prisoners in the hands of Conrad of Montferrat, who flatly refused to send them to King Richard. After a confidential interview with the king in which he made this report, Bishop Hubert explained the failure of his mission before the leaders as a whole. Both King Richard and a number of leaders were so angry with Conrad that they swore to go for the prisoners and to punish Conrad for his refusal to co-operate.[32] However, the duke of Burgundy persuaded them to give him a chance to talk with Conrad before they took any drastic action. He wisely chose several close friends of Conrad to accompany him to Tyre, and after some delay they returned with the hostages on August 12. A few days later the talks with Saladin broke down in spite of the increased weight given Richard's position by having all the hostages under his own control, and the crusaders accused Saladin of not meeting the first instalment of the payment agreed to in the surrender agreement. In a rage, Richard and the duke of Burgundy ordered that the Moslem hostages be beheaded. Despite their allegations that Saladin had treated Christian prisoners in the same cruel fashion, they thereby committed one of the worst atrocities of this crusade.

But concern with the terms of surrender or even with the execution of the hostages did not weigh most heavily in king Richard's thoughts. With the initial obstacle of Acre overcome the decision as to how best to effect the reconquest of Jerusalem the true goal of any crusade, had to be made. The biggest problem was that of maintaining supply lines, and for this a more convenient port nearer to Jerusalem was needed as a base from which to launch an attack on the Holy City. Not only was Acre too far from Jerusalem, but also the country in between was too dangerous

32. *Ibid.*, II, 186-189; Stubbs, *Itine-* lation), pp. 224-225.
*rarium*, p. 242; Ambroise (English trans-

to establish the lines of communication that Richard needed between himself and the sea. Clearly his next objective must be to seize the port of Jaffa lying to the south of Acre. The crusading army therefore gave up the relative comfort of the captured city of Acre and pushed south along the coast, keeping contact with the fleet as they went. Saladin's forces followed a parallel course somewhat further inland along a line of march that would allow them to take advantage of any false move by the crusading army and to harass the crusaders continuously with hit-and-run attacks. But the heavy armor worn by the crusaders gave them protection from the arrows shot by their enemies during such attacks and their discipline remained firm so that they resisted the fatal temptation of breaking ranks to crush their more lightly armed tormenters and thus expose themselves to being outmaneuvered and cut down piecemeal by a more swiftly moving adversary.

Saladin had judged that Jaffa would be unable to withstand a siege and had ordered the defenses torn down in order that they might not be useful when they fell into enemy hands. However, this meant that he was forced to seek a full-scale engagement in the field if he were to stop the crusaders before they could obtain their objective. For this reason he selected his ground carefully. Choosing a place where the route of the crusaders narrowed between the sea and a forest, he concealed the main body of his forces in the forest while a smaller force attacked and then retreated in an attempt to lure the crusaders into the ambush. In spite of these plans, the battle of Arsuf on September 7, 1191, was a serious defeat for Saladin. King Richard avoided the ambush and managed to inflict such losses on Saladin's men that the Saracens were convinced from that time on that they could not hope to win an open battle against the more heavily armed Westerners.

After the battle of Arsuf, neither side gained such decisive position that it could force an end to the conflict. In this period King Richard took Ascalon to the south of Jaffa; rebuilt the fortifications as a permanent threat to Saladin's communications with the most important part of his empire in Egypt; gained, lost, and regained Jaffa; suffered from disagreements on strategy with many of the French leaders; and failed to win a position from which Jerusalem could be attacked with a reasonable chance of success. Various negotiations with Saladin by Richard and by some of his opponents among the crusaders pointed the way to an ultimate negotiated settlement, for Saladin's followers also were becoming less reliable and had little interest in prolonging the war indefinitely.

The extent of Hubert Walter's active participation in the various monotonous skirmishes which mark this period is largely unknown. None of the chroniclers specifically mentions him for over nine months after the battle of Arsuf. Finally, on June 12, 1192, his name appears in accounts of one of the skirmishes typical of this phase of the crusade. With the crusaders near Beit Nuba, only some twelve miles from Jerusalem, the French camp was attacked. Only the action of the count of Perche and of Bishop Hubert saved it from being overwhelmed by the Saracens; half-hearted moves by the former bolstered by the quick response of the latter saved the day, according to the witnesses.[33]

Two months later Hubert's position becomes more clear. King Richard became seriously ill, and panic began to spread through the ranks of the crusaders until the quiet counsel of Hubert was able to prevail and restore calm. With King Richard too ill to make any decisions, Hubert called a council of the English leaders and made a truce with Saladin to which he obtained the consent of Henry of Champagne, who now had claim to the title of king of Jerusalem by inheritance through his wife's right. However, when the king recovered somewhat, he wished to resume the fighting and Hubert feared the truce would be broken. But when many English knights balked and refused to heed his orders, Richard authorized Bishop Hubert and Henry of Champagne to seek out a truce such as they had already negotiated without his knowledge.[34] A more lasting agreement was finally reached on September 2, 1192, when both sides approved a treaty providing for a three-year truce from the previous Easter. The treaty also provided that the Christians should continue holding the strip of land they had reconquered along the coast from Tyre to Jaffa and that Western pilgrims were to have the right to travel freely throughout Palestine.

The final act of the Third Crusade was a pilgrimage to Jerusalem now

33. Stubbs, *Itinerarium*, p. 372.

34. Richard of Devizes, "De rebus gestis Ricardi Primi," in Howlett, III, 444, 448, 451-452. The negotiations for a truce are also discussed by Behâ ed-Dîn, *The Life of Saladin* (English translation, London, 1897), p. 381 or in Arabic with French translation in *Récueil des historiens des croisades*, III, 342. One would naturally assume that the "Huât" who led the embassy was Hubert Walter, but I am informed by an Arabic specialist that this deformation of the name is contrary to the nature of the language rather than a mistake to be expected in transferring a name from French to Arabic. Nevertheless, Hubert is most likely meant in this context.

made possible by terms of the treaty, but King Richard took no part personally in this act of devotion. Instead, he sent Bishop Hubert, who had been his "inseparable and faithful comrade and wise colleague," to fulfil his vow and lead the last of three groups of crusaders who now made the pilgrimage. Some of his advisers had warned Richard of possible danger to himself if he made the pilgrimage, but the pilgrims who did go arrived safely, although the main body was placed in considerable danger through the negligence of messengers sent ahead to notify the Moslems and secure safe conduct for the unarmed throngs that followed. Stopping to rest these messengers fell asleep. Meanwhile, the main body overtook them and passed on without suspecting that they were entering enemy territory with no advance planning to insure safe passage. When the messengers were seen riding up from the rear, the unarmed pilgrims were terrified by the danger to which they had unwittingly been exposed. Safe conduct was quickly arranged and the journey completed without injury. In Jerusalem the pilgrims visited the holy places and saw the True Cross, where some placed offerings, but most preferred to give their offerings to Western and Syrian prisoners being held in Jerusalem because they knew that the Saracens would later take any offerings made before the Cross.

Saladin himself received Bishop Hubert, possibly, as one chronicler says, because of Hubert's reputation and wide renown, but more likely because he came as representative of King Richard. Saladin also offered him the use of a house during his visit. This Bishop Hubert refused because he came as a pilgrim, but a long conversation took place between the two leaders. Saladin asked questions about King Richard and also wanted to know what the crusaders thought of his Saracens. In the course of this interview carried on through interpreters, Saladin offered to grant any request that Hubert might make, and Hubert cautiously asked for a day to consider the matter. Next day his request was that two Latin priests and two Latin deacons be allowed to serve along with the Syrian priests both at the Holy Sepulchre and in Bethlehem and Nazareth, with their maintenance to come from the gifts of pilgrims. It is easy to agree with the chronicler who suggested that the bishop should have been proud to give back to God the Latin chants that had been lacking in these churches.[35]

Both Hubert's request and his fulfilment of the king's vow of pilgrim-

35. Ambroise (English translation), pp. 434-435, 438-439, 443; Stubbs, Itine- rarium, pp. 432-438; William of New- burgh, in Howlett, I, 378.

age, which made it possible for him to talk with Saladin, are typical of the dual role that he had had throughout the crusade—royal adviser and military leader on the one hand, and spiritual leader of the English forces. When the English returned to Acre after the pilgrimage and sailed for home on October 9, 1192, those who had accompanied Hubert Walter in the first contingent had spent just over two years in the Holy Land. The crusade had confronted Hubert with the challenge of more formidable administrative problems than he had faced as dean of York or bishop of Salisbury, had introduced him to the practice of diplomacy, and had brought him into contact with such shrewd personalities as Saladin and Philip Augustus, king of France. From this trial by battle Hubert emerged unscathed with his reputation enhanced, especially where it counted most, in the eyes of King Richard.

# 3 IN SERVICE OF A CAPTIVE KING

After having experienced the responsibilities of leadership and suffered the hardships of the Third Crusade, Hubert Walter would probably have viewed a return to the regular duties of bishop of Salisbury as something of an anticlimax particularly if it had been accompanied by a retirement from royal service. However, this prospect of comparative tranquility ended abruptly when King Richard fell into the hands of his enemies even before Hubert reached Italy on his return to England.

By crossing through German territory in disguise, Richard had hoped to circumvent his French enemies, who were rumored to be planning to seize him on his return from the crusade. However, he only succeeded in falling prisoner to the Duke of Austria, with whom he had quarreled at Acre; and, subsequently, he was turned over to the emperor for settlement of the latter's old grievances against him. This was the unwelcome news that greeted Hubert when he reached Sicily, probably sometime in March 1193. Immediately, he abandoned his own homeward journey and hastened to the king in his German prison, pausing only at Rome, where he attempted to rally papal support to obtain Richard's release.[1] Not for long did Hubert commiserate with the captive king. About the first of April

1. William of Newburgh, in Howlett,   p. 363.
I, 388; Stubbs, *Epistolae Cantuarienses,*

he was sent on to England to care for the realm and make arrangements to obtain the money needed for Richard's ransom.[2]

Although Hubert returned to England with his special commission from the king, there is no indication that he was given any official position. Just as it had been since King Richard sailed for the Holy Land, the government remained in the hands of justiciars, with Richard's mother, Queen Eleanor, also taking a very active role. Hubert's authority must simply have rested on the fact that he was known to have come directly from the king and could best represent his views, although he no doubt carried from the king some letter of general instruction and authorization that is no longer extant. Certainly King Richard placed complete confidence in him, because, as one chronicler noted, there was no one else whose faith, wisdom, and sincerity had been tested so many times in various trying situations.[3]

The royal council meeting the first week of June at St. Alban's clarified Hubert's status in regard to the specific task of raising money for the ransom. Along with Richard, bishop of London, the earl of Arundel, the earl of Warenne, and the mayor of London, he was named as one of the trustees to receive the money, acting under the seal of Queen Eleanor and the principal justiciar, Walter of Coutances, archbishop of Rouen.[4] Once again the qualities of leadership that had been displayed so conspicuously on the crusade during the months of famine and later when King Richard had fallen ill were demonstrated as Hubert set about rallying support for the king. According to Gervase of Canterbury, he spoke brilliantly, clearly, and earnestly, first with the monks of Canterbury and then to all the churches and people of England, emphasizing the necessity that all difficulties that divided the country, such as the differences between those loyal to King Richard and those who supported his brother John, must be quickly overcome in order that with much labor the king might be redeemed within a year. To further these goals, Hubert negotiated a truce with Prince John in regard to Windsor Castle, which John was holding against his brother's officials. All effort could thenceforth be concentrated on raising the first payment on the ransom.[5]

Suitable reward for such loyal service—past, present, and expected—

2. William of Newburgh, I, 388; Gervase of Canterbury, II, 407; Landon, *The Itinerary of King Richard I.*
3. William of Newburgh, in Howlett,
I, 388.
4. Roger of Hoveden, III, 212.
5. Gervase of Canterbury, I, 516; II, 407.

lay within King Richard's power in the vacant archbishopric of Canterbury. Several letters from the king arranged to bring his influence to bear in securing this prize for Hubert Walter. After the death of Archbishop Baldwin on the crusade, the monks of Christ Church had elected the bishop of Bath as his successor, touching off a controversy that might have become serious if the elect had not died within a month. Since that time no further attempt at election had been made. On March 30, 1193, three letters written by King Richard from his place of captivity set the election process in motion again.[6] To the monks he gave instruction to hold an election with the advice of Queen Eleanor and William de Ste. Mère Eglise, without mentioning any candidate by name in order not to seem to be interfering with the actual election. In a letter to his mother, however, he cited the service Bishop Hubert had rendered during the crusade and Hubert's present efforts to speed his release as principal reasons for managing his election. A third letter to the justiciars urged their support of Hubert in the election for similar reasons. Hubert probably knew of this nomination from the time that he left King Richard for England, for these letters were then being carried by William de Ste. Mère Eglise, his traveling companion on that journey, who was also instructed to aid in managing the election. The letters emphasize that Hubert enjoyed the complete confidence of the king and that he returned to England as the king's special representative. The king also made quite explicit his belief that the election of Hubert would speed up the collection of the ransom and strengthen the defense of the realm. In fact, Richard urged his mother that Hubert's election was second only to his own liberation in the business he had entrusted to her. Such preparations by the king produced the desired result. On May 29, 1193, the monks of Canterbury elected Hubert, anticipating by one day the same action by the suffragan bishops of Canterbury, who claimed to have a right to participate in the election of an archbishop. The deputation of monks sent to Rome to secure the pallium returned without incident in October to complete the formalities of election and papal approval.[7]

It fell to the chronicler, Gervase of Canterbury, who was also at this time sacrist, to deliver the archiepiscopal cross to Hubert, a task which he performed on November 3 with a short formal exhortation that he

6. Stubbs, *Epistolae Cantuarienses*, pp. 362-365; Gervase of Canterbury, I, 517.
7. Gervase of Canterbury, I, 518, 522; Roger of Hoveden, III, 213, 221, 223; Ralph de Diceto, II, 108-109, 111; Landon, p. 74.

recorded in his book as a model for such occasions. The archbishop-elect was enjoined to receive the church of Canterbury from God, to care for it in faith, and to take his cross "willingly, and bear it faithfully, that you may rejoice in eternity with your saintly predecessors as patrons of the Church of Canterbury. Amen."[8] Hubert was shortly after received at Canterbury with the kiss of peace and honored there by the bishops of England and the monks of Christ Church. On November 7, clothed with alb and hood, he led a procession of the monks and advanced with bare feet to receive the pallium from the papal nuncio. Then, wearing the pallium and the vestments of a bishop, he was enthroned and celebrated mass for the first time as archbishop of Canterbury. The solemnity of the occasion was marred only by an indecorous dispute between the bishops of London and Rochester as to which should have the place of honor, but calm was restored when a compromise was arranged. Later in the day the new archbishop visited St. Augustine's monastery close by the cathedral where he again was received with the kiss of peace and where he celebrated mass.[9] If William of Newburgh is correct in his description of the day's events, Archbishop Hubert also assumed the religious habit of the canons of Merton as a mark of the dedication with which he undertook his new position. Even then, however, the cares of secular responsibility seemed certain to intrude upon his ecclesiastical vocation.[10]

The month after his enthronement as archbishop, sometime before Christmas, Hubert Walter was appointed justiciar, an appointment that placed him at the head of the machinery of government directly under the king. In his efforts to collect the ransom, Hubert for some months had already assumed many of the functions of a justiciar, and King Richard's letter written at Speyer on December 22 to announce that the date for his release had been fixed was addressed to Hubert, implying recognition of his pre-eminent position in England by that date, even though the formal title of justiciar was not yet his.[11] With this appointment Hubert followed in the tradition of his uncle Ranulf Glanvill, who had been one of the great justiciars of the period, and he brought to bear upon the office the basic training that he had received years before in his uncle's household. The significance of this office has been examined by H. G. Richardson,

8. Gervase of Canterbury, I, 521-522.
9. *Ibid.*, pp. 522-523.
10. William of Newburgh, in Howlett, I, p. 392. See the comment by Cheney,

*From Becket to Langton*, p. 39.
11. Roger of Hoveden, III, 226; Landon, p. 81.

who writes: "The central fact in the administrative history of England and Normandy under the Angevins is the delegation of authority to the justiciars, who acted as viceregents in the king's absence." The same writer points out the broad responsibility of this official:

The justiciar then is supreme over finance and the administration of justice, which are centralized at the exchequer, and he may use the exchequer seal, or his own, for the many writs that must be issued for these and other purposes of government. Now all these functions are functions of the *curia regis.* . . . The king's justices sit at the exchequer at Westminster: their head is the justiciar and he often presides over them, but they are in the king's court, whether the king is in England or, as he more often is, overseas.[12]

In preparation for the governing of England during his crusade, King Richard had divided the authority exercised by Glanvill and appointed two men to succeed him; later, other justices were associated with the two and all were expected to work together as a group. This scheme of government failed to work as planned, and further revision resulted in a system by which the justices, now headed by Walter, archbishop of Rouen, were reinforced by consultation with the magnates on crucial matters.[13] After Richard's capture, Queen Eleanor had taken a more active part in the government in an effort to protect the throne for her elder son. When John threatened to invade England in March 1193, orders for the defense of the coast were dispatched in the name of Queen Eleanor, who was described as ruling England at that time.[14]

The appointment of Hubert Walter as justiciar marked a return to the practice of having a single justiciar and was accompanied by a summons to Queen Eleanor, Archbishop Walter, and many others to join the king in Germany, thus leaving the government completely in the hands of the newly appointed "summus justitiarius in Anglia."[15] Something of his work is shown in the allowances on the Pipe Roll authorized by Archbishop Hubert, or "per breue H. Cant' archiepiscopi per breue R. de ultra mare."[16] In fact, perhaps the easiest way to gain an impression of the all-pervading activity of the justiciar is to look at the extremely large number of entries under Hubert's name in the index for the printed volume of the Pipe Roll.

12. Introduction to *Memoranda Roll 1 John*, pp. xi, xv.

13. Bertie Wilkinson, "The Government of England during the Absence of Richard I on the Third Crusade," *Bulletin of The John Rylands Library*, xxviii (1944), 485-509.

14. Gervase of Canterbury, I, 515.

15. Roger of Hoveden, III, 226.

16. *P.R. 7 Ric. I*, pp. 113, 119, 226.

A few surviving examples of writs of *liberate* prove beyond any doubt that by the end of 1193 the new justiciar had also reverted to the older practice of the justiciar's issuing writs in his own name.[17]

At first glance, such references to the activities of the justiciar may be confusing because he is normally designated by his ecclesiastical title. Of course, the holding of important secular office by a bishop was not new, although the combination of the highest ecclesiastical and the highest secular office in one man was unique for England. Hubert himself had served as a justice both while dean of York and while bishop of Salisbury, and during the reign of King Henry II seventeen bishops, about one-third of the episcopate, were also royal judges.[18] F. W. Maitland commented on this development:

Henry's greatest, his most lasting triumph in the legal field was this, that he made the prelates of the church his justices. . . . English law was administered by the ablest, the best educated, men in the realm; nor only that, it was administered by the selfsame men who were 'the judges ordinary' of the church's courts, men who were bound to be, at least in some measure, learned in the canon law. . . .[19]

Within the church, however, there was some opposition to the merging of responsibilities. A contemporary, writing in 1190 just before Archbishop Hubert became justiciar, complained about the bishops' desire for secular office and their involvement in secular business. He was reminded of Roger, bishop of Salisbury, who had been King Henry I's justiciar. In that day, however, Roger would not become justiciar until he had obtained approval by the pope and was urged to do so by several archbishops.[20] A lawyer might also have pointed out that canon law, reiterated as recently as 1175, in canon three of the council of Westminster, prohibited clerks in holy orders from becoming involved in court sentences prescribing death or mutilation. Another principle of canon law, that clerks should avoid positions that made them answerable to laymen, was reinforced in 1179 by the twelfth canon of the Third Lateran Council, which provided for the deposition of clergy who undertook secular jurisdiction under princes or laymen.

However, it is notable that in the same year three out of the four

17. *Memoranda Roll 1 John*, p. lxxiv.
18. Cheney, *From Becket to Langton*, p. 24.
19. Frederick Pollock and Frederic William Maitland, *The History of English Law before the Time of Edward I* (2nd ed.; Cambridge, 1923), I, 132.
20. Ralph de Diceto, II, 77.

chief justices appointed by King Henry II were bishops and that Richard, archbishop of Canterbury, defended them in a letter to Pope Alexander III, insisting that secular office had not caused them to neglect their duties as pastors and that it was an advantage to the church to have ecclesiastical influence around the king. All in all, it is clear that the bishops of England differed among themselves in their views on this prohibition and that it was never enforced in the later twelfth century.[21] In Archbishop Hubert's case, the particular office of justiciar was almost certain to involve him in making the prohibited judgments of blood, even if the prohibition against holding a position answerable to laymen need not be observed. But the issue was not raised until it was later incorporated in charges made against him by his opponents in his quarrel with the monks of Christ Church, Canterbury.

The most vocal critic in Hubert's day of the custom of combining secular and ecclesiastical offices was the saintly Hugh, bishop of Lincoln. When during the previous reign King Henry II had asked that a vacant prebend at Lincoln be given to one of the men of his court, Bishop Hugh had refused, with the withering comment that ecclesiastical benefits were for clergy who served the altar, not for those who served in the palace, treasury, or the Exchequer. He later clashed with Archbishop Hubert. When Hugh ordered one of his deacons to desist from charging a certain knight with a felony because it involved dragging a man into a secular court and a possible judgment of blood, Hubert invoked ecclesiastical censure to prevent Hugh from restraining the deacon. In his refusal to obey, the bishop made a distinction between the obedience he owed Hubert as archbishop and that he owed him as justiciar, basing his refusal in the immediate case on the biblical principle that one must obey God rather than man. On other occasions Bishop Hugh, who was an older man than the archbishop, exhorted Hubert to spend more care on his ecclesiastical office than in the governing of the realm but succeeded only in provoking the archbishop's anger. When King Richard attempted to extort service from some rich canons at Lincoln through orders sent by the archbishop, Bishop Hugh threw himself into the fray in defense of the canons. Asserting a position that clearly conflicted with that of Hubert, he stated that time after time he had forbidden even clerks who were not in his service but who held a benefice in his church to take part in ad-

21. Cheney, *From Becket to Langton,* pp. 16-26.

ministrative activities in which they would oppress the laity.[22] Perhaps it is unfair to judge the career of Hubert Walter by the standards of a saint, especially when the majority of English bishops by their actions showed themselves more in agreement with the archbishop than with their colleague. Nevertheless, Bishop Hugh's opposition demonstrates that at least one bishop was aware of the danger in the heavy involvment of the English episcopacy with the burdens of secular government and administration.

As for immediate problems confronting the new justiciar, the question of finance was to loom large for several years because of the necessity of raising money, first for King Richard's ransom and then for the renewed war with France. Of scholars working over the records of this period, perhaps the one closest to the subject of finance in its intimate detail is Lady Stenton, who has edited the Pipe Rolls for the years 1194 through 1197. In one of her informative introductions she writes: "Despite the obvious and often successful attempts to get the money owed the king paid in full, and as quickly as possible, continuous exactions resulted in a largely extended Pipe Roll.... Taken together the rolls of these years [1194-1197] give the impression of a country taxed to the limit."[23] This is true in spite of the fact that the Pipe Rolls have little direct information on the collection of the ransom itself. A fragment of a Receipt Roll seems to indicate that the ransom was handled entirely separately from other sums collected.[24] Perhaps the special Exchequer board that was dealing with arrears in payments for the ransom in 1198 was established already in 1193, even though there is no record to verify this assumption. The impression of a separate board is strengthened by a reference in the Pipe Roll of 1195 under the heading of "Nova Promissa" levied by Hubert Walter; one debtor claimed that he had already paid the sum in question at the exchequer of the ransom. Certain sums enrolled as *auxilia* in the Pipe Rolls represent the personal activity of the justiciar, who visited some of the great towns after the king's return as part of his effort to get the money needed to complete payment of the ransom.[25] Among other evidence bearing on the collection of the ransom is a letter from King Richard sent from the Continent to the justiciar on April 15, 1196, authorizing an inquest into the amount raised for the ransom but leaving the decision

22. *Magna vita*, II, 28-30, 96, 110-113, 188-189.
23. *P.R. 9 Ric. I*, p. xiii.
24. *P.R. 7 Ric. I*, pp. xv, xxxi.

25. Sydney K. Mitchell, *Taxation in Medieval England* (New Haven, 1951), pp. 25-27, 286.

whether to make the inquest to the discretion of Hubert Walter.[26] The monks of Christ Church, Canterbury, took the precaution of obtaining a letter of assurance from the king that their free gifts for the ransom would not be held as precedent against their liberties and of having this letter confirmed by Pope Celestine III.[27] At the same time, even the Jews of Canterbury were contributing heavily to the ransom in an amount surpassed only by the Jews at London and Lincoln.[28]

As is so frequently the case, the dull statistics of financial records and the almost equally colorless phraseology of official letters come to life in the chronicle written by Jocelin of Brakelond. Many of the precious ornaments at St. Edmund's were alienated in order to help ransom the king, and Abbot Samson determined to concentrate his building activity on the feretory of the martyr St. Edmund as the one thing not likely to be taken away whatever the royal financial extremity. Those dark days of exactions for the king's ransom were recalled by Jocelin in this way:

For when King Richard was taken captive in Germany, there was no treasure in all England that was not given or redeemed, but the feretory of St. Edmund remained untouched. None the less the question was raised before the judges of the Exchequer, whether the feretory of St. Edmund should be stripped at least in part for the ransoming of King Richard; and the Abbot arose and said, "Know this for the truth that it shall never be done if I can prevent it, nor is there any man that can force me to consent thereto. But I will open the doors of the church. Let him enter who will, let him approach who dare!" And each of the judges replied with an oath, "I will not approach, nor will I. For the fury of St. Edmund can reach those who are absent and far away; much more will it strike those who are present and desire to strip his shirt off him." This said, neither was the feretory stripped nor was anything taken therefrom.[29]

Since Hubert Walter was still involved with the problem of raising the king's ransom at the outset of his tenure as justiciar, no radical change in personnel or administrative policy could be expected. The justiciar continued to be supported by the same sheriffs who had been in office under the former justiciars, and even in 1195, when a number of the sheriffs were changed, the new appointees had no special ties with Hubert

26. Stubbs in his introduction to Ralph de Diceto, II, lxxix.

27. Lambeth Palace Library, Lambeth MS.1212, pp. 241-242. Printed in Walther Holtzmann, *Papsturkunden in England* (Berlin and Göttingen, 1930-52), II, 468 from Canterbury, D. and C. Mun., Register A.

28. Michael Adler, "The Jews of Canterbury," *Jewish Historical Society Transactions*, VII (1911), p. 26.

29. Jocelin of Brakelond, p. 97.

Walter, although he had known most of them during their careers in royal service. Several who had been especially close to King Richard must have benefited from the king's personal interest in their appointments. However, the justiciar's prodding may very well have been behind the complete accounting at the Exchequer at Michaelmas in 1194. At that time the counties that King Richard had granted to John before going on the crusade again appear on the Pipe Roll firmly in the hands of faithful custodians for half, or at least part, of the previous year.

Hubert's influence upon the itinerant justices is much more immediately apparent. Of the thirty-five justices known to have been involved on the eyre at some time in 1192, the new justiciar retained fifteen in 1194. Those retained include Gilbert Glanvill, bishop of Rochester, and men whom Hubert had known in royal service since his days in Glanvill's household: Geoffrey fitz Peter, Osbert fitz Hervey, Hugh Bardolf, William de Stuteville, Richard fitz Nigel, and William de Warenne. Most of the twenty-four justices added in 1194 were also closely connected with the justiciar. William Glanvill, Ralph de Ardene, Theobald de Valoines, and William de Aubervill were related by family or marriage through Ranulf Glanvill. Members of Hubert's archiepiscopal *familia* were Geoffrey de Bocland, Simon of Scales, and Henry de Castellion, who was archdeacon of Canterbury. William de Ste. Mère Eglise and Abbot Samson of Bury were old friends, and the abbots of Malmesbury and of Hyde likely had some connection with Hubert in ecclesiastical administration. The names of Roger Bigot, earl of Norfolk, and one or two others hint at connections in Norfolk, a region always strongly represented in the men associated with both Ranulf Glanvill and Hubert Walter. The obvious conclusion is that within a year the administration of the new justiciar, while still firmly anchored on men with experience in government, had begun to reflect his personal influence and the strong ties of family and friendship that had been established during his apprenticeship in the household of Ranulf Glanvill.[30]

With the ransom that would free King Richard in the process of being raised and the new justiciar firmly in control, the opportunity that Richard's capture had given his brother John to seize the throne seemed rapidly to be fading away. Before leaving on the crusade, Richard had conferred upon his brother a large territory, consisting of several honors with their

30. Based upon an analysis of the  Pipe Rolls for 1191-95.

castles, the shire of Derby, and four other shires in southwestern England, making him virtually independent of royal authority in this area. During the crusade, John had shown his disloyalty and the folly of the king's generosity to him. When Richard dispensed both his brothers from the oath that they must stay out of England for a period of three years during his absence on the crusade, only the solidarity of the justiciars and the magnates acting jointly had prevented John from grasping regal power.[31] Now, informed of Richard's captivity by King Philip Augustus of France, no friend of the English king, John hastened first to the Continent, where he declared himself king. Then he set about trying to secure the homage of the nobility in Richard's possessions there, only to have his hopes dashed against the rock of obstinate loyalty that the Norman barons had for Richard. No more successful in subverting English loyalties, he continued to intrigue with Philip Augustus against the day of Richard's release. In February 1194 he made his bid for England, sending his confidential clerk, Adam of St. Edmund, to England with secret letters to his castellans to furnish his castles for the coming struggle with those who supported the king.

Adam crossed to England without difficulty and moved on to London, where he had the incredible audacity to dine at the house of Archbishop Hubert. During the evening, he boasted of the prosperity of his lord and of John's close relations with the king of France. Naturally, Hubert and other men loyal to the king were outraged by such treasonable comments, but the rules of hospitality prevented them from taking immediate action. Nevertheless, when the clerk returned to his lodgings, he was arrested on February 9 by the mayor of London, undoubtedly under instructions from Hubert, and his letters were seized and sent to the justiciar. These letters provided the damning evidence of John's disloyalty which Hubert presented before a royal council hastily convoked the following day to deal with the threatened rebellion. The council pronounced its decision that John should be dispossessed of all his lands in England and that any of his castles not surrendered in accordance with this decision should be taken by siege. Later that same day Archbishop Hubert joined many bishops, abbots, and clergy from the Canterbury diocese in excommunicating John and his followers.[32]

The enforcement of this decision against John was well advanced

---

31. Wilkinson, pp. 500-507.      32. Roger of Hoveden, III, 236-237.

before King Richard himself returned to England. Three castles held by John's partisans had surrendered and the other two, Nottingham and Tickhill, had been placed under siege. Archbishop Hubert resumed a martial role for the first time since the crusade and commanded the operations against Marlborough Castle, which fell within a few days. Some details of this short siege can be seen in record entries: on February 14 Hubert ordered a petrary transported from Reading to Marlborough, the expenses of serjeants in charge to be paid by the custodian of the vacant see of Salisbury; another petrary and mangonel were prepared in Winchester along with other siege paraphernalia and returned there after the castle fell; and the damages caused in the fighting later had to be repaired at royal expense.[33] The situation at Lancaster Castle was different, for it was held for John by Theobald Walter, the brother of the justiciar, and he surrendered it into Hubert's hands without a siege.[34]

It might be noted that Theobald was no latecomer to the side of Count John. He had been part of his household at least since 1185, when King Henry II had sent his youngest son on an expedition to Ireland. Probably they had become friends during the time that the king had entrusted his son John to the care of Ranulf Glanvill, with whom both the Walter nephews were then living. In fact, Glanvill accompanied the impetuous young men with John into Wales at the time of the Irish expedition but apparently did not sail with them. John was generous with Theobald in his grants of land in Ireland and, in addition, made him his butler, an office Theobald probably still held when he surrendered Lancaster Castle.[35]

Archbishop Hubert also played an important part in the struggle against John's men elsewhere. Henry de la Pomerai, who had driven the monks from St. Michael's Mount in Cornwall and garrisoned it, was forced to surrender that position. If Henry died of fright at the news of King Richard's approach, as one chronicler has it, he was a victim of poor military intelligence, for it was Hubert Walter who received the surrender of the Mount in the name of the king, who had not yet reached England.[36]

Not until March 13, 1194, did the king land at Sandwich. Proceeding to Canterbury, he gave thanks to the martyred St. Thomas Becket for his

33. B. M., Egerton MS. 3031 printed by H. G. Richardson in *Memoranda Roll 1 John*, p. lxxiv; *P.R. 6 Ric. I*, p. xv; Roger of Hoveden, III, 237.
34. Roger of Hoveden, III, 237.
35. Lambeth Palace Library, Carew MS. 613, fos. 20, 20 v., 21; Gilbert, pp. 51-55; Giraldus Cambrensis, "Expugnatio Hibernica," in *Opera*, V, 380; *P.R. 31. Hen. II*, p. 2; Orpen, II, 93-105.
36. Roger of Hoveden, III, 237-238; *P.R. 6 Ric. I*, p. xvj.

deliverance from his enemies and to the monks of Christ Church for a more concrete form of aid in their contributions to his ransom. Next day on the road to Rochester and London, the king met Archbishop Hubert, who hastened joyfully to join Richard when he heard of his return. As the two parties approached each other, the king dismounted and knelt before the primate, and Hubert with tears in his eyes raised him again to his feet.[37]

Under the circumstances, with castles at Nottingham and Tickhill still holding out against royal forces and the temper of the country at large somewhat uncertain, there was little time wasted in either ecclesiastical or social amenities. Even Canterbury had gone through a scare; the city government, ignoring the immunities of Christ Church monastery in the emergency, had forced some of its men to help strengthen the city walls against possible attack by partisans of John.[38] The king assumed command and summoned his barons to meet him at Southwell, a manor in mid-Nottinghamshire belonging to his brother, the archbishop of York, and conveniently located for attack upon either of the rebel castles.[39]

After accompanying the king on his journey northward, Hubert then went on to Tickhill, where Hugh, bishop of Durham, was conducting the siege, and may have arrived there before the constable surrendered that castle. When the defenders at Nottingham heard that King Richard had joined the siege and that Tickhill had surrendered, they entered into negotiations that shortly resulted in the capitulation of this last armed group holding out for John against royal authority.[40] On March 30 a great council was held at Nottingham to pass sentence on John and his followers, a council at which Archbishop Hubert sat at the king's right hand and used his influence to obtain clemency so that most of John's followers were allowed to redeem their lands by payment of fines. Gerald de Camvill was disseized of the castle and county of Lincoln, Hugh Bardolf was replaced as sheriff of York, and some other sheriffs were shifted around. John and the bishop of Coventry were given forty days to make their peace with the king. Three weeks after the council, Jollan de la Pomerai, who had been with his brother Henry at St. Michael's Mount, chose to go into exile rather than be tried by the *curia regis*. Among those listed in

37. Gervase of Canterbury, I, 524.
38. Canterbury, D. and C. Mun., Register A, f. 84; Register B, f. 406.
39. *P.R. 6 Ric. I*, p. xvj.

40. *Ibid.*, p. xvij; Gervase of Canterbury, I, 524; Roger of Hoveden, III, 238-240.

the Pipe Rolls as having paid fines for their connection with John's rebellion is Adam of St. Edmund, whose mood as he paid his one hundred marks to atone for his offense must have been far different from that of the evening when he sat boasting at the table of Archbishop Hubert.[41]

With the fall of the last of John's castles and the surrender of his partisans, England was restored to complete obedience to King Richard. His resumption of the full powers of the kingship after a long absence and humiliating captivity was marked by a second coronation. The form that was followed on the occasion suggests a revival of the custom of crown-wearing used by the Norman kings of England, rather than the form normally used in coronations during the twelfth century, and there is a hint that the ceremony was planned to erase some taint of dishonor that was thought to linger from the period of captivity. In contrast to the troubles of the previous weeks, the scene at Winchester Cathedral on April 17, 1194, when Archbishop Hubert placed the crown on King Richard's head, was a brilliant one with enough pomp and ceremony to make anyone forget days when the crown had not sat so securely on the royal head.[42]

Having completed this ceremony, King Richard remained in England less than a month before proceeding to the Continent to take up the war against the king of France. This short interval was marked by numerous confirmations of charters and the issuing of many new grants. Among the grants was a charter to Theobald Walter for the wapentake of Amounderness to be held for three knights' service.[43] Because Theobald's ties heretofore had been to John, hardly qualifying him as a recipient of the king's gratitude, this gift must represent the influence of Archbishop Hubert with the king, and indeed the archbishop's name heads the list of witnesses to the charter. Theobald had also been allowed to remain as sheriff of Lancashire.[44] After some delay caused by bad weather in the Channel, King Richard left England for the last time on May 12, leaving the government of England once again in the capable hands of his justiciar, Hubert Walter.

41. Roger of Hoveden, III, 241-242, 249; *P.R. 6 Ric. I*, pp. xv, xviij.

42. Gervase of Canterbury, I, 525-526; Roger of Hoveden, III, 247-248; Ralph of Coggeshall, p. 64; H. G. Richardson and G. O. Sayles, *The Governance of Mediaeval England from the Conquest to Magna Carta* (Edinburgh, 1963), pp. 139, 153.

43. Farrer, *Lancashire Pipe Rolls*, p. 434.

44. *P.R. 6 Ric. I*, p. xviii.

# 4 "BY THE GRACE OF GOD, ARCHBISHOP OF CANTERBURY"

One of Hubert Walter's principal characteristics, which became evident in every position he ever held, was his industry—the vigorous way in which he met each challenge and problem and the sheer quantity of work that he seemed able to dispatch. Such an impression is no less true of his work as archbishop of Canterbury than of the various secular offices he held, even though at the same time he held the archbishopric he had heavy administrative responsibilities first as justiciar and later as chancellor. In fact, as C. R. Cheney has commented, anyone examining the extant records of his activity as archbishop could scarcely guess from them that he was ever troubled by other responsibilities.[1] The explanation of this seeming paradox can be found in the ability of the men who made up his household, or *familia,* upon whom he must have been forced to rely for much of the work of the archbishopric. Evidently Archbishop Hubert had learned the lesson of a successful administrator in choosing capable subordinates and being willing to delegate responsibility to them. In this, his own training and observation in the household of Ranulf Glanvill and at the court of King Henry II must have proved valuable in ecclesiastical as well as in secular affairs.

Much about the composition and the work of Archbishop Hubert's *familia* has been described by Professor Cheney in his book on English bishops' chanceries during this period. He has thoroughly demonstrated the value of careful attention to such things as the names of men who witnessed the various *acta* of a bishop or archbishop. One interesting conclusion from his study of Hubert's *acta* is the importance of an academically trained element in the archbishop's *familia:* of the thirty-eight clerks who often witnessed for Hubert, twenty-four held the academic title of *magister;* of the thirty who were almost certainly regular members of his household, some twenty were *magistri.*[2]

Some additional information about three of these learned clerks is found in an incidental reference by Master Thomas of Marlborough. In pleading a case for the monks of Evesham before Archbishop Hubert in 1203, he noted that Honorius, John of Tynemouth, and Simon of Southwell,

1. Cheney, *From Becket to Langton,* pp. 35-36.
2. C. R. Cheney, *English Bishops'* *Chanceries 1100-1250* (Manchester, 1950), p. 11.

who supported his position in the case, were "magistri mei in scholis," apparently during his canon law studies in England.[3] Master Honorius, who passed from the service of Geoffrey, archbishop of York, to that of Hubert at Canterbury, was archdeacon of Richmond and is otherwise known as the author of a work on canon law. He successfully argued a case for the archbishop in an appeal to Rome before Pope Innocent III in 1202, helped to reconcile the lengthy dispute between Hubert and Gerald of Wales, and after Hubert's death was sent to Rome by King John as one of the proctors in connection with the disputed election at Canterbury. As for the other two masters, John of Tynemouth and Simon of Southwell, many of the contemporary glosses on a late-twelfth-century copy of the *Decretum* are attributed to them; these show that they frequently took issue with each other and were clearly rivals in their interpretations of canon law. Although there is no certain trace of Master John in the *familia* until 1198, his frequent appearance thereafter indicates that he attained a position of importance. Master Simon came to the archbishop's service about 1195 from the household of Hugh, bishop of Lincoln. He had been appointed as a papal judge delegate by Pope Celestine III and represented the archbishop at Rome in two important cases. When Archbishop Hubert was on the Continent in 1202, Simon administered the archbishopric as *officialis generalis,* and in 1203 he became treasurer of Lichfield, holding a canonry there until 1209. Although Master Simon had formerly lectured at Bologna and at Paris, the evidence seems to indicate that the three masters were teaching at Oxford when Thomas of Marlborough studied with them.[4]

It is typical of Hubert Walter that, although he had no scholarly pretensions himself, he surrounded himself with men who did have the best academic training available and who could supply the learned counsel he needed as archbishop.[5] Unlike some self-made men, he did not despise learning. His practical interest in it is evident in his appropriation of the church of Lower Halstow for the precentor in Christ Church monastery to

3. *Chronicon abbatiae de Evesham,* ed. William D. Macray (R.S., London, 1863), p. 126; Stephen Kuttner and Eleanor Rathbone, "Anglo-Norman Canonists of the Twelfth Century," *Traditio,* VII (1949-51), p. 316.

4. Kuttner and Rathbone, pp. 304-305, 308, 316-318, 326-327; Cheney, *English Bishops' Chanceries,* pp. 12-14; C. R. Cheney and W. H. Semple, eds., *Selected Letters of Pope Innocent III Concerning England (1198-1216)* (London, 1953), p. 42.

5. Wilmart, p. 227, commented on this educated group.

use in repairing books.[6] He also exerted his influence with the king to obtain a subsidy of ten marks to send Robert de Vermeilles to school at Oxford.[7]

Like Master Honorius and Master Simon, the clerks of the archbishop sometimes came from other dioceses; other members of the *familia* passed through his household to serve elsewhere later. Hubert brought Master Simon of Scales with him from Salisbury. They had been working together since Hubert's days in Glanvill's household, and Simon had been one of the men who had administered the see at Salisbury during Bishop Hubert's absence on the Third Crusade. Other clerks who transferred from Salisbury were Ranulf, who remained treasurer of Salisbury but often handled important business for the archbishop, Roger of Basingham, Robert of Ruddeby, and William of Neketon. From his predecessor at Canterbury, Hubert took over the services of Robert of Bristol, who attested twenty-six of the new archbishop's *acta* and lived to serve Stephen Langton after Hubert's death. Clerks David and Robert of Ruddeby, whose names may indicate a family relationship, appear later in the service of John de Gray, bishop of Norwich.[8] Master William de Calna and a Master Gervase also witnessed for the Bishop of Norwich, but it is not certain that this Gervase is the man who was in Hubert's *familia*.[9] William de Bosco was still serving the bishop of Rochester in 1201 when he appeared in the king's court to verify a decision taken in the bishop's court.[10] Because of the disputed election at Hubert's death, it is difficult to trace the degree of continuity between his household and that of Stephen Langton, but Kathleen Major, who has studied the *familia* of Archbishop Langton, has found that Robert of Bristol, Aaron of Kent, William de Bosco, William de Beauton, and Elias of Dereham did stay on at Canterbury. Possibly James Savage and John of Kent should be added to that list, but the evidence is not clear in their cases.[11]

Because of Hubert's position as justiciar under King Richard and as chancellor for King John, there was considerable overlap in the clerks

6. Canterbury, D. and C. Mun., Register A, f. 165 v.; Gervase of Canterbury II, 413.

7. *P.R. 10 Ric. I*, p. 190.

8. Windsor, D. and C. Mun., MS. XI.G. 11, #4, 7; Cheney, *English Bishops' Chanceries*, pp. 15-16.

9. Norwich, D. and C. Mun., Register I, f. 31; Register 4, p. 32; B.M., Cott.

MS., Titus C. VIII, f. 11. A "Master Gervase" also witnessed a charter of Bishop Seffrid of Chichester, B.M., Cott. MS., Claudius A. VI, f. 54 v.

10. *Curia Regis Rolls*, I, 458.

11. Kathleen Major, "The 'Familia' of Archbishop Stephen Langton," *The English Historical Review*, XLVIII (1933), p. 530.

who served the king and those who served the archbishop. Four of the archbishop's men who also served as royal justices were Master Simon of Scales, in 1195; Henry de Castellion, the archdeacon of Canterbury, who sat as a royal justice on the bench with Archbishop Hubert in 1196; Ranulf, treasurer of Salisbury, in 1197-1198; and Master Godfrey de Insula in 1201 and after. Others mentioned as carrying out various Exchequer business were Master Gervase of Hubbridge, Master William of Neketon, and Master William of Hatfield.[12] Along with King Richard's admiral, Alan Trenchemer, and two other men, Master Gervase accounted for property of the king's enemies which they had sold in Flanders and various ports.[13] In 1202 William de Bosco was one of two men appointed by the king to view the work being done on the king's houses at Corfe.[14] On the other hand, Geoffrey de Bocland, who witnessed for successive justiciars and also served as a royal justice, frequently accompanied the archbishop and also placed his name on some twenty of the archbishop's acts. Other clerks who served both king and archbishop were Simon de Camera and Richard of Ringstede.[15] When the archbishop had cases come for judgment before the *curia regis,* he could name as his attorneys men who had considerable experience in royal service, for he usually was represented in such actions by James Savage, William of Neketon, or Ranulf, the treasurer of Salisbury.[16]

The internal organization of the archiepiscopal household appears only incidentally—when, for example, some clerk lists the office he holds in affixing his name to a document. One of the charters of Archbishop Theobald has an unusually complete list of such offices, which includes a chancellor, steward, chamberlain, chaplains, cross-bearer, dispenser, master cook, porter, and marshal.[17] For Archbishop Hubert, we have the name of Master Richard as chancellor. His office is much more frequently mentioned than it is in previous pontificates,[18] probably an unconscious reflection of the growing importance of that office, which can be seen in the increasing output and professionalism shown in extant documents of

12. Cheney, *English Bishops' Chanceries*, p. 17; *P.R. 7 Ric. I*, p. xxj. West, *Justiciarship*, pp. 165-166, discusses the later career of Godfrey de Insula, but he is not aware of the earlier career in the archbishop's household.

13. *P.R. 8 Ric. I*, pp. 93, 138 and following years.

14. *P.R. 4 John*, p. 85.

15. Cheney, *English Bishops' Chanceries*, pp. 18-19. West, *Justiciarship*, pp. 122-123, describes Geoffrey de Bocland's later career.

16. *Curia Regis Rolls*, I, 281; IV, 15.

17. Major, "The 'Familia,'" p. 531.

18. Cheney, *English Bishops' Chanceries*, p. 35.

the archbishop. About Elias of Dereham, who filled the office of steward, more will be said later.[19] The question of chaplains is complicated by the use of *capellanus* in the broad sense of "priest" as well as in its more specific meaning, and by vague statements such as Gerald of Wales's comment that Gilbert, bishop of Rochester, was a chaplain of Archbishop Hubert.[20] Of the chaplains in his household, one is known only because of a misfortune that brought him into a royal court in 1198. Chaplain William laid claim to a horse that had been sold by a certain Lucas after one of the chaplain's boys had been killed when riding on this horse near the town of Stanes.[21] Undoubtedly Archbishop Hubert had servants in the other jobs mentioned in Theobald's charter, but the names of those who held them do not happen to occur in his extant *acta*. However, a physician may also have been part of his household since Jordan the physician witnessed a number of his acts and two other men who were physicians are at other times mentioned in connection with the archbishop. When the archbishop was abroad in 1202, Simon of Southwell served as his *officialis,* remaining in England, where he issued letters in the name of the archbishop and with his seal.[22]

Although references to the archbishop's clerks are to some extent dependent upon the accidental survival of documents, William de Bosco, one of the clerks already mentioned, seems to illustrate the axiom that some people manage to have their names recorded only when they are in trouble. More often than not it was something to do with his family that caused his name to be entered in the legal records. In 1198 his nephew Nicolaus owed a half-mark for disseisin. Three years later, William himself and his brother Robert ran afoul of the forest law and were assessed some three marks. On other occasions he appeared in royal courts pressing claims to land, including an appearance in 1205 as attorney for his mother in her suit for eighty acres.[23] In spite of such legal difficulties, however, his position in the household of the archbishop was a source of

19. A. Hamilton Thompson, "Master Elias of Dereham and the King's Works," *The Archaeological Journal* (London), XCVII (1940), p. 2 thought it likely that Elias was Hubert's steward but could not find evidence for this. Elias is specifically identified as steward in Lambeth Palace Library, MS. 1212, p. 92.

20. Cheney, *English Bishops' Chan-ceries,* p. 9; Giraldus Cambrensis, III, 304.

21. *Curia Regis Rolls,* I, 49.

22. Major, "The 'Familia,'" p. 536; *P.R. 2 John,* p. 132; Giraldus Cambrensis (English translation), p. 147.

23. *P.R. 10 Ric. I,* p. 205; *P.R. 3 John,* p. 30; *Curia Regis Rolls,* I, 315, 375; II, 5; IV, 10.

influence, as a letter to him reminds us. The writer, addressing him as Master William de Bosco, clerk of Lord Hubert, archbishop of Canterbury, asks him to obtain the patronage of the archbishop for his niece and her sons. It seems the lady had married the butler of Glastonbury Abbey and that both expected their son to succeed his father in that post, but the bailiff of the abbey had dismissed the son at the death of his father and put one of his own nominees into the job.[24] Presumably, a man with such strong family ties as William was touched by this appeal and did what he could to help the poor widow, but the letter with its little human drama reminds us that for all their virtual anonymity as mere names on lists of witnesses to the acts of greater men these clerks of the archiepiscopal household were not unimportant in the eyes of their contemporaries. There must have been similar pleas to other clerks which could reveal another side to life in the household that can now only be a subject for conjecture.

Better known and more important than William de Bosco among the clerks of Archbishop Hubert was Master Elias of Dereham, whose later career in architecture brought him some recognition in his own right. The connection with Dereham probably explains why he came to the attention of the archbishop, whose interest in the abbey he founded at West Dereham gave him some continued contact with the place of his birth. Elias' name is found on a number of Hubert's *acta,* and he was one of the executors of the archbishop's will and custodian of the vacant archbishopric from 1205 to 1207 during the dispute over election of a successor. Later he continued as steward for Stephen Langton, was executor of his will in 1228, for the will of Langton's successor two years later, for the bishop of Durham in 1237, and for the bishop of Winchester in 1238. In June 1215 he played a small role in a famous event at Runnymede when he was named as one of the commissioners to distribute copies of Magna Carta.

Elias' connection with master masons and architecture began at Wells, where he may have been general surveyor for the completion of the nave and the west front. His main claim to fame rests upon the tradition that he was the architect of Salisbury Cathedral. The date at which he became a canon at Salisbury is not known, although it is tempting to think he may have been named to a canonry by Hubert Walter. But in 1222 he was

24. Canterbury, D. and C. Mun., Christ    Church Letters, II, -02.

clearly one of the senior canons there and in 1225 was keeper of the fabric fund, as he may have been from its inception in 1220. During the building of Salisbury Cathedral, he also worked for King Henry III on the hall of Winchester Castle in 1233 and on the gatehouse of the castle in 1236, and was keeper of the king's works at Clarendon in 1234. Roger of Wendover says he was one of two men responsible for making the shrine of St. Thomas Becket in Canterbury Cathedral and for handling the technical details of the translation of the body of England's most famous saint; royal records also show him in charge of preparing the tomb of King Henry III's sister in Salisbury Cathedral.[25] In spite of the fact that he is usually said to have been the architect of Salisbury Cathedral, the records would seem to indicate that his work was more administrative and financial than that of a designer. His position appears to have been much like keeper of the works, a title he held officially at Clarendon. His other architectural work was probably also of the same nature, and his title of "master" was the academic one of a clerk, not the practical title of a master mason.[26] His being one of the executors of Archbishop Hubert's will raises the question of whether he was also responsible for Hubert's tomb at Canterbury, but there is no evidence on which to judge.

In gathering such learned men into his household Hubert would seem to have been following the precedent of his predecessors at Canterbury, whose households had been notable as centers of patronage and learning, especially that of Archbishop Theobald (1139-1161).[27] However, closer examination of the type of men who made up these households reveals fundamental differences indicative of the profound changes that had been taking place in ecclesiastical administration since the middle of the century. A trend, of which there was only a hint at the time of Theobald, had completely transformed the archiepiscopal household by the time of Hubert. Men trained in letters, like John of Salisbury, had given place to men whose training was focused on Roman and canon law. To be sure, the third most famous member of Theobald's household (after Thomas Becket and John of Salisbury) was Master Vacarius, who did much to establish the study of canon law in England. Hubert's household, however, had many lawyers and several who were authorities on canon law.[28] This

25. Josiah C. Russell, "The Many-Sided Career of Master Elias of Dereham," *Speculum*, V (1930), p. 379.

26. A. H. Thompson, pp. 2-33.

27. Avrom Saltman, *Theobald Archbishop of Canterbury* (London, 1956), is a recent biography.

28. *Ibid.*, p. 175. See also Vacarius.

trend toward a growing legal element in the archiepiscopal household, so evident at the time of Archbishop Hubert, paralleled the growing interest and expertise in canon law reflected in the number of English decretals in the codes then being formulated with a significant contribution by English canon lawyers.[29]

To some whose career extended throughout the period, such as Peter of Blois, this growing emphasis upon legal professionalism became intolerable. Peter, whose letters show him to have been one of the most accomplished writers of the time, served Archbishop Richard and Archbishop Baldwin. Then for a time after the death of Baldwin, he entered into the household of Queen Eleanor. When she left for Germany in 1194 to meet her son, King Richard, just released from his captivity, Peter stayed in England and for a short time joined the household of Hubert Walter, the new archbishop of Canterbury.[30] Gerald of Wales tells of an incident that is intended to illustrate the ignorance of the archbishop. After hearing Master Peter of Blois preach, Hubert asked:

"Whence, Master, came that store of wisdom with which to-day you have refreshed us, discoursing so admirably concerning the properties of the Three Persons and teaching us so well and clearly that our Lord Jesus Christ is Father, Son and Holy Ghost?" And he with downcast face and full of shame, answered never a word. But this utterance of the Archbishop, spoken in the hearing of many, made some to flush for shame, while in others it wakened unrestrainable laughter and gave occasion for mockery.[31]

Peter's retirement from the uncongenial surroundings of the new model household and the rather pathetic letter in which he expresses continued obedience but pleads illness to justify a two-year absence mark the triumph of a practical and narrowly professional spirit at Canterbury.[32] Yet it was this very professional element in Archbishop Hubert's house-

29. Charles Duggan, *Twelfth-century Decretal Collections and Their Importance in English History* (London, 1963), p. 141.

30. J. Armitage Robinson, "Peter of Blois," *Somerset Historical Essays* (London, 1921), pp. 121, 125-126. Other pertinent writings about Peter are E. S. Cohn, "The Manuscript Evidence for the Letters of Peter of Blois," *English Historical Review*, 41 (1926), pp. 43-60; R. W. Southern, "Some New Letters of Peter of Blois," *ibid.*, 53 (1938), pp. 412-424; and R. W. Southern, *The Making of the Middle Ages* (New Haven, Conn., 1961), pp. 210-217.

31. Giraldus Cambrensis (English translation), pp. 283-284.

32. Peter of Blois, "Epistolae" in J. P. Migne, *Patrologiae cursus completus* (Series latina, 207; Paris, 1904), col. 332.

hold that enabled him to function as archbishop while at the same time bearing a heavy burden of secular responsibility.

One of the problems in maintaining a highly trained household was providing sources of income. This was most often solved by the use of Hubert's influence as archbishop to obtain ecclesiastical benefices for his clerks. For example, he conferred the church of Tarring (West Tarring, Sussex) with its dependent chapel of Patching upon Master Honorius, his clerk learned in the canon law, with the additional proviso that another clerk of the archiepiscopal *familia*, John de Bedingeham, be made vicar at Patching for an annual rent of one mark paid to Honorius.[33] Master Reiner of Stanford held the tithes of some houses for a fixed annual payment to the abbot and monks of Peterborough, the prioress and convent of St. Michael extra Stanford granted two houses to William de Sumercote, and in 1200 the king granted a church that he held because of a vacancy in the office of abbot at Ramsay to Richard de Ringestede.[34] Possibly the influence of the archbishop explains the royal grant of income from land in Cornwall made to Jordan the physician in 1195 and continued throughout the lifetime of the archbishop.[35] Sometimes efforts to secure such preferments failed, as happened in 1201, when the king attempted to present Simon de Camera, who served both king and archbishop, to the church at Faversham and thereby touched off a controversy with the monks of St. Augustine's, Canterbury, who finally managed to block the move by an appeal to Rome.[36] The following year Archbishop Hubert petitioned the king to give Simon custody of royal houses in Westminster, of Flete Prison, and of the son and heir of Robert of Leveland, who was preparing to go on a crusade.[37] The lifetime tenure of William de Calna in the church of Elmstead (Kent) was carefully protected when the archbishop transferred this church to the small house of St. Gregory at Canterbury.[38]

33. Canterbury, D. and C. Mun., Chartae Antiquae, P50. Tarring was one of the eight deaneries in the immediate jurisdiction of the archbishop. See Irene J. Churchill, *Canterbury Administration: The Administrative Machinery of the Archbishopric of Canterbury Illustrated from the Original Records* (London, 1933), I, 62-64.

34. Peterborough, D. and C. Mun., MS. 1, f. 105; P.R.O. Exchequer, Augmentation Office, Miscellaneous Books, 35/1; *Rotuli chartarum*, I, Pt. 1, 43b.

35. *P.R. 7 Ric. I*, p. 132 and following years.

36. Eric John, "The Litigation of an Exempt House, St. Augustine's, Canterbury, 1182-1237," *Bulletin of the John Rylands Library*, 39 (1956-7), p. 401.

37. *Rotuli de liberate ac de misis et praestitis, regnante Johanne*, ed. Thomas D. Hardy (London, 1844), p. 26.

38. Cambridge University Library, MS. LL. #15, f. 7.

At Canterbury this problem of making suitable provision for the professional element in the archbishop's *familia* was complicated by the monastic organization of the cathedral chapter and by the position of the archbishop as abbot over the monks of Christ Church. Bishops whose chapters were made up of secular clerks and who thus controlled a number of prebends were in a much more favorable position to meet the growing need for a more professional body to carry on the business of the see. The attempt of Archbishop Baldwin to establish a collegiate church at Hackington staffed by secular canons was in accord with developments within the English church and might in part have provided a solution to the problem posed by the limited value of monks as administrators. But the monks of Christ Church had seen in that move a fatal threat to their prestige and had opposed such a plan with all the force they could muster. The resulting controversy has been mentioned earlier in connection with the involvement of Hubert Walter in the efforts of Glanvill and, later, of King Richard to bring about a settlement. Victory had come for the monks against Archbishop Baldwin with a papal mandate requiring him to destroy the buildings he had begun at Hackington, and his death on the Third Crusade had seemed to mark the end of his project for all time.

Yet, in spite of the trouble that had arisen in Archbishop Baldwin's time, Archbishop Hubert in 1196 revived his predecessor's plan. In taking this step, he ignored the advice of Hugh, bishop of Lincoln, who repeated the warning that he had earlier given Archbishop Baldwin. Such a plan, he said, would cause trouble with his monks, force the archbishop to use royal authority to support the plan, and expose him to the greed and political maneuvers of the Roman *curia,* a threefold prediction that could serve as a capsule summary of the developments that followed.[39] As Dom David Knowles has commented, "it is difficult . . . to comprehend why a man of such great practical wisdom should have so deliberately revived a proposal which had already caused such bitter and unprofitable strife."[40]

The difficulty arises chiefly because we expect a man with Hubert Walter's background to act always in a calculated and "practical" manner. It is true that while he was trying to decide whether to renew the building effort, the bishops and clerks urged him to do so because such a move would weaken the monks, who were their ecclesiastical rivals. Moreover, there was some practical benefit in the plan, for at least one of his *familia*

---

39. *Magna vita*, I, 122-123.     40. Knowles, p. 326.

—Simon, archdeacon of Wells—was installed as rector of one of the churches appropriated to the new church at Lambeth.[41] But his own conciliatory approach to the monks—he had proposed the foundation of a church at Maidstone when they objected to the building that had been started by Baldwin at Lambeth—is an indication that he had no inflexible political objective in mind. At least three times Hubert made proposals that would have secured the monks of Christ Church against any damage from the new foundation, but these were summarily rejected. His persistence, even after the final adverse decision of the pope, in trying to build an entirely new church dedicated to St. Stephen and St. Thomas with whatever safeguards the pope should specify is further indication that he did not have political motives in mind.[42]

What, then, were his real motives? Gervase of Canterbury, who strongly supported his fellow monks in the quarrel with the archbishop, reports Hubert's answer to a monk who asked him why he intended to revive Baldwin's plan. Hubert explained to his interrogator that he found it hard to oppose the monks who had called him to become archbishop but that he likewise found it shameful to leave a work like that started by Baldwin unfinished; he would pray for divine guidance in making his decision in the matter.[43] This answer should be taken at face value. If we find it difficult to believe that Hubert may have acted from religious motives, we should nevertheless remember that he had close ties with Archbishop Baldwin, whose hope it had been to build a chapel dedicated to St. Thomas Becket, and that Hubert had served as executor for the last will of his friend when he died on the crusade. The circumstances suggest that Hubert was acting in this instance from rather nobler motives than those of political expediency.

Even though some allowance must be made for the fact that most of the evidence concerning the renewed struggle between monks and archbishop comes from sources favorable to the monks, it is evident that once Archbishop Hubert had decided to proceed he used all the means of persuasion available to him to secure papal and royal support for his plan. First, he obtained authorization from Pope Celestine III to proceed with the buildings at Lambeth, a permission given in a papal letter of June 9, 1197, which carefully provided that the church should not interfere with

---

41. Gervase of Canterbury, I, 534-537. Stubbs, *Epistolae Cantuarienses*, p. 513.

42. Stubbs, *Epistolae Cantuarienses*, p. 491.

43. Gervase of Canterbury, I, 543.

the rights of Canterbury, especially in regard to ordinations.[44] Land for the new church was secured in 1197 by an exchange of the archbishop's manor and church at Darenth for the manor and church of Lambeth, which belonged to the monks of Rochester.[45] When he returned from Normandy on November 3, 1197, Archbishop Hubert took up his plan in earnest, but at the same time he offered security to the monks of Christ Church that no damage should come to them from this work.[46]

The monks remained adamant in their opposition and wrote Pope Celestine III for his support, reporting to him that the archbishop had proceeded with his organization at Lambeth by naming a dean, a provost, and forty canons chosen from noble families, rich men, or relatives of the king or the pope, and by supporting them from revenues that belonged to the church of Canterbury. Other canons were selected from men involved in administration at the Exchequer or in the households of various bishops. In an obvious attempt to frighten the pope into taking action against the new foundation, the monks further charged that this organization would place the bishops in the status of cardinals and make the archbishop into an English pope.[47]

After these preliminaries, both sides sent representatives to Rome to pursue the contest, those of the archbishop bearing many gifts by which they hoped to obtain a favorable hearing, according to charges made by their opponents. At home, the archbishop visited Canterbury in March 1198 and excommunicated the two monks who had gone secretly to represent the monastery at Rome on the ground that they had not obtained his consent to leave their monastery.[48] Nevertheless, the first real battle was won by the monks, who persuaded the new pope, Innocent III, to issue a mandate in their favor on April 24, 1198. On June 9 the arch-

44. Stubbs, *Epistolae Cantuarienses,* pp. 371-372.

45. Rochester, D. and C. Mun., Title Deeds B 307 a-c, on deposit in the Kent County Archives, Maidstone, with reference DRc T60/1-3; Registrum temporalium, fos. 124 v, 125, also on deposit; John Thorpe, *Registrum Roffense* (London, 1769), I, 270-272; Lambeth Palace Library, Carte Miscellane, XI, 17-18, 21-22; Lambeth MS. 1212, pp. 135-137; *Rotuli chartarum,* I, Pt. 1, 68 a-b; B.M., Cott. MS., Vespasian A. XXII, f. 64 v.

46. Gervase of Canterbury, I, 545.

47. Stubbs, *Epistolae Cantuarienses,* p. 380. Some original documents that have survived show that only minor variants have crept into the compilation made by the monks and printed by Stubbs, thus insuring the general accuracy of the transcription: Canterbury, D. and C. Mun., Chartae Antiquae, H102 (equals Stubbs p. 340), H 103 (Stubbs, p. 339), L 133 (Stubbs, p. 514), L 134 (Stubbs, p. 514), L 135 (Stubbs, p. 497), L 138 (Stubbs, p. 496). L 129a gives evidence on the dispute, but is badly decayed.

48. Gervase of Canterbury, I, 550-551.

bishop accepted the papal command to annul everything that had been done at Lambeth: the buildings had to be torn down, the clergy suspended, any property taken from the monks during the dispute restored, and all sentences of excommunication annulled. All aggressors against the property or rents of the monks were ordered to be excommunicated.[49]

At this point, King Richard once again intervened as he had in the time of Archbishop Baldwin, but this time in complete support of the archbishop, rather than as a mediator. Having failed in his ecclesiastical position, the archbishop was using his special position at the court to call in royal support for his cause. On June 14, King Richard ordered the monks to desist from their efforts at Rome and to support the archbishop. At the same time, he took the new church at Lambeth under his royal protection and ordered the suffragan bishops of Canterbury not to obey the papal order, which he believed came from a pope not properly informed of the situation. In a letter to the pope on the next day he renewed the request for approval of the new foundation, pointing out that the law of England gave the archbishop the right to build a chapel on his own land, just as the king and the nobles had such a right.[50]

Demonstrating his political experience, Archbishop Hubert followed up the royal intervention by securing letters to the pope from the English bishops and abbots who favored his case—the letter from the Cistercian abbots being especially strong in its praise of the archbishop—and having these letters sent along with relics of English saints as gifts to the pope. When the monks refused further conciliatory moves from the archbishop and would not accept mediation, the king ordered his agents to seize the possessions of the monastery, but the archbishop, when he heard that the justices had made the seizure, persuaded the king that such a course would be offensive to the pope and harmful to their cause. Early in November, the archbishop went to the monks with the assertion that he had returned good for evil in persuading the king to restore their manors and properties and made a final attempt to persuade them to come to an agreement, pointing out that their quarrel caused evil to them and to the whole church in England and promising to show great kindness to them in the future if they would agree to his proposal.[51]

49. Stubbs, *Epistolae Cantuarienses*, pp. 391-393.

50. *Ibid.*, pp. 403, 405-406; Gervase of Canterbury, I, 557-558.

51. Gervase of Canterbury, I, 559-561, 566-571, 574; Stubbs, pp. 423, 437, 439-440, 445-447.

Shortly thereafter, on November 20, 1198, the final papal decision in the case was made and on January 2 Archbishop Hubert received the mandate containing the order that the chapel at Lambeth was to be destroyed.[52] Although the archbishop accepted the order with good grace, many among the secular clergy would have agreed with the bitter comment of Ralph de Diceto: "There was given to Peter the power of building, the power of multiplying, and the power of transferring sees, but by what law, by what canon or indulgent permission a sacred place may be destroyed must be left to His judgment who gave the power of building."[53]

There was considerably more trouble over other differences between the monks and the archbishop which were submitted to arbitration by a panel of bishops and abbots. It does not seem necessary to review the rather petty details of this struggle, which continued up to the moment when the arbiters gave their final award on November 6, 1200. This award modified the papal decision by allowing the archbishop to build a church at Lambeth for Premonstratensian canons, but this permission was never acted upon. One of the copies of this award preserved at Canterbury is in its outward appearance the most impressive of all the manuscripts that survive from the controversy; it is especially noteworthy for the seals of Archbishop Hubert and many of the arbiters which remain intact.[54]

Gervase of Canterbury relates that at the conclusion of the long quarrel Archbishop Hubert spoke to the monks with such good grace that he persuaded them that in the future no dispute should come between them that could not be settled by arbitration. After this, according to Gervase, there was so much love between the archbishop and the monks that it was as if by the grace of God their heart and souls were one.[55] Curiously, one of the minor incidents in this extended controversy, the acquisition of Lambeth manor and church by Archbishop Hubert, has left the most lasting legacy, and Lambeth Palace as the residence of the archbishops of Canterbury has to some extent overshadowed Canterbury, although not precisely in the sense feared by the monks of Christ Church in 1197.

52. Canterbury, D. and C. Mun., Register A, fos. 57-59; Gervase of Canterbury, I, 576-584; Stubbs, *Epistolae Cantuarienses*, pp. 463-468.

53. Ralph de Diceto, II, 165.

54. Chartae Antiquae, L 130. Other references bearing on this arbitration are A 5, C 175, L 131, L 132, L 136, L 137; Stubbs, *Epistolae Cantuarienses*, pp. 512-514, 517; and Cheney, *From Becket to Langton*, pp. 73-74.

55. Gervase of Canterbury, II, 409-410, 412.

# 5 SHEPHERD OF HIS FLOCK

Those who have written about the ecclesiastical history of England in the twelfth century have usually given their attention to a few famous controversies, such as the Becket affair or the dispute between Archbishops Baldwin and Hubert and the monks of Christ Church. A few notorious controversies, however, are hardly representative of developments within the church in this period.[1] Certainly Hubert Walter as archbishop of Canterbury had far wider jurisdiction and far more important responsibilities than those involved in his relation with the monks of Christ Church, even if for the present we omit consideration of the secular responsibilities he had as justiciar under King Richard and as chancellor under King John. In fact, so widespread were his ecclesiastical activities that there is often some difficulty in determining by what authority Archbishop Hubert was proceeding in a particular instance—as diocesan, metropolitan, or papal legate. To these purely ecclesiastical responsibilities was added the administration of the archiepiscopal lands and properties, which were as extensive as those of most barons.

In 1166 the archbishopric had been returned as owing the service of 84¾ knights, and this number remained the same in the survey of 1212 shortly after Hubert's pontificate. Most of the fees were concentrated in Kent, but there was one fee in Buckinghamshire, two in Suffolk, two and three-fourths in Middlesex, and other smaller holdings in Surrey and Suffolk. In 1212 these fees were shared among 106 persons who held of the archbishop.[2] By comparison, King John had 123 fees in Kent, but the royal fees were much less subdivided than those of the archbishop, with only one holding of less than a full knight's service and the total number of royal fees in Kent in the hands of only twenty-three persons.[3] The same inquisition shows that the total lands of the archbishop were greater than those of any other ecclesiastical tenant. They may be compared with the holdings of an earl, being almost the same as the number of fees held by the earl of Arundel, greater than those of earl Warenne, and not

1. An admirable exception to this approach is provided in Cheney, *From Becket to Langton.*

2. Chew, p. 19; *Red Book of the Exchequer,* II, 469-473, 724-727. A good account of the lands of the medieval archbishop may be found in F. R. H. Du Boulay, *The Lordship of Canterbury* (London, 1966).

3. *Red Book,* pp. 474-475.

many fewer than those of the earl of Clare. To these surveys that show the important feudal position of the archbishop of Canterbury may be added a record of the value of the Canterbury temporalities as reported to the Exchequer during the vacancy after Archbishop Hubert's death when royal custodians accounted for the period from June 24, 1205, to May 30, 1207. When the thousand marks that the custodians had received from the treasury is deducted and the total for the period divided by two to obtain an approximate figure for one year, the report shows an annual income from the temporalities of approximately £2,250.[4] This may be compared with the vacant bishopric of Lincoln, where the sum of just over £1,838 was entered for the year 1206-1207, although some sums included in that figure were collected in a period slightly longer than a year. Similarly the income from the bishopric of Exeter was just over £655 in that year.[5]

One fact that immediately stands out about Hubert is that he was particularly careful in the management of these lands and other property. When he first took over the responsibility of the archbishopric, he secured letters of protection from King Richard for the property and liberties of Canterbury, a routine but necessary precaution for any archbishop to take; later, he obtained the same guarantees from King John.[6] The scattered figures for income from the temporalities of Canterbury during periods when they were in royal hands also show that there had been an increase in annual income by the time Archbishop Hubert died. In 1171 the king received £1,172 19d. for three-fourths of a year, and the following year the account shows an income of £9 7s. 3d. from the old farm and £1,558 7d. from the new farm with some amounts still outstanding.[7] Closer to the time of Hubert Walter—in 1184—the custodians rendered account of £1,135 17s. 6d. for farm of the manors, £11 5s. 6d. for rent of mills, and £68 16s. 2d. for pleas and other sources.[8] Since these figures are recorded at such irregular intervals and since they may have been influenced by exceptional conditions during the short period of any one account, they should not be overemphasized. Nevertheless, it seems fair to conclude that the increase from something over £1,200 in 1184 to an annual income of about £2,250 at Hubert's death provides con-

---

4. *P.R. 8 John*, pp. xi, 54.
5. *P.R. 9 John*, pp. xxi, 13, 222.
6. Lambeth Palace Library, MS. 1212, pp. 38, 55, 56; Canterbury, D. and C.
Mun., Chartae Antiquae, C 30, C 1305.
7. *P.R. 17 Hen. II*, pp. 142-143; *P.R. 18 Hen. II*, pp. 139-140.
8. *P.R. 30 Hen. II*, p. 151.

firmation for general statements that Hubert built up the properties of Canterbury.

Although they are not particularly significant in themselves, some transactions may be cited which show something of the detail by which Archbishop Hubert proceeded in his successful efforts to increase the temporal income of the archbishopric. A subordinate part of the dispute with the monks of Christ Church involved monastic lands seized by the archbishops during the controversy. This gain was only temporary, however; for when agreement was reached, these lands were returned with the exception of two churches that seem to have escaped the notice of all participants, remaining among the holdings of the archbishops until they were belatedly restored to the monks in 1365.[9] Still, the controversy had lasting effects upon the management of the lands of the archbishop. For example, in 1199 the monks complained to the pope that Hubert had sent his officials to seize the marsh of Appledore, which they claimed had been attached to their manor by custom, a point left to be determined by a local jury in the final arbitration award.[10] And the charter recording an exchange of woods for all the lands in the marsh held by the prior and monks of Dover was probably part of Hubert's efforts to clarify and consolidate lands in that area.[11] Similarly, we find Archbishop Hubert, after he had obtained Lambeth, making agreements that added to the value of that manor: he acquired houses located next to the Thames in London which had formerly been used by the archdeacon of Rochester for his town house but then belonged to Boxley Abbey, and he added some reclaimed land along the river to his holdings in the area.[12] It is ironic to find the monks of Christ Church being given possession of land in Southwark by a man who held that land from the archbishop, making them responsible for paying rent to the archbishop as well as the mediate tenant for property in the vicinity of the nascent chapel at Lambeth over which they had so long disputed.[13]

In 1199 King John granted the archbishop license to hold a fair at Lambeth, but the citizens of London were afraid their interests might be damaged and were able to have the terms of the grant changed in a

9. Historical Manuscripts Commission, *Fifth Report* (London, 1876), Appendix, p. 440.

10. Stubbs, *Epistolae Cantuarienses*, pp. 490, 513-514.

11. Lambeth Palace Library, MS. 241, f. 175.

12. *Ibid.*, MS. 1212, pp. 207-209.

13. Canterbury, D. and C. Mun., Chartae Antiquae, S 302, S 303.

manner satisfactory to all concerned.[14] Archbishop Hubert's interest in such matters had already resulted in a license for a weekly market for his manor at Maidstone in 1195, and in 1201 he gave King John four palfreys for the privilege of holding a ten-day fair at Northfleet, an area within the archbishop's personal jurisdiction.[15] In 1194 King Richard granted him a tenth of all the silver mined in Careghofa in Shropshire, and one of his clerks was soon busily at work reopening the mines and strengthening the castle there to protect the workings. Soon coins were being minted at Shrewsbury from the new silver, with profits presumably coming to the coffers of the archbishop from this source.[16]

Such activities in strengthening the property of the archbishopric were pronounced enough to warrant a comment by Gervase of Canterbury in his brief sketch of Hubert's pontificate. He notes that after the accession of King John, the archbishop recovered the estates of Canterbury that had been alienated: Saltwood Castle, Hythe, Rochester Castle, the fief of Geoffrey de Ros of five knights, the homage of the Earl of Clare for Tonbridge Castle, and others.[17] When we consider the fact that some of these represent old claims and disputes in which even Archbishop Thomas Becket had failed, the accomplishment of Archbishop Hubert is placed in a more meaningful perspective. One factor in his success was that he got royal co-operation. In one instance King John sent an order to his justices to give any help the archbishop might request when he sought the testimony of free and legal men in the areas involved in his attempt to recall parts of his demesne that had been alienated unjustly.[18] This close relation with the monarchy also resulted in the renewal of the right held by the archbishop's predecessors to receive any amercements made by royal justices against any of the men who were of the Canterbury fief. This privilege was to be entered in the records of the Exchequer so that the men could be exempted from payment there. How this worked in practice is illustrated by the Pipe Rolls for 1196 and 1197, which list amercements of more than twenty-five marks against the men of the archbishop for various kinds of offenses as adjudged before the itinerant

14. Lambeth Palace Library, MS. 1212, p. 91; Carte Miscellane, XI, 15; *Memoranda Roll 1 John*, p. xlv.

15. Lambeth Palace Library, MS. 1212, pp. 38, 45, 194, 198; *Rotuli de oblatis et finibus . . . tempore regis Johannis*, ed. Thomas D. Hardy (Rec. Comm., London, 1835), p. 126.

16. Lambeth Palace Library, MS. 1212, p. 35; *P.R. 6 Ric. I*, p. xxxiv.

17. Gervase of Canterbury, II, 409, 411.

18. Lambeth Palace Library, MS. 1212, pp. 49, 201; *Rotuli litterarum patentium*, ed. Thomas D. Hardy (Rec. Comm., London, 1835), p. 6a.

justices. The sheriff of Kent duly reported the sums involved but noted that they remained unpaid because the archbishop had claimed he was entitled to these sums by virtue of the liberty of Canterbury.[19]

Saltwood, one of the properties mentioned by Gervase, had been a fief held by Henry of Essex from the archbishop of Canterbury until Henry had been convicted of a felony for deserting King Henry II in his campaign in North Wales in 1157. The king had seized the fief into his hands, and in spite of the efforts of the archbishops it had remained in royal possession until Hubert persuaded King Richard to return it in 1197. Upon Richard's death, King John confirmed his brother's charter, a move that reflects Archbishop Hubert's shrewd estimate that a fief held in royal hands for such a long period and only recently returned to him would hardly be safe from the ambitions of a new king unless the king himself had been persuaded to confirm the restoration.[20] In another move affecting Saltwood, Hugo de Montfort pledged not to alienate any of the land he held from the archbishop there; on another occasion he sold his rights over land in Saltwood to the archbishop for fifty marks of silver.[21] Although the sequence of these charters and their exact significance is obscured by the fact that private charters in the twelfth century usually were not dated, the general picture of the archbishop working to consolidate his control of properties returned to him in the area around Saltwood emerges clearly enough.

King John's order that Rochester Castle was to be put into the custody of the archbishop is dated July 20, 1202, but Hubert had already accounted at the Exchequer for the farm of the city of Rochester for a half year in 1200 (which perhaps extended into the early part of 1201).[22] Possibly the privilege of farming Rochester was a temporary measure until the king could arrange for the archbishop to get custody of the castle, but the account given in the Pipe Roll as usual gives no explanation as to why Hubert should have acted in place of the sheriff for that period of time. If we assume that the fief of William de Ros is the same as that mentioned by Gervase as belonging to Geoffrey de Ros, an assumption made probable

---

19. Lambeth Palace Library, MS. 1212, p. 202; *P.R. 8 Ric. I*, p. 286; *P.R. 9 Ric. I*, pp. 29, 32.

20. Lambeth Palace Library, MS. 1212, pp. 34, 43, 194, 218; *Rotuli chartarum*, I, Pt. 1, 23a.

21. Canterbury, D. and C. Mun., Chartae Antiquae, S 352; Lambeth Palace Library, MS. 1212, p. 76. Another reference to the restoration of Saltwood is found in Windsor, St. George's Chapel, D. and C. Mun., XI. G.39.

22. *Rotuli litterarum clausarum*, ed. Thomas D. Hardy (Rec. Comm., London, 1833), I, 14b; *P.R. 2 John*, p. 211.

because William is mentioned as a minor heir, some details of the process by which the archbishop reclaimed the fief are also available in surviving records. Claims to this fief made on behalf of the king and on behalf of the archbishop were brought before an inquisition in a royal court in 1200 and then transferred to the court of the archbishop as being within his jurisdiction. Later, King John confirmed the right of the archbishop to the fief, and the archbishop named Peter de Stokes as custodian during the minority of the heir.[23] Since this same Peter was one of the witnesses to the king's charter and a year later was a steward of the royal household, the custody of the fief may have been part of the bargain struck between the king and the archbishop.

For fifteen marks of silver Archbishop Hubert added lands in Pagham, Sussex, to those already belonging to the see. In the same area he also exchanged a messuage in the city of Chichester for land in Pagham. Altogether, he seems to have had a shrewd business sense in building up the property of the see. He did not lose such opportunities as the one presented when William Parnel had to convert some of his land into cash. The deal was closed with Parnel's statement that "for this concession and confirmation and because of my urgent need the aforementioned Hubert gave me fifty marks of silver and a palfrey."[24] A charter of Henry de la Pomerai to Archbishop Hubert is interesting both for the persons involved and the complicated financial arrangement. Henry's father, who had held St. Michael's Mount for Count John during his revolt against King Richard, died just before the siege ended with surrender of the island to Hubert Walter as representative of King Richard. For the land being transferred in this charter Archbishop Hubert agreed to pay £200 Angevin to acquit a debt Henry owed the king for having his inheritance in Normandy.[25] Among the other surviving charters granting land or privileges to the arch-

23. Lambeth Palace Library, Carte Miscellane, XI, 12; XI, 16; MS. 1212, p. 91; *Curia Regis Rolls*, I, 215. The fief might have been known as that of Geoffrey de Ros either from the Domesday tenant of that name or the second Geoffrey of the early twelfth century mentioned in the Pipe Roll of 1130. The next member of the family was William, who died in 1190 leaving a son also named William. The latter would be the minor heir named in this case, for he does not seem to have come of age until 1211. See I. J. Sanders, *English Baronies* (Oxford, 1960), pp. 105-106. Peter de Stokes became a household steward in 1201, according to F. M. Powicke and E. B. Fryde, *Handbook of British Chronology* (2nd ed., London, 1961), p. 73.

24. Lambeth Palace Library, MS. 1212, pp. 22, 49, 75, 91-92, 112, 204.

25. *Ibid.*, pp. 98-99; Canterbury, D. and C. Mun., Register B, f. 392 v.; Edward Powley, *The House of de la Pomerai* (London, 1944), pp. 19, 23.

bishop are several made by King John, including a renewal of his father's gift of the priory of St. Martin in Dover, which, according to John's charter, was done for the benefit of the souls of his father and his brother Richard.[26] Somehow this pious purpose seems completely incongruous when one considers how John treated both these men when they were alive. On another occasion King John authorized Hubert to convert lands held of him in gavelkind to military fiefs. However, not all arrangements between king and archbishop favored the latter, for the king got Hubert to grant William Marshal a half-knight's fee for an annual rent of 100s.[27]

Most of the other economic activities of Archbishop Hubert can be glimpsed only through chance references. An early thirteenth-century charter refers to land that Archbishop Hubert had made into a park, probably by enclosing it, near Burstow in Surrey.[28] In 1201 the archbishop obtained the privilege of buying hawks and falcons wherever in England he might find them for sale, and in 1205 he had a letter giving royal protection for ships he sent to Cologne to get wine.[29] Gervase of Canterbury gives Hubert credit for the erection of splendid buildings not only in Canterbury but also in the various archiepiscopal manors and for carrying out a large number of repairs and reconstruction of other buildings.[30] The documentation for one of Hubert's economic activities is somewhat fuller. In 1199, King John confirmed the privilege that King Richard had restored to Baldwin of having a mint at Canterbury with three moneyers to work there. Shortly thereafter the right to operate an exchange was added to the privilege of operating the mint, and, later, Archbishop Hubert accounted at the Exchequer for some funds in connection with this exchange. The exceptional nature of this latter privilege is shown in the terms of a general monetary reform that was instituted in January 1205. At that time coins could be exchanged only at the royal exchange or that belonging to the archbishop of Canterbury.[31]

When the activities of Archbishop Hubert in building up the lands and privileges of Canterbury are considered, it is small wonder that some of his contemporaries called him avaricious. True, not much credence can be given the more detailed charges hurled against him by Gerald of Wales

26. Lambeth Palace Library, MS. 241, fos. 6 r-v; 8 r-v.

27. *Ibid.*, MS. 1212, pp. 19, 48, 195.

28. B.M., Additional Charter, 7620.

29. *Rotuli chartarum*, I, Pt. 1, 102b; *Rotuli litterarum patentium*, p. 51b.

30. Gervase of Canterbury, II, 412.

31. Lambeth Palace Library, MS. 1212, pp. 44, 45, 202, 203; *Rotuli chartarum*, I, Pt. 1, 24a-24b; *Rotuli de oblatis et finibus*, p. 239; *P.R. 5 John*, pp. 10, 25; *P.R. 7 John*, pp. xxvij-xxix, xxxi.

in his venomous work entitled *De Invectionibus*, but there may be some significance to the fact that almost half the specific charges have to do with his greed for money. Contemporaries with some vague knowledge of the archbishop's zeal for increasing the holdings of Canterbury may have believed Gerald when he said that the archbishop had proclaimed himself the sole person allowed to buy and sell grain in the lands belonging to Canterbury in order that he might buy cheap and sell dear, that he sent merchant ships with grain to areas of famine in order to get extortionate prices, that he used inside information to buy arms all over England in order to sell them at a huge profit when a royal order was issued for everyone to procure arms, that he made loans through Jewish agents, and that his every ecclesiastical promotion smelled of simony.[32] Today there is no way of investigating some of the charges, and since other charges from the same list can be shown to twist the facts or to be completely false—some were later retracted by Gerald himself—there seems little point in paying much attention to the detailed charges. Furthermore, it might be said that Hubert's activity is simply characteristic of a man who threw himself into any job and that building up the property of the church should be considered a meritorious action in any event. Nevertheless, there is something incompatible about the hard, businesslike, and somewhat ruthless way in which he acquired land and wealth for his diocese and the spiritual leadership implicit in his position as an archbishop. Worldly success and saintliness rarely coexist in the same person. Canterbury had already had its saint earlier in the century, and Archbishop Hubert was not the man to follow in that path.

Even so, the scattered evidence that remains of his activities in his diocese of Canterbury and the more complete information about his work in the province prohibit the opposite conclusion that he neglected his duties as archbishop because of his involvement in secular responsibilities. It is often difficult to determine by what authority Archbishop Hubert was proceeding in a particular instance—as diocesan, metropolitan, or papal legate—and there is little hope that the modern scholar will be entirely successful in solving this problem when Hubert's contemporaries sometimes were confused; but for the sake of clarity there is some advantage in discussing his relationship with his subordinates and his activity in each sphere separately, beginning with his basic responsibility over the diocese of Canterbury.

32. Giraldus Cambrensis, III, 38.

There is almost no evidence about Archbishop Hubert's performance of the routine ecclesiastical functions of a bishop, such as preaching, ordination, and confirmation. Presumably he fulfilled his duties in this respect or arranged to delegate some of the work to other bishops. In the next century, when more evidence is available, preaching and confirmation were neglected or given very little emphasis, and these are not the kinds of activity that would have been mentioned by contemporaries in the twelfth century unless something very unusual was involved. Such exceptional notice did occur when Archbishop Hubert violated canon law by ordaining a clerk as a deacon without giving him title to a specific benefice. A letter from Pope Innocent III, which was necessary to correct the error, decreed that if the clerk were found suitable for the position by a committee of papal delegates in England, the archbishop was to secure a suitable benefice for him.[33]

Another aspect of Archbishop Hubert's responsibility in his diocese, as judge ordinary for ecclesiastical cases either in the diocese or in the few exempt parishes over which he had immediate jurisdiction, is better documented. Of course, he also presided over ecclesiastical cases under his metropolitan and legatine authority. There is some indication that even contemporaries were not always clear as to which authority was involved, but the difficulties more often arise for us in the cases where no dispute occurred and the archbishop never bothered to spell out the basis for his authority.[34] Many cases that came to his court raised the question of presentations to churches, because such presentations could only become effective when the clerk named by the patron of a church had been confirmed by the bishop of the diocese in which the church lay.[35]

A rather unusual situation developed when the church of Northfleet, near Gravesend on the Thames, fell vacant at the death of the incumbent in 1200. The monks of Rochester presented Adam, rector of Dartford, to the church and sought confirmation from the archbishop. However, Hubert, believing the church was in his own patronage, had already con-

33. Canterbury, D. and C. Mun., Chartae Antiquae, A 191. Printed in Cheney and Semple, p. 35. The principle that ordinations should not be made without a specific benefice was embodied in the decrees of the Third Lateran Council in 1179 and was being enforced by Pope Innocent III in areas outside England also. See Innocent III,

*Opera Omnia* in J. P. Migne, *Patrologiae . . series latina* (Paris, 1844-65), vol. 214, 68.

34. Churchill, I, 6.

35. J. W. Gray, "The Ius Praesentandi in England from the Constitutions of Clarendon to Bracton," *The English Historical Review*, 67 (1952), p. 491.

ferred it upon Stephen Ridel, a clerk in royal service, thus raising the question of the right to present to this church. After an examination of the charters of his predecessors, the archbishop determined that the right belonged to the monks and conceded the church to them, at the same time confirming their rights in a number of other churches.[36]

Evidence for the appropriation of tithes and other income from churches to support monasteries, a process that had reached the proportions of a general trend in the later twelfth century, can be found among the records of Hubert's pontificate. He approved the gift of the church of Eastchurch to the monks of Dover by its patron King Richard I, the appropriation of the tithes and annual payments from the church of Acrise to Leeds Priory, the grant of the church of Postling to the canons of St. Radegund at Bradsole, and other gifts of this type.[37] Part of the routine business of an archbishop and his clerks was to examine and confirm grants made by his predecessors. Thus, Archbishop Theobald's grants of a church and demesne tithes to the canons of South Malling and of tithes to Leeds Priory were confirmed.[38] Sometimes, in approving appropriations of churches, Archbishop Hubert seems to have played a more active role, as is illustrated by a charter of Hamo de Valoignes, who gave Leeds Priory an annual rent from a church because he had been warned by the archbishop that he should do something for the safety of his soul and the souls of his ancestors.[39]

Ecclesiastical cases before the court of the archbishop involved similar questions about rights of patronage and rights to income from particular churches. When Hubert ordered the dean of Bocking, an area under his immediate jurisdiction, to notify two parishes to prepare for visitation by the archbishop, proctors who represented the bishop of Rochester objected that Hubert should not visit these particular parishes except by metropolitan right because they belonged to the see of Rochester. They produced charters in support of this claim, and the archbishop after in-

36. Rochester, D. and C. Mun., Title Deeds, B 1309, B 131 on deposit in Kent County Archives (Reference T 53/9-10); Thorpe, I, 505-506.

37. Cambridge University Library, Register of Prior Henry de Eastry, fos. 7, 24, 32, 152 v. For a general discussion, see Giles Constable, *Monastic Tithes from the Origins to the Twelfth Century* (Cambridge, 1964), pp. 99 ff.

38. Canterbury, D. and C. Mun.,

Chartae Antiquae, L 376; Lambeth Palace Library, Carte Miscellane, V, 97, XI, 45; Register Warham, f. 97; P.R.O., The Treasury of the Receipt, 15418; Kent County Archives, Cartulary of Leeds Priory, fos. 7-8; *Calendar of the Charter Rolls*, V, 201.

39. Cambridge University Library, Register of Prior Henry de Eastry, f. 153.

specting the charters decided that the claim dating back to the time of Archbishop Lanfranc was valid.[40] Visitation was one of the first duties of a conscientious bishop, for it provided the principal means by which the church on a local parish level was kept free from scandal and the parish priests encouraged to do a competent job. Consequently, it is valuable to have even this indirect reference to Hubert's efforts in regard to visitation because episcopal registers and other records which in the next century begin to make it possible to follow the efforts of bishops in regard to visitation or, on the contrary, their neglect of this responsibility are completely absent for the earlier period. This case also provides an insight into the operation of the archbishop's household. That he arrived at his decision only after consultation with his chapter and men learned in the law substantiates the natural assumption that the *magistri* of his household were used in reaching decisions in his court.

The execution of such decisions normally fell to the archdeacon of Canterbury, who was the chief administrative official of the diocese. In addition to being the agent of the archbishop, the archdeacon had broad jurisdiction in which he was more or less independent. This was sometimes responsible for conflict between archdeacons and their bishops in regard to the scope of their respective jurisdictions. However, the presence of the archdeacon of Canterbury, Henry de Castellion, as a witness to many of Hubert's *acta* is an indication that these two men worked closely together. One letter from Henry to the archbishop provides a brief picture of the archdeacon at work. At the command of the archbishop he had associated himself with the abbot of Boxley, the prior of Leeds, Master William de Calna of the archiepiscopal *familia,* his own official Master Everard, and many others to make an inquiry of the abbot of St. Augustine's, Canterbury. The abbot, however, had refused to answer the inquiry on the grounds that some of the chapter, including several of the obedientiaries of the monastery, were absent.[41] The particular point of the inquiry was to determine the right of patronage to the church of St. Peter in Sandwich, a point that was part of a larger dispute with St. Augustine's that will be discussed later. The archdeacon in his letter made an urgent plea to Hubert to uphold the rights of the archdeaconate in this church with the

40. Thorpe, I, 444-445. A similar reference to consultation is Lambeth Palace Library, MS. 1212, p. 111.
41. Canterbury, D. and C. Mun., Chartae Antiquae, S 269. Master Everard is called "vicearchdiaconus" in Stubbs, *Epistolae Cantuarienses,* p. 467.

warning that otherwise his office would be lowered in prestige and his retention of other churches in Sandwich would be threatened. A point of minor interest is the mention of the archdeacon's official, or vice archdeacon, who served as his deputy and provided another link in the administrative chain joining the archbishop to the local clergy.

Another point referred to only incidentally in the archdeacon's letter as support for his claim is the definition of the jurisdiction of the archdeacon that had been made by Archbishop Richard in 1184. By that definition the archdeacon was to have institution and dismissal of rural deans in consultation with the archbishop, custody of vacant churches not in the gift of the archbishop and the fruits of these, pleas and profits from those churches in the demesnes of the archbishop and the monks of Christ Church within the archdeaconry of Canterbury, and all emoluments of pleas throughout the archdeaconry. By the thirteenth century, and possibly earlier, the archdeacon also had certain visitation rights over parishes, separate from the visitation rights of the archbishop, and some independent court jurisdiction.[42] Nevertheless, the archbishop could and did make changes in the jurisdiction of the archdeacon. In organizing the endowment for the new churches at Hackington and Lambeth, both Archbishop Baldwin and Archbishop Hubert apparently provided that a number of churches were to be exempted from the jurisdiction of the archdeacon. Some years later in 1227 Archbishop Stephen Langton again made changes when he issued a mandate in favor of his brother Simon, then archdeacon, which nullified these exemptions and stated that all parish churches in the diocese in the donation of the archbishop or the monks of Christ Church and the rectors or chaplains of such churches were subject to the archdeacon in the correction of morals, in visitation of churches, and in other rights pertaining to the office of archdeacon.[43]

The archbishop's authority as diocesan applied to monasteries except those specially exempt from that authority. In addition, he had special relations with three monastic foundations: he was abbot of the cathedral chapter of Christ Church; he appointed the prior of St. Martin in Dover, a priory subordinate to Christ Church; and the priory of St. Gregory in Canterbury was an archiepiscopal foundation. In spite of the long dispute with his chapter over Lambeth chapel, Archbishop Hubert took his position as abbot seriously enough to have been concerned about the internal

42. Churchill, I, 44-45.
43. Canterbury, D. and C. Mun.,  Chartae Antiquae, A 43.

organization of the monastery. In a letter in 1198 he urged the monks to remember that "we are the head of your church and your principal rector, under whose jurisdiction you are and whose counsel you should follow in everything, just as in your necessity you expect to find protection and patronage from us."[44] A year later the monks complained that the archbishop wanted to change the status of the monastery including even the ordering of monastic discipline established by the fathers Gregory and Augustine. Perhaps these complaints resulted from presentiments of the revision of Archbishop Lanfranc's constitutions for Christ Church which Archbishop Hubert carried out in 1203.[45]

Hubert displayed a similar paternal attitude toward the monks of Dover, who had been under direct control of the archbishop since Theobald sent monks from Christ Church to replace the canons. Hubert used the authority of his office on their behalf on a number of occasions.[46] He ordered Prior Robert to hold an inquiry into the alienation of any lands or possessions by his predecessor, to be carried out with the aid of the archbishop's clerk, Master William de Neketon, and authorized the prior to reclaim any unjust alienations that might be found. Again, he helped the monks by ordering the dean and clergy of Dover to pay the tithes due the monastery and by reinforcing this mandate with a second when the first failed to produce results. Similarly, when the burgesses of Dover failed to pay their tithes to the priory as they had been accustomed to do since the time of Archbishop Theobald, Hubert warned them of the danger to their souls in failing to fulfil this pious obligation and ordered them to make payment. In the twelfth century as in the twentieth Dover was the most popular port for those who crossed the Channel, and the monks at Dover Priory found themselves overburdened with providing hospitality for the hordes of clerks who stopped there in their comings and goings on business for the church, the king, or nobles in whose households they served. Solicitous as ever for the monks, Archbishop Hubert granted them exemption from the obligation to provide such hospitality.[47] Furthermore, the archbishop's responsibility included his general oversight of the financial organization of the priory, as is shown by Hubert's confirmation

---

44. Stubbs, *Epistolae Cantuarienses*, p. 447.

45. Lambeth Palace Library, MS. 1212, pp. 81-83. A modern copy of this is found in B.M., Cotton MS., Vespasian C. XIV, vol. I, f. 240.

46. Saltman, p. 75.

47. Lambeth Palace Library, MS. 241, fos. 37 v., 38, 59 v., 189 v.

of a charter by which the prior and monks added certain lands in Cheriton to estates allotted to the almoner of the monastery.[48]

The small priory of Augustinian canons of St. Gregory in Canterbury had claim to Hubert's special attention because their house was an archiepiscopal foundation. Several times he found himself having to resolve conflicts between members of his own *familia* and the priory. In one instance, he granted the church of Elmstead (Kent) to the priory with the provision that they might dispose of it freely only after the death of Master William de Calna, one of his clerks who then possessed the church. Again, the prior and canons brought to the archbishop's court a dispute over tithes between themselves and one of his clerks, Robert of London. A similar settlement was reached, which provided that Robert might have the tithes during his lifetime in return for payment of an annual rent of six shillings to the priory and that the canons were to have full rights after his death. The closeness of Hubert's relationship with the priory was shown also when after depriving the nuns of Ramestede (possibly Ramscombe, Sussex) of their lands because of their scandalous life, he granted their holdings to the canon of St. Gregory's.[49]

On the other hand, one of the disputes that marred his pontificate involved the monks of St. Augustine's Abbey close by his own cathedral. It was part of a seemingly never ending controversy involving the control of certain churches by St. Augustine's Abbey and the exercise of ecclesiastical jurisdiction over the parish priests and parishioners. The first phase of the struggle had ended with a composition between the monks and archbishop in 1183, but a vacancy in Faversham church in 1201 caused the whole question to flare up again. King Henry II had presented a royal clerk, Osbert de Camera, to the church, and this had been tolerated by the monks with no objection until his death that year. King John, exercising the same right as his father, presented another royal clerk, Simon, archdeacon of Wells, who was also a clerk to Archbishop Hubert. In fact, Simon was sometimes referred to by his opponents as "vice-chancellor of the archbishop," a phrase that lacks official precision but probably describes with some accuracy his position when Hubert was royal chancellor. The monks appealed to Rome protesting the king's right

48. *Ibid.*, MS. 1212, f. 99v.
49. Audrey M. Woodcock, ed., *Cartulary of the Priory of St. Gregory, Canterbury* (Camden Society, 3rd Ser., 88, London, 1956), pp. 5-7.

to make a presentation.[50] Although the archbishop wrote a careful letter advising them to agree to the appointment, indicating his own interest in Simon's career, and promising to obtain royal confirmation of their charters and favorable attention to the business of their house if they agreed, the monks remained unmoved.[51]

The sheriff of Kent, having attempted to drive the monks from the church in Faversham, besieged them from July 31 to August 16 until Roger, the abbot of St. Augustine's, brought a strong band of men and drove off the besiegers. Meanwhile, the official of the archdeacon, who claimed ordinary jurisdiction over the church, had refused to institute the candidate named by the monks and had suspended the church. When the parishioners appealed to the pope against the suspension, Archbishop Hubert excommunicated certain elders of Faversham by name. When he passed through the town, he also refused his blessing to the people of Faversham because they had harbored excommunicated persons. On September 24 the sheriff returned with a larger following and forcibly ejected the abbot and monks from the church, polluting it by spilling blood in the process. Two proctors sent by the monks to the archbishop were trying unsuccessfully to win his support when news arrived of this latest turn of events. The monks later described Hubert's reaction:

Having heard this, the archbishop with consternation of mind greater than would be believed, fearing that what had been done in his name although without his knowledge, and without his ratification, would somehow in time be visited on his own head, immediately passed sentence of excommunication in general on all who had inflicted the said violence on the abbot and monks, saying that so horrible and outrageous a deed had not been perpetrated in England since the murder of St Thomas the Martyr.[52]

Two separate cases emerged from this controversy. One involved the king's seizure of the temporalities of the abbey into his hands as punishment for infringement of his right of patronage. To conciliate the king and receive confirmation of their charters, the monks offered him two hundred marks and a palfrey, but he would give them no answer until he

---

50. This dispute has been discussed by John, pp. 390-415. King John's charter in favor of Simon is in P.R.O., Exchequer, Miscellaneous Books, I/27, f. 95. The men of Sandwich were attempting in the same year to prevent the abbot of St. Augustine's from appointing his choice for parson of St. Peter's Church in Sandwich: *Curia Regis Rolls*, II, 36.

51. Thorne, p. 140; John, p. 402; P.R.O., Exchequer, Miscellaneous Books, I/27, fos. 95-95 v.

52. Thorne, p. 145.

had consulted the archbishop. Hubert advised that there was do doubt of the abbey's right to the patronage of Faversham (thus pronouncing on a matter that was determined by the common law, on which he was an acknowledged authority), and he recommended that the abbey's lands be restored. Going beyond the legal considerations, he used the further practical argument that the king's officials might have profited by the seizure but the king himself had profited little; as the chronicler has Hubert put it, the king had shaken the bushes but others had caught the birds. Hubert added, somewhat gratuitously:

As to whether you should receive an offering for this same restitution and money for your favour, we shall give you no advice since it seems to us that restitution ought rather to be made for nothing than for money and restoration of what was taken away done for its own sake, not for profit. You, no doubt, will do what seems good to you.[53]

King John took the proffered fine and confirmed the charters on June 15, 1203.

The second case which arose from the controversy involved the jurisdiction of the archdeacon. Archbishop Hubert continued to support the jurisdiction of his archdeacon over the church at Faversham as the ecclesiastical case followed the tortuous path of appeals to Rome, hearings by judges delegate, and eventual compromise. Although the dispute ended with a compromise made in 1206, after the death of Archbishop Hubert, the main question was not settled until 1237.[54] At that time, the position that Hubert had taken was vindicated, and the archdeacon retained the right to institute rectors and vicars in the churches over which St. Augustine's had the right of patronage.

Not all cases tried in the archbishop's court were strictly ecclesiastical cases, for in addition to his presidency of an ecclesiastical court, he was also a great landholder whose position in relation to the king and, in the opposite direction, to the men who held lands from him was that of a lord over a fief. Some of the cases in which Archbishop Hubert took part arose from this function as feudal lord. When William de Lesnes obtained a writ in a royal court to proceed against the prior of Christ Church in 1200, the prior attempted to get the case removed to his own court, but Hubert intervened with a claim of jurisdiction for his court. The royal

53. Thorne as translated by John, p. 404 (p. 156 in Butler's translation).

54. A copy of several charters prob- ably made in connection with later aspects of the case is: Canterbury, D. and C. Mun., Chartae Antiquae, F 85.

justices fixed a date for the proctors of both prior and archbishop to produce their charters in support of their divergent claims in a manner not different from that followed when any feudal lord claimed jurisdiction for his court.[55] Judgments made in the archbishop's court for those holding lands from him were also placed in evidence in proceedings in royal courts. His court might be called to warrant such decisions by a procedure like that followed when he sent six men to report his decision about land in a case of *novel disseisin* being tried in royal court.[56]

The archbishop might be cited to appear in royal court to defend his claim to rights over land, and he might appear to seek jurisdiction for his court.[57] In one case in which he had successfully managed a transfer of jurisdiction to his court, the plaintiff who had raised the issue in royal court was fined for not attending the archbishop's court to press his case.[58] Cases might also pass from the archbishop's court to a royal court. One such case in 1198 would seem to modern eyes to raise a definite question of conflict of interest because the case was transferred from the archiepiscopal court to a royal court over which Hubert Walter presided as justiciar and in which the final concord that settled the case was arranged.[59]

The complexities of jurisdiction over criminal cases are illustrated in the brief notice given by Gervase of Canterbury to the visit of the itinerant justices sent out by the justiciar in 1195. Arriving in Canterbury in December, the three justices for this circuit took up crown cases in which the defendants either cleared themselves or perished as a result of a judgment by water. Those cases in which the jurisdiction fell within judicial privileges of the archbishop were put to the test "in the ditch of the archbishop near the Westgate." Those within the jurisdictional liberties belonging to Christ Church monastery were sent to the same ditch, but with ministers of the prior and monastery presiding over the ordeal.[60]

King John granted the archbishop additional privileges that increased the jurisdiction of his court. He authorized Hubert and his successors to hold grand assizes in their court for lands in Kent held of them by gavelkind tenure. The procedure was for the archbishop to request the king or his justiciar to send justices to the archbishop's court to hold these assizes.

55. *Curia Regis Rolls*, I, 238. Other examples are *Rotuli curiae regis*, ed. Francis Palgrave (London, 1835), I, 131, 328.

56. *Curia Regis Rolls*, III, 79; *Rotuli de oblatis et finibus*, pp. 298-299.

57. *Curia Regis Rolls*, I, 223, 238, 438.

58. *Ibid.*, III, 79.

59. Canterbury, D. and C. Mun., Chartae Antiquae, S 231.

60. Gervase of Canterbury, I, 531.

Any fines assessed there against men holding of the archbishop would go to him and fines assessed against other men would go to the king.[61]

It is clear that the administration of the diocese of Canterbury in itself presented Hubert Walter with a challenging task, without considering his broader ecclesiastical duties and his responsibilities in the royal government. On the whole, the evidence from the surviving documents gives the impression that he was not only a hard-working prelate in building up the property of the archbishopric and administering both ecclesiastical and feudal justice in the diocese, but that he used his service to the king as a means of obtaining royal support and greater privileges for the see of Canterbury.

61. Lambeth Palace Library, MS. 1212, pp. 48-50, 202; B.M., Cotton MS., Vespasian C. XIV, vol. I, f. 300 is a modern copy. One of the relevant charters is printed in Rymer, I, Pt. 1, p. 83. The relation of knight service and gavelkind tenure is discussed by Du Boulay, pp. 67-72.

# 6 PRIMATE AND METROPOLITAN

Turning from the consideration of Archbishop Hubert's activities in administering his diocese of Canterbury, we find more evidence for his work in the broader jurisdiction of the southern province. The official style he used—"Hubert, by the grace of God archbishop of Canterbury, primate of all England"—carried a resounding note of authority even without the addition of "and legate of the Apostolic See," which he used from 1195 to 1198. Yet the source of his authority over the bishops in the province of Canterbury—his position as metropolitan—even though expressed by his suffragan bishops in a letter to Pope Innocent III in 1198— in which they referred to Hubert as "pater et metropolitanus noster"— never officially became part of the diplomatic title used either by Hubert or his medieval successors.[1] True, some archbishops in the thirteenth century seem to have considered "primate" as virtually synonymous with "metropolitan," but the title of primate had broader implications that were the source of frequent misunderstandings with the archbishops of York until the fourteenth century.[2]

In the summer of 1193 when everyone's nerves were on edge through-

1. Stubbs, *Epistolae Cantuarienses*, 420.  2. Churchill, I, 154.

out England because of the efforts that were being made to raise the ransom for King Richard, councils of both laymen and clergy were held in London to discuss the question of the remaining sums that must be raised. During one such meeting in Westminster at which Hubert Walter, the archbishop-elect of Canterbury, was not present, Geoffrey, the archbishop of York, to the consternation of all present entered preceded by his crucifer. In the face of this intrusion, Gilbert Glanvill, bishop of Rochester, informed Geoffrey that if he had appeared in the meeting in a proper manner they would have saluted him with honor for the office he held, but by having his cross carried before him he dishonored the elect of Canterbury. Then, more formally, Bishop Gilbert appealed to the pope against this violation of the ancient privilege that no archbishop of York was to have his cross borne erect in the province of Canterbury, that is south of the Humber. Herbert, archdeacon of Canterbury and later bishop of Salisbury, rushed to the side of the bishop of Rochester, and the other bishops present acclaimed the stand he had taken. Even the Londoners had warned Archbishop Geoffrey that displaying his cross might cause violence in London. Having firsthand evidence of the hostility his action had provoked, the archbishop withdrew from London with his cross covered up and when he returned to York made his own appeal to the pope.[3] Thus was played out one more of the numerous scenes in the drama that had begun with the exaction of an oath of obedience from the archbishop of York by Lanfranc of Canterbury before he would perform his consecration in 1070.

The question of primacy erupted again when on March 25, 1194, Archbishop Hubert accompanied King Richard to the siege of Nottingham Castle and had his cross carried before him. Archbishop Geoffrey had not had his cross carried and complained to the king about Hubert's action since it occurred within the province of York. Hubert's retort was that as primate he ought to use his cross and that perhaps Geoffrey should not have his cross carried. A month later the positions of the two were reversed with Hubert complaining of Geoffrey to the king. Recognizing the type of decision in which there would be no pleasing either party, King Richard refused to be drawn into the dispute, saying that it belonged within the jurisdiction of the pope, not the king.[4] Had he known that the issue

3. Gervase of Canterbury, I, 519-520.
4. Roger of Hoveden, III, 239, 250; F. Makower, *The Constitutional History* *and Constitution of the Church of England* (London, 1895), pp. 282-283, 289-290. Canterbury, D. and C. Mun., Reg-

would be settled by a compromise not reached until the middle of the fourteenth century, he could not have made a better answer.

The judgment made against Geoffrey by Hubert Walter, acting as justiciar in the absence of King Richard I in 1194, which resulted in seizure of Archbishop Geoffrey's lands and the administration of them by royal custodians was characterized by William Stubbs as "one of the most arbitrary and high-handed proceedings of Hubert's ministry. . . ."[5] If anything, this incident simply illustrates the complicated intermingling of lay and ecclesiastical functions. Both men also held secular office, and Geoffrey was most likely judged for default of his duties and responsibilities toward the king, perhaps as sheriff of York or possibly for the debt he owed the king, rather than for ecclesiastical troubles in the case between him and his canons pending at Rome simultaneously.[6] Still, the ecclesiastical rivalry was real. A draft letter among the records of Archbishop Hubert at Canterbury seems to foreshadow Hubert's intercession with Pope Innocent III for the priory of Newburgh in York against the alleged oppressions of the archbishop of York.[7] There continued to be debate about the question of primacy, but when in 1195 Pope Celestine III bestowed on Hubert the authority of legate over the province of York as well as Canterbury the practical balance of power shifted to the south.[8]

If the title of "primate" represented some vague claims to authority, the surviving records allow us to see the archbishop as metropolitan actively at work in harmony and close co-operation with the suffragan bishops of his province. The duties of the archbishop acting as metropolitan can be classified under five headings: consecrating suffragans, hearing appeals, convoking provincial councils, visiting in the suffragan dioceses within his province, and administering such dioceses during vacancies.[9] Although some of the functions are illustrated more thoroughly than others, the surviving records from Hubert's time do show him performing all these duties. This evidence of varied ecclesiastical activities reinforces the evidence for his work as diocesan to prove that his opponents were wrong

ister A, fos. 171 v.-173 has a copy of the compromise reached in 1352 and the papal confirmation.

5. Intro. to Roger of Hoveden, IV, lxii.

6. *P.R. 6 Ric. I*, pp. xxviij-xxxii; Jolliffe, p. 113.

7. Canterbury, D. and C. Mun., Christ Church Letters, II, 214.

8. Foreville, *L'Église et la royauté*, p. 556, is too sweeping in her statement of this point.

9. Robert Brentano, *York Metropolitan Jurisdiction and Papal Judges Delegate (1279-1296)* (Berkeley and Los Angeles, 1959), p. 6.

in their allegations that he neglected his clerical duties because of his absorption in secular office as justiciar and, later, as chancellor.

The official beginning of the relation between a new bishop and his archbishop was the ceremony in which the archbishop, assisted by the bishops of the province, consecrated a newly elected bishop and received his profession of obedience to Canterbury. These ceremonies were usually noticed by the chroniclers. Gervase of Canterbury provides a summary list of fifteen bishops consecrated by Archbishop Hubert and adds that a sixteenth, who had been consecrated at Rome, made his profession of obedience during Hubert's pontificate.[10] However, the inclusion of Savaric of Bath, who was consecrated in 1192 at Rome, is an error, and the correct total of consecrations made personally by Hubert is fourteen. Normally the archbishop presided during the consecration of a new bishop, but his presence was not absolutely necessary. When Archbishop Hubert found himself too ill in 1203 to come to Canterbury for the consecration of the bishop of Lincoln, he wrote to his suffragan bishops gathering at Canterbury and delegated his authority to the group with instructions for them to work out the details of the ceremony among themselves.[11]

One of the complaints made in 1198 by the monks of Christ Church against Archbishop Hubert was that he had held no consecrations at Canterbury. In fact, when the place of consecration is given by the chroniclers, Hubert seems to have used the chapel of St. Catherine at Westminster most frequently for this purpose, although he did consecrate two bishops at Canterbury at the beginning of his pontificate and, later, he again held consecrations at Canterbury.[12] The monks feared a loss of prestige to their church and charged that the archbishop planned to perform consecrations in his new chapel at Lambeth, perhaps foreshadowing the time when the see would be translated to Lambeth. According to the monks, the bishops already complained that Canterbury was too remote and difficult to reach.

The pagentry of an episcopal consecration caught the interest of the crowd, of course, but all was not ceremonial about the archbishop's right to consecrate the bishops of his province. He might also defer or veto the candidate presenting himself for consecration or use his position as metro-

---

10. Gervase of Canterbury, II, 410.

11. Canterbury, D. and C. Mun., Chartae Antiquae, C 106. William Stubbs, *Registrum Sacrum Anglicanum* (Oxford, 1897), p. 53, follows Matthew Paris and mistakenly lists the place of consecration as Westminster.

12. Stubbs, *Registrum*, pp. 52-54.

politan to influence an election. When King Richard secured the election of his physician to the see of Worcester, Archbishop Hubert refused immediate consecration, raising questions about the legality of the election because the bishop-elect was not of legitimate birth. Finally, he referred the question to the pope for guidance. The fact that he commended the merits and learning of the particular candidate indicates that he was acting on principle, not personal animus. In fact, Pope Innocent III ruled that such an election was against the canons of the Third Lateran Council; but since dispensations had been made and since the archbishop had given the candidate a favorable recommendation, he suggested that the monks of Worcester revert to a correct procedure and petition for a dispensation to allow for an election in spite of canonical disabilities.[13] The influence exercised by the English kings when elections to bishoprics and arch-bishoprics were held in their presence is perfectly obvious, and Archbishop Hubert was placing himself in a similar position to wield his influence when he wrote the dean and chapter of St. Paul's, London, on November 9, 1198, ordering them to send seven canons to him for the purpose of electing a new bishop. His position in regard to this election was made possible by the absence of the king, for whom he substituted, and was strengthened by a letter from the king to the canons to the same effect as that by the archbishop.[14]

The occasion of the consecration of a bishop also provided a good opportunity for consideration of business for the province because a consecration meant the gathering of the suffragan bishops. In 1198 Hubert sent letters to all his bishops notifying them that the pope had decided against him in the Lambeth controversy with his monks and asking them to be prepared to give him their advice and counsel when they came to Canterbury for the consecration of the bishop of Coventry.[15] This instance is typical of the generally cordial relations that existed between Hubert and his bishops, who supported him as a group throughout the Lambeth controversy. In fact, there was a considerable sense of a community of interest among the suffragans of Canterbury so that it was not unusual for them to be found co-operating in the furtherance of a common policy. Without much success the bishops even claimed a share in the election of

---

13. Gervase of Canterbury, II, 410; Cheney and Semple, pp. 16-22.
14. Ralph de Diceto, II, 164.
15. Gervase of Canterbury, I, 554; Stubbs, *Epistolae Cantuarienses*, pp. 394-395 and pp. 405, 413, 420-422 for other examples of collective support of the archbishop by his bishops.

an archbishop, and did, in fact, assemble and hold an election when Hubert became archbishop. But any controversy that might have embroiled them with the monks was averted by the fact that both parties had chosen the same man.[16] Nevertheless, this custom of collective action by the suffragans of Canterbury was a source of strength to Archbishop Hubert when the bishops supported his policies, as they did in his quarrel with the archbishop of York and in his opposition to the claim that St. David's in Wales should have metropolitan status separate from Canterbury, two of the better-known problems faced by Archbishop Hubert.

The archbishop, in turn, co-operated with his bishops by confirming their charters and lending the approval and authority of his office to their actions. In 1199 King John confirmed the possessions of the almonry of Peterborough Abbey to be held "just as reasonably witnessed by the confirmations of our venerable father H., archbishop of Canterbury, and Lord Hugh, bishop of Lincoln."[17] An agreement between the bishop of Lincoln and the earl of Leicester about some land in Leicester was made in the presence of the archbishop and with his assent.[18] Another charter recording a grant of lands made by Walter fitz Robert assumes a joint responsibility by being addressed to the archbishop and the bishops of London and Norwich.[19] Hubert also confirmed the charters of his suffragans by which they granted lands, instituted clergy to churches within their dioceses, or approved exemptions from the jurisdiction of the archdeacon.[20]

Archbishop Hubert had the doubtful privilege of having one of the few saints of this period in the history of the English church among his suffragans. The character of Hugh of Avalon, bishop of Lincoln, was in sharp contrast to the general air of businesslike efficiency that characterized his colleagues and the archbishop as well. In spite of their differences, however, there seems to have been a spirit of friendly opposition between the two men based upon a mutual respect rather than similarity of views.

16. Gervase of Canterbury, I, 519; Ralph de Diceto, II, 108-109; Roger of Hoveden, III, 213.

17. F. M. Stenton, *Facsimiles of Early Charters from Northamptonshire Collections* (Lincoln and London, 1930), pp. 46-47.

18. C. W. Foster, ed., *The Registrum Antiquissimum of the Cathedral Church of Lincoln* (Lincoln Record Society, 27, Lincoln, 1931), I, 140-141. Bishop Hugh's biography commented on his conduct of a case against the Earl over some land in *Magna vita*, II, 83-85.

19. B.M., Harley MS. 662, f. 6 v.

20. B.M., Cotton MS., Galba E. II, f. 44 v.; Vespasian E. XXIII, f. 23 v., Harley Charter, 43 G. 25; P.R.O., The Exchequer, Treasury of Receipt, 14000; Thorpe, I, 508; Foster, p. 253.

The case in which Bishop Hugh used ecclesiastical censure against a deacon who had brought a false charge of felony against a knight in secular court has already been mentioned. The bishop was trying to draw a line between the obedience he owed Hubert Walter as justiciar and the obedience he owed him as archbishop. When the bishop suspended the man from his office and benefice, the archbishop as papal legate relaxed the suspension; when the bishop excommunicated, the archbishop absolved. Whether Bishop Hugh would really have excommunicated the deacon a hundred times if necessary (as he threatened to do) was never tested, for the unfortunate cause of the dispute was killed at this point as a result of other circumstances and the case was closed. On another occasion, probably late in 1198 or in 1199, when Bishop Hugh had come to London during a quarrel he was having with the king, Archbishop Hubert advised him to soothe the king's anger with a gift of money. The archbishop's supporting argument was probably more valuable for its insight into the king's character than for its medical lore: "Don't you know, lord bishop, that as a person with dropsy craves water, so the lord king craves money?" But this was not the way of Saint Hugh, who rejected the suggestion out of hand with the quip, "Even if he has the dropsy, I will not be water for him to swallow." When Hugh was on his deathbed, the archbishop visited him and in the course of the interview suggested that it might be advisable for him to ask pardon for having so often provoked his spiritual father and primate. True to form to the last, Hugh declared that, on the contrary, if he lived he would provoke him oftener than before.[21] And it must have been with a sense both of relief and of loss that Archbishop Hubert honored the memory of his intractable bishop by his presence at the funeral on November 23, 1200. Rarely was such honesty shown in the court of King Richard or King John.

One of the letters preserved at Canterbury from Hubert Walter's time, addressed to the archbishop by Bishop Herbert of Salisbury, is especially valuable for the glimpse it gives of the routine interaction between the archbishop and one of his bishops. A rather detailed summary will give something of the flavor of the letter, although the particular business mentioned is of no special concern. The bishop tells Hubert that he has studied his letters containing instructions about resident and non-resident clerks, especially the forms prescribed for aiding paupers and for giving

21. *Magna vita*, II, 30, 124, 188-189, 274, 336.

an aid to the king. He reports some hesitation on what he should do about the second article on alms because he was not able to have a tenth part of the clergy in his see present in one chapter. In the absence of the greater and wiser part, those present refused to give him a definite response to the archbishop's letters. He suggests that the archbishop may want to instruct him by a letter concerning what should be done about the absent clergy. Further, he has detected some dissatisfaction with his conduct in regard to the election of an abbess at Wilton, for which he has no one in mind, and asks the archbishop to let him know if he has some definite wish in the matter. He complains that since the archbishop has neither written nor instructed him orally about this he should not be blamed for lack of diligence. Finally, he reports that he has made a careful investigation of the charge that Master Roger de Winesham spoke against the archbishop and can find nothing that should displease him. On this point, he asks the archbishop to suspend the anger that he has exhibited against Roger until Bishop Herbert can show him sufficient excuse for Roger either orally or by arranging any other acceptable satisfaction.[22]

Of all the bishops in the province, Rochester had an especially close relationship with Canterbury—a relationship that depended neither upon the circumstances of geographical proximity nor upon the personal ties between Hubert Walter and Gilbert Glanvill, the bishop of Rochester during his pontificate, who was probably the brother of Ranulf Glanvill. The unique fact about Rochester was that the archbishop of Canterbury had feudal rights over that see, rights which were held by the king in other dioceses, and, for that reason, during a vacancy at Rochester the archbishop held both the temporalities and spiritualities. In addition, the archbishop was the patron of the see, issuing a license to elect when a vacancy occurred and being present when an election was held at the chapter house in Canterbury.[23] When Archbishop Baldwin went on the Third Crusade, he committed both the spiritualities and the temporalities of Canterbury to the bishop of Rochester with instructions to consult certain members of his household for advice in each sphere.

However, Baldwin seems to have committed his metropolitan authority

22. Christ Church Letters, II, no. 225. Printed in Historical Manuscripts Commission, *Report on Manuscripts in Various Collections* (London, 1901), I, 233-234.

23. John Moule, "Gilbert Glanvill, Bishop of Rochester, 1185-1214 and the Relationship of the See of Rochester to Canterbury to 1238" (University of Manchester, Unpublished Master's thesis, 1954), pp. 109-111, 114.

to the bishop of London in accordance with the custom that had been followed since the time of Lanfranc.[24] Actually, such a procedure was but an extension of the normal procedure by which the archbishop communicated with his suffragan bishops by having the bishop of London as dean of the province convey his wishes to them. Perhaps something happened during the years of this division of authority between the two bishops or during the vacancy after Archbishop Baldwin's early death on the crusade, when the Bishop of Rochester continued to exercise the powers delegated to him. At any rate, the two men were in open dispute as to who should sit at the right hand of the archbishop when the newly chosen Hubert Walter was enthroned in 1193. The bishop of London claimed that privilege because he was dean of the province; Rochester countered on the grounds that he was chaplain.[25] Three years later these two, joined by the bishop of Winchester, who as sub-dean of the province put forward his own claims, disputed among themselves concerning the right to consecrate bishops, crown a king, and occupy the principal seat in the convocation of the province during an absence of the archbishop. Finally, this rather scandalous dispute reached the ears of Pope Celestine III, probably by a complaint from the bishop of Rochester, and the pope issued a letter to Archbishop Hubert in which he referred to quarrels that had occurred when the suffragans of Canterbury were convoked and commanded that disputes over precedence should be prevented by observing the rule followed at Rome that the order be determined by the date of their ordination.[26] With the same three bishops contending with one another for authority in the absence of the archbishop in 1203, it is obvious that the question remained an issue even after the papal intervention.[27]

Far more famous is the dispute between Archbishop Hubert and that fiery and articulate defender of Welsh independence, Gerald of Wales. The contemporary impact of such a *cause célèbre* was somewhat exaggerated, but it formed a part of the assessment of Archbishop Hubert's career in his own time. It was as a loyal monk of Christ Church that Gervase of Canterbury wrote: "Others may say what they wish of the work of Hubert, I count this his greatest work that he retained seven bishops [in Wales]

24. Stubbs, *Epistolae Cantuarienses*, pp. 324-325; Thorpe, I, 50; Churchill, I, 26, 285 n; Moule, pp. 174-175.
25. Gervase of Canterbury, I, 522.
26. Rochester, D. and C. Mun., Registrum Temporalium, fos. 132-132 v.

printed in Thorpe, I, 51; Holtzmann, II, 480-481; Moule, pp. 186, 192.
27. Giraldus Cambrensis, III, 304. Date is provided by Stubbs, *Registrum*, p. 53.

in subjection to the church of Canterbury and handled the cunning rebellion of Gerald."[28] The controversy that began with the death of the bishop of St. David's in Wales on June 16, 1198, led to a five-year vacancy and raised the question not only of the disputed election of Gerald to the bishopric but also of the claim of St. David's to metropolitan status independent of Canterbury. The archbishop rejected the names of Gerald and three others on a list submitted to him by the chapter of St. David. His comment that the king would not have a Welshman, especially one related to the prince of Wales, reveals the political implications of an independent ecclesiastical province, which might have aided a move for political independence for Wales.[29]

The issue of metropolitan status that Gerald raised had been argued about 1130, again about 1147, and last in 1176, with no success. In explaining his rejection of Gerald, Archbishop Hubert wrote to the pope that Gerald would not be content with consecration but would seek exemption from Canterbury, and with the restraining influence of Canterbury removed, unrest and rebellion might be expected in Wales.[30] Gerald's own vivid and highly colored account of his calamities in pursuit of this case in England and in Rome, which he visited three times during the course of the litigation, need not be followed in detail, nor all of his charges against his formidable opponent listed, but a few incidents not previously mentioned in other connections might be described.

On June 17, 1202, Gerald appeared before papal judges to argue his case against the archbishop's proctors—Master Simon of Southwell, Master John of Tynemouth, and Master William of Calna. He charged that the archbishop had misused his position as King John's chancellor by sending the justiciar orders under authority of the royal seal to seize the lay tenements and escheats of the canons of St. David's. Later, he himself admitted this charge was not true.[31] In another place, he charged that on

28. Vol. II, 412.

29. J. Conway Davies, ed., *Episcopal Acts and Cognate Documents Relating to Welsh Dioceses 1066-1272* (Historical Society of the Church in Wales, [n.p.], 1946), I, 210-211; Lloyd, II, 625 and for further discussion pp. 480-482, 486 n., 559-562, 624-630. Canterbury, D. and C. Mun., Chartae Antiquae, C 137 is a document from an earlier phase of the controversy over metropolitan status.

A lecture on Gerald of Wales, chiefly as a writer, is printed in F. M. Powicke, *The Christian Life in the Middle Ages and Other Essays* (Oxford, 1935). Roger of Hoveden, IV, 103-106, discusses the controversy.

30. Giraldus Cambrensis, I, 120-122, dated Nov.-Dec. 1199 by Davies, I, 308.

31. Giraldus Cambrensis, III, 218-219. Nearly all relevant parts of Gerald's own account have been arranged in chrono-

the advice of his clerks Hubert had given £45 sterling to witnesses for their expenses and in other payments to them, first exacting an oath from them that they would testify against Gerald when they appeared in court. In Gerald's opinion, the extent to which the archbishop employed bribery was shown by his comment that the case against Gerald had cost him 11,000 marks, plus the loss of several clerks who had died at Rome while representing him there.[32]

Gerald may well have been right about the archbishop's use of bribes and gifts to secure a favorable decision, for the monks of Christ Church made similar charges. But these charges speak more eloquently of the corruption of the Roman curia than of Hubert's character.[33] It is true that whether contending for secular or ecclesiastical objectives the archbishop showed a thorough knowledge of the means needed to win his cause and that his employment of these means made him successful in his own day. Gerald was aware of the political influence that his opponent might use. The archbishop was able to have money Gerald had received as a royal subsidy from the farm of Hereford cut off and to get a letter from the king not only denying support to Gerald but also forbidding anyone else to aid him.[34] On another occasion Hubert solicited the support of his friend, Gilbert Glanvill, bishop of Rochester, to write the pope his testimony to facts he had witnessed in contradiction of the "lies" that Gerald had told the pope.[35] On December 7, 1203, a compromise was reached in which the archbishop paid Gerald the money the pope had awarded him and conferred on him ecclesiastical revenues worth sixty marks. Gerald later had the grace to note that Hubert had fulfilled his part before his death.[36] In return, Gerald in a charter sealed before an impressive number of witnesses agreed to give up all claims to the church of St. David's and its metropolitan status, and never again to even give counsel or aid to anyone who might raise the question.[37] The chapter of St. David's then elected Geoffrey, prior of Llanthony, a candidate favored by the archbishop, and presented him to the archbishop for consecration without further resistance.[38]

logical order and translated by H. E. Butler. His "Retractiones" is printed in *ibid.*, I, 426.

32. *Ibid.*, III, 247, 264.

33. Stubbs, *Epistolae Cantuarienses*, pp. 457, 484.

34. *P.R. 5 John*, pp. xix-xx, 55; *Rotuli*

*litterarum patentium*, I, 7a.

35. Canterbury, D. and C. Mun., Eastry Correspondence, Group VI, #1.

36. Giraldus Cambrensis, III, 323-324.

37. Canterbury, D. and C. Mun., Register A, f. 73 v.

38. Chartae Antiquae, C 105.

The exercise of a metropolitan's right and duty of visitation brought him into continuing contact with the suffragan bishops and monastic houses of his province and provided more opportunity than the right of consecration for exercising his authority. Unfortunately, evidence for Hubert's visitations is fragmentary. Despite the numerous references to a visitation he carried out after returning from a legatine visitation of York, the evidence is not complete enough to work out itineraries or even to delineate clearly the source of the authority by which he was acting in each instance. In 1195 he was at Thorney and Lichfield, as well as York. Probably another tour took him to East Anglia, where he visited Norwich, Castle Acre, and Ely. Accompanied by Hugh, bishop of Lincoln, and several abbots, he visited Ramsey Abbey and delivered injunctions for the management of the possessions of that abbey. On several journeys to the west country he visited Evesham and Llanthony. In fact, since no regular visitation by bishops was established in England until the late thirteenth century, his conscientiousness as a visitor, was probably the reason for an attempt to discredit him with the pope as an oppressive and extortionate visitor. This charge he was able to answer simply by asking the clergy of York to report on his visitation in that province.[39]

The main reason for Hubert's visitation at Thorney was to execute the mandate of Pope Celestine III that the abbot be deposed and held in custody until further instructions were sent from Rome. Later, when Pope Innocent III reconsidered the case, he upheld the actions taken by Archbishop Hubert, who had also imposed silence on the abbot and imprisoned him in a monastery at Gloucester. However, Innocent did modify the sentence to provide that money from the revenues of Thorney be used to support the deposed abbot in some other religious house.[40] At Lichfield the archbishop was faced with the problem of canons who did not reside at the cathedral city where they held prebends. In fact, the pluralism fostered by both the secular and ecclesiastical administration made non-residence a necessity for some canons, and several of Hubert's own *familia* would have been numbered among such offenders while they served him and the king. Of the various types of benefices that provided financial support for such clerks, cathedral prebends, which did not require cure of

39. Ralph de Diceto, II, 147; C. R. Cheney, *From Becket to Langton* (Manchester, 1956), pp. 140-141; Dom David Knowles, *The Monastic Order in Eng-* *land* (Cambridge, 1940), p. 651.

40. Ralph de Diceto, II, 151; Cheney and Semple, pp. 41-45.

souls, were most convenient. In accordance with canon law a man having a prebend could still hold one other benefice requiring cure of souls and other benefices without that responsibility at the same time. The arrangements that Archbishop Hubert made for Lichfield were the same as those used at Salisbury. They required three months' residence of all canons with the aim of having at least one-fourth of the canons resident at all times, but exceptions were made for clerks in service of king, archbishop, or bishop, and for university students.[41]

The relationship between Archbishop Hubert and heads of monasteries within his own diocese began with a ceremony in which he blessed the abbots in a manner analogous to his consecration of bishops. Gervase of Canterbury lists only three abbots thus blessed by Archbishop Hubert during his pontificate, two for Langdon and one for St. Radegund's, both Premonstratensian houses in Kent.[42] In the case of some monasteries that had secured exemptions from the diocesan bishop, the newly elected abbots preferred to make their professions of obedience to the archbishop rather than appear to concede any degree of control over their monasteries to the bishop of the diocese, but there is little evidence of such actions during the pontificate of Hubert. This may be the reason that Archbishop Hubert instituted John as abbot of St. Albans in July 1195 to fill the place of his deceased predecessor, but the chronicler does not give enough information to make the situation clear.[43]

When the bishop of Worcester died in October 1195 and the bishopric came temporarily into the hands of the archbishop by virtue of his right as metropolitan during a vacancy in one of the suffragan dioceses, he found the monastic chapter in disorder. Some of the monks were sent to other houses in England, and two monks from Canterbury were sent to Worcester to reform the monastery and restore order there.[44] In co-operation with the bishop of Lincoln, several heads of monasteries, and the *maior et sanior pars* of the monks, Archbishop Hubert on another occasion issued a charter establishing constitutions for the governing of Ramsey Abbey.[45] When the lay brothers at the Cistercian abbey of Garendon rebelled against a reforming abbot and wounded him in a fray, disciplinary measures were

41. David Wilkins, ed., *Concilia Magnae Britanniae et Hiberniae* (London, 1737), I, 497, 500-501; K. Edwards, pp. 36-38, 53.

42. Gervase of Canterbury, II, 410.

43. Saltman, p. 83; Churchill, I, 121;

Gervase of Canterbury, I, 529.

44. Gervase of Canterbury, I, 530.

45. W. H. Hart and P. A. Lyons, *Cartularium monasterii de Rameseia* (R.S., London, 1884-1893), II, 204-207.

taken by the general chapter of the Cistercians to disperse the lay brothers to remote Cistercian houses, and notice of this action was given in letters to the king, the earl of Leicester as patron, and the archbishop of Canterbury.[46] This notification implies a general interest and jurisdiction that appears also in a number of Hubert's acts in regard to monasteries. Indirect though it may have been, this sort of authority, which went with a powerful office, appeared to contemporaries to have practical value. The abbot of Hyde, for example, gave King John thirty marks to obtain letters interceding with the archbishop to remove some monks who were opposed to the abbot.[47] Just as Jolliffe has shown that we should not underestimate the personal authority of the king's will in twelfth-century royal government, perhaps the influence of Archbishop Hubert beyond areas in which he had clearly defined jurisdiction should not be underemphasized. Along with the bishop of Ely and the justiciar, Archbishop Hubert mediated a dispute between the abbot of Cluny and the patron of Lewes over the method of choosing a prior for that foundation; he confirmed the restoration of the patronage of Walden Abbey to its rightful holder, who had been deprived when the abbot had persuaded King Richard to give the patronage to the abbey itself; and he took a rather minor and ineffectual role in a particularly wearisome case involving the monks of Evesham against their abbot and both against the bishop of Worcester.[48]

In addition to his role as a stern father correcting monastic irregularities, Archbishop Hubert could also serve as a wise and valuable counselor. A man named Brian had been brought before the court of the abbot of Reading, where he confessed that he was a thief. After this confession, Brian made some charges against others which involved violations of the forest law, and the bailiff of Windsor requested the surrender of the prisoner in order to produce him in the royal court at Windsor. The abbot of Reading, who was presiding in the case in his own court, asked the archbishop for advice and was told to surrender Brian in order not to seem to be impeding forest justice. Later Brian was returned for judgment in the abbot's court. Archbishop Hubert's personal experience in the administration of royal justice enabled him to possess a unique authority for giving advice in this case, and his letter as archbishop, addressed to "all to whom

46. Knowles, p. 657.

47. *P.R. 5 John*, p. 148.

48. J. H. Round, *Calendar of Documents Preserved in France Illustrative of the History of Great Britain and Ireland* (London, 1899), I, 516; P.R.O., Records of the Duchy of Lancaster, D. L. 25 #8; *Chronicon abbatiae de Evesham*, pp. 106-107, 117, 119, 125-126, 128-129; Knowles, pp. 334-336.

this present writing shall come," provided assurance for the abbot that nothing in the handling of the case should be construed in such a way as to diminish the right and dignity of the abbey.[49]

The archbishop's general supervision of monasteries in his province is shown in numerous chance references to his activity in this field. After Hubert's death a man offered the king two palfreys to hold a formal inquiry concerning whether Archbishop Hubert had caused Michael to become prior of St. Peter's, Ipswich, against the right of election belonging to the ancestors of the petitioner, but two years later he still was listed as owing the palfreys to the king.[50] Charters of Archbishop Hubert contain an *inspeximus* of St. Thomas' confirmation of the transfer of a church from the abbot of Ramsey to the bishop of Lincoln, a grant of two houses by the prior and convent of Lewes to Humphrey de Bohun and his mother, and confirmation of Henry de Pinken's gift of a meadow to Biddlesden Abbey.[51] Apparently the Archbishop sometimes paid the king for confirmations of the possessions of monastic establishments. This would seem to be the explanation for the two palfreys he owed the king in 1203 for two confirmations, one for the prioress of Ikelinton (Ickleton, Cambridge?) and the other for the prioress of Campessei (Campsey Ash, Suffolk?), but, as usual, no explanation is given for the entry in the Pipe Roll.[52] In 1201 the archbishop aided the monks of Daventry by issuing an indulgence for the remission of fifteen days' penance throughout the dioceses of Lincoln and Coventry to anyone giving alms to help toward the repair of the monastic buildings.[53]

At other times, Archbishop Hubert was called upon to arbitrate claims put forward by monasteries. Although the division between Llanthony in Wales and Llanthony in Gloucester had first occurred in 1136, there was still a dispute between them in regard to both possessions and debts, and the archbishop had to issue a mandate to the bishops of Worcester, Hereford, and St. David's in Wales outlining the terms for the division. He also confirmed an agreement about burial privileges between the Llanthony canons at Gloucester and the monks of Gloucester in 1197 and confirmed

49. B.M., Egerton MS 3031, f. 91 v.
50. *Rotuli de oblatis et finibus*, p. 324; P.R. 7 John, p. 237.
51. P.R.O., Exchequer Augmentation Office, Misc. Books, 31/45; Records of the Duchy of Lancaster, Cartae Miscellaneae, I/203, Deeds, 27/4; B.M., Harley Charter, 84. C. 42.

52. *P.R. 5 John*, p. 27.
53. Oxford University, Bodleian Library, MS. Charters, Northants a. I #2; N. Denholm-Young, *Cartulary of the Medieval Archives of Christ Church* (Oxford Historical Society, XCII, Oxford, 1931), p. 49.

the canons there in their possessions.[54] In 1199 Hubert successfully arbitrated another long-standing controversy between the canons of Wells and the monks of Bec-Hellouin. This dispute originated when Robert fitz Gerold, as patron of the church of Cleeve, Somerset, gave the church to the monks of Bec and apparently overlooked existing claims by the canons of Wells. Bec got papal confirmation of the appropriation of the church in 1190, the papal legate intervened the following year, and in 1192 the bishop of Wells twice confirmed the claims by Bec, but still the controversy remained unsettled. Several charters that mark the final settlement in 1199 show that Hubert dealt with the controversy on more that one occasion and that he finally managed to solve it to the satisfaction of both parties.[55]

Thus, in the normal administrative activity of the province both bishops and heads of monasteries came under the authority of the archbishop of Canterbury. The most important way in which these subordinates could be brought together by an archbishop was by the calling of a provincial council. Archbishop Hubert held one such council at Westminster starting on September 19, 1200. Bishops present were London, Rochester, Salisbury, Exeter, Ely, Coventry, Bangor, Llandaff, St. Asaph, and the bishop-elect of Hereford. Those of Lincoln, Winchester, and Chichester were too ill to attend. Many abbots and priors also attended.[56]

The fourteen canons of this council were mostly drawn from the canons of the Third Lateran Council of 1179, but the evidence for provincial councils suggests that the legislation usually was drawn up to meet the needs of the province and was not designed to be a systematic code of law.[57] The subjects of the Westminster canons were (1) and (2) the mass, (3) baptism and confirmation, (4) penance, (5) visitations, (6) ordination, (7) ecclesiastical justice, (8) ecclesiastical fees and benefices, (9) tithes, (10) clerical duties, (11) marriage, (12) persons of bad

---

54. P.R.O., Chancery, Master's Exhibits, Cartularies and Registers of Llanthony Priory, A 2, fos. 246-247; A 1, fos. 27, 33 v.-34; A 4, fos. 203-204.

55. F. A. Cazel, Jr., "Norman and Wessex Charters of the Roumare Family," in P. Barnes and C. F. Slade, eds., A Medieval Miscellany for Doris Mary Stenton (P.R.S., London, 1962), pp. 83-84, 88. Documents from this case are

also printed by Marjorie Chibnall, Select Documents of the English Lands of the Abbey of Bec (Camden Society, 3rd ser., LXXIII, London, 1951), pp. 13, 20-21.

56. Ralph de Diceto, II, 169.

57. C. R. Cheney, "Legislation of the Medieval English Church," The English Historical Review, L (1935), pp. 206-207, 388-389.

character, (13) churches for lepers, and (14) religious orders.[58] Professor Cheney has pointed out the general significance of these canons:

These drew largely upon the decrees of the Third Lateran, but they are much more than mere reiteration of papal decrees. . . . They contain more of the didactic element than is found in earlier English conciliar law: they are the precursor and exemplar of synodal statutes of the thirteenth century, in particular those of Salisbury c. 1220.[59]

The bishops returning from such a provincial council published the canons in their own synods, and the canons of Westminster seem to have passed from one diocese to another without any mark of origin, thus giving some influence to the work of a provincial council that would otherwise be little known. In addition to the Salisbury statutes, later statutes drawn up by synods at Winchester and Chichester show some dependence upon Hubert's council of Westminster.[60]

Some reference has been made to the normal business of the archbishop as metropolitan in connection with the previous discussion of his relationships with the bishop and heads of monasteries in the province, but the surviving records from the time of Archbishop Hubert allow us an even fuller picture of the metropolitan at work. Inspection and confirmation of charters looms large, especially in monastic cartularies, but the actual work would have been done by the archbishop's clerks, and the essentially repetitious nature of such documents needs little comment. Sometimes such confirmations involved a rather elaborate chain of authority, as in Hubert's confirmation of his predecessor Baldwin's confirmation of Richard's charter confirming the bishop of Chichester's confirmation for the monks of Boxgrove.[61] Other types of confirmation charters by Archbishop Hubert include charters of his suffragans for a general confirmation of possessions, confirmation of a gift, approving a vicar presented to a church, and regulations made by the bishop of Coventry for the deanery of Lichfield.[62] The charters of monasteries, several examples

58. Roger of Hoveden, IV, 128-136.
59. Cheney, *From Becket to Langton*, p. 142.
60. Cheney, "Legislation," p. 209; Cheney, *English Synodalia of the Thirteenth Century* (Oxford, 1941), pp. 55, 76, 87.
61. B.M., Cotton MS., Claudius A. VI, fos. 61-61 v.
62. B.M., Additional Charter 33596; G. H. Fowler and Joyce Godber, *The Cartulary of Bushmead Priory* (Bedfordshire Historical Record Society, 22, 1945), pp. 20-21; Lambeth Palace Library, Carte Miscellane, XI, 32; H. E. Savage, *The Great Register of Lichfield Cathedral* (The William Salt Archaeological Society, 1924, Kendal, 1926), p. 118.

of which have already been mentioned, comprised another class which the archbishop was expected to confirm. At other times he was merely present and acted as a witness when benefactors made grants or confirmed grants to monasteries.[63] Just as in the archbishop's charters for his diocese, the purpose in many of the charters which as metropolitan he confirmed for monasteries was the appropriation of churches by which a monastery obtained the income from a church, usually placing a vicar to serve the church at small cost and enjoying the difference between the salary of the vicar and the income of the church.[64]

The court of the archbishop in his jurisdiction as metropolitan was still in the formative stage in the twelfth century. Pope Alexander III wrote the suffragan bishops sometime between 1166 and 1170 setting out the double nature of the authority of the court by virtue of the archbishop's position as metropolitan and as legate. The bishops had maintained that the archbishop should not hear any cause except by appeal from their courts. The pope answered that although this might be true under the archbishop's authority as metropolitan, as legate he could hear all causes by appeal or by complaint.[65] Certainly Archbishop Hubert heard both types of cases. By the mid-thirteenth century the "Official of the Court of Canterbury" presided over that court as a court of appeal for the province. But the archbishop might also use the court as a court of audience by his personal attendance and might; on the other hand, he might exercise a superior jurisdiction by virtue of his legatine power. Miss Churchill, in her study of the administration of Canterbury in the thirteenth century and later, has written that the existence of the official and the court of Canterbury in the twelfth century is likely but that there is no direct evidence for this.[66] At least one letter from the time of Archbishop Hubert seems to provide some support for her assumption, but caution must be exercised against reading into a single reference all the details of an institution known more fully only from later evidence.[67]

The court of the archbishop served as a place where anyone injured by the arbitrary or illegal actions of a bishop or his subordinates could appeal and as an institution through which the archbishop could take disciplinary measures if necessary. On one occasion, the bishop of

63. Lancaster, I, 436.
64. B.M., Harley MS. 391, fos. 102-102 v.; P.R.O., Exchequer Augmentation Office (Misc. Books), 61, f. 104; Ely, D. and C. Mun., Papal Legates, #81.

65. Churchill, I, 424-425.
66. *Ibid.*, 425-426, 499.
67. Canterbury, D. and C. Mun., Sede Vacante Scrap-book, I, 133, #3.

Chichester appointed one of his clerks to defend his actions in this court, but at other times the bishops did not bow so easily.[68] Certain clerks in the diocese of Llandaff appealed to Archbishop Hubert against their bishop, and the archbishop delegated two men to hear the case for him. Not only did the bishop refuse to appear, but he also had the bearer of the letters citing him to appear in court seized and beaten, and he proceeded to excommunicate the clerks in spite of their appeal.[69] The principal weakness in the archbishop's power over his bishops is demonstrated in this case. When Hubert absolved the clerks from their bishop's excommunication, the bishop took the whole matter out of his hands by an appeal to the pope. Whatever the final outcome of such a case, an appeal often had the effect of delaying the execution of justice for an indefinite period of time.

When a dean refused to pronounce a sentence of excommunication as ordered by his bishop, even though the bishop was in fact transmitting the mandate of the archbishop in this case, all parties were cited to appear in the archbishop's court for final judgment.[70] The obverse of this relationship between a bishop and his subordinate is illustrated when a clerk charged the bishop of Exeter with molesting him in his vicarage and appealed to the archbishop for judgment in the case.[71] When the same bishop excommunicated a group of men even though they had not been convicted and had appealed their case to Rome, the action was brought before the archbishop, but the bishop defended his excommunication on the grounds that the men had resisted his authority and stirred up a riot in Plympton church during which several clerks had been killed.[72] In another case the archbishop had to decide whether to support the bishop of Coventry in his suspension of one of his subordinates who failed to appear in the bishop's synod or to decide in favor of the subordinate and his chaplain, who supported this defiance of episcopal authority by continuing to celebrate mass in the face of the bishop's pronouncement of excommunication.[73] There are several points of interest in a dispute in which the archbishop had to decide between the bishop of Norwich and the cathedral priory: the decision is explicitly stated to have been made at Lambeth in the presence of the archbishop; the question in dispute was

68. Chartae Antiquae, D 111.
69. Christ Church Letters, vol. II, #250; Sede Vacante Scrap-book, I, 133, #3.
70. Sede Vacante Scrap-book, I, 132, #1.
71. *Ibid.*, p. 51, #1.
72. Christ Church Letters, vol. II, #238.
73. *Ibid.*, #230.

the right of presentation to the church of Martham; the dean of Norwich, who made the presentation by right of the bishop, had installed Adam of Walsingham, one of Archbishop Hubert's clerks, as vicar; and three bishops are among the witnesses to the settlement, probably indicating the need to bolster the decision with the authority of impartial judges.[74]

Several other cases also concerned members of the archbishop's *familia* as principals with questions raised about their rights to churches to which they had been named by the archbishop as a way of providing income for his clerks. For example, when the archbishop conferred the church of Lindefeld on Master William de Bosco, the latter refused to pay the monks of Lewes five shillings annual rent which they claimed from a chapel dependent on his church and thus reopened an old dispute. Earlier the dispute over the parochial rights of the chapel at Sotenesberi had been carried by the canons of Malling and the monks of Lewes to the point of appeal to Rome and had finally been settled by papal judges delegate in favor of the monks of Lewes. When the case was brought to his court, Archbishop Hubert, after hearing the testimony of the canons of Malling on the outcome of the old dispute, ordered Master William to continue the payments.[75] This practice of taking sworn testimony from witnesses in the locality of a disputed church was used in other instances to clear up the facts in a case.[76]

Although the surviving records represent only bits and pieces in the handling of cases in the archbishop's court, some points of procedure do emerge to show something of the pattern followed in such cases. Most of the cases mentioned above came to the court on appeal from the decision or action of one of the suffragan bishops, and other cases were appealed from the court of a dean or an archdeacon.[77] Such appeals could work for the benefit of the defendant insofar as they meant delay in final determination of the case, as occurred when the poor minister of the church at Leveston attempted to deal with a problem. He was about to begin Sunday mass when some men who had been drinking entered the church, and one of them caused an interruption of the mass. Yet when he attempted to bring the offender before the dean of Lincoln, the man appealed

74. Norwich, D. and C. Mun., Temporary #953, original archbishops' charters.

75. L. F. Salzman et al., *The Chartulary of the Priory of St. Pancras of Lewes* (Sussex Record Society, 38, 40, supp. vol. for 1943, n.p., 1932-43), II, 131-132.

76. Canterbury, D. and C. Mun., Christ Church Letters, vol. II, #248.

77. *Ibid.*, #243; Sede Vacante Scrapbook, I, 154, #2.

to the archbishop.[78] Many of those involved in suits before the court of the archbishop were represented by proctors, and there are a number of surviving letters that notify the archbishop when such proctors were chosen.[79] One letter from Robert of Bocland to the archbishop is different from the usual formalities because Robert had to beg additional time in order to prepare his defense against the charges made in court.[80] Decisions of the court were always couched in the form of a mandate from the archbishop. Sometimes he certainly was present, but many letters (like those already discussed that concern appeals from bishops) are reports to the archbishop of the disposition of cases which he had given to delegates to try in his stead. Some of these in which the delegates had been unsuccessful indicate that a further direct intervention by the archbishop might be required.[81]

The process of reaching a decision and, even more, of enforcing that decision was often far from simple. For example, one case in Lincoln was tried in a minor court, appealed to the bishop, appealed from him to the archbishop, delegated by the archbishop to commissioners for hearing, and then with the testimony taken by the commissioners referred to the archbishop for final decision.[82] Even those men involved in administering the system sometimes were at a loss about how to proceed. When one of the parties summoned to appear before Hubert's delegates failed to do so, the delegates were confused and asked the archbishop for further instructions.[83] In addition, there was always the possibility that the unsuccessful party in a suit before the archbishop might be tempted to appeal to Rome, thus initiating a further step which, at the least, would mean considerable delay and could mean an almost indefinite postponement of decision.

A good example of a case in which the appeal to Rome meant a long delay in the final decision was the famous dispute between Archbishops Baldwin and Hubert and the monks of Christ Church, but the situation was not greatly different in less important cases. The difficulty of enforcing decisions is illustrated in each step of a case in which the rector of a church was trying to force his chaplain to make certain payments to him. Al-

---

78. Christ Church Letters, vol. II, #253.

79. Sede Vacante Scrap-book, I, 50, #2, #5; II, pp. 177, 204.

80. Christ Church Letters, vol. II. #241.

81. *Ibid.*, #235-236; Sede Vacante Scrap-book, I, 50, #4; B.M., Harley MS., 391, f. 140.

82. Christ Church Letters, vol. II, #228.

83. *Ibid.*, #254.

though the chaplain admitted he had no right to retain the payments, he refused to end his defiance even when the archbishop instructed his delegates to inflict canonical punishment on him. Instead, he obtained papal letters and the case was placed under papal jurisdiction. Only time could be gained by this procedure, for Archbishop Hubert was then also papal legate and the dispute again came into his hands in that capacity. For a second time he returned it to the two delegates, who now were able to take final action on the basis of papal authority.[84] Although the process of appeal to Rome meant delay, the practice of the popes in arriving at their decisions through the use of judges delegate chosen from the English clergy and the conferring of legatine authority on the archbishop of Canterbury helped to keep such appeals from seriously undermining the authority of English ecclesiastical courts.

Both the problems raised by appeals to Rome and the relation of this system to English courts are illustrated in actions coming before Archbishop Hubert. One defendant wrote the archbishop complaining that the subordinates of the bishop of Salisbury interfered with his possession of certain chapels in spite of the writer's appeal to Rome. Another requested the archbishop's protection for his churches while he perfected an appeal to Rome. Similarly, some monks asked protection against the archdeacon of Worcester while their case against the abbot of Westminster was being appealed. Even papal judges delegate sought the aid of the archbishop in disciplining several of his clergy who resisted their decision and continued to celebrate divine service even though the judges had ordered excommunication.[85] Clearly the power of the archbishop, although sometimes impinged upon by the practice of appeals to Rome, remained central in the enforcement of ecclesiastical justice in England, and during the years that Hubert Walter was papal legate, or when he was appointed as a judge delegate by the pope, his co-operation was absolutely essential.

When we turn from questions of procedure to the substance of the cases that came before the archbishop in his capacity as metropolitan, it becomes evident that there was no lack of variety. Dispute over rights to benefices was the source of many actions. An example of this type was Hubert's decision on the right of William de Wrotham to a canonry at

84. Exeter, D. and C. Mun., MS. #810-813; Cartulary #3672, p. 36. Historical Manuscripts Commission, *Report on Manuscripts in Various Collections*, IV, 57 prints excerpts from #810-811, 813.
85. Canterbury, D. and C. Mun., Christ Church Letters, vol. II, #232, 242; Chartae Antiquae, M 263, P 46.

Wells in a dispute that developed early in the career of a man who later had a rather distinguished administrative career under King John.[86] Although the question of patronage was a matter for the royal courts, disputes over presentation to churches frequently came before the archbishop. Two such suits named clerks of Hubert's *familia,* Roger of Basingham and William de Bosco, when they became involved in litigation over churches they held.[87] Similar questions about tithes produced considerable difficulty.[88]

Because certain questions impinged upon both ecclesiastical and common law, it also became necessary for royal courts to decide such questions as that posed by the writ *utrum,* concerning whether the priory of Coventry held its lands by free alms or by lay fee, before a case could be decided by the appropriate court, lay or ecclesiastical.[89] Other cases before the court of the archbishop resulted from the same kind of overlapping jurisdiction. For example, if the question of legitimate birth arose in a case being tried in a royal court, this question was referred to the appropriate ecclesiastical court for determination. One of the cases referred to Archbishop Hubert in 1200 involved a difference in interpretation of illegitimacy between canon law and common law. Although by canon law any children born prior to a marriage and recognized at the time of the marriage were considered legitimate, the interpretation in common law, as expressed in the treatise that bears Glanvill's name, holds to a ruling made by the justiciar Richard de Lucy that only those children born after marriage are legitimate. For this reason, Archbishop Hubert reported to the royal justices that the finding of his court in a case of bastardy was that the son in the case had been born before marriage, the daughter after.[90]

In other business before his court dealing with questions arising from marriage, Hubert had to decide whether Henry of Winchester's mother had taken the habit of a nun before he was conceived. Again, the nature of the relations between the consort of Margaret of North Wales and

86. Canterbury, D. and C. Mun., Ecclesiastical Suits, #1.
87. Christ Church Letters, vol. II, #231; Jones, I, 299-300.
88. Canterbury, D. and C. Mun., Christ Church Letters, vol. II, #244, 245, 246 (printed in Historical Manuscripts Commission, *Report on Various Collections,* I, 240), 249; B.M., Harley Charter 43. I. 18; 83. C. 27; H. E. Salter, *Newington Longville Charters* (Oxfordshire Record Series, III, Oxford, 1921), pp. 37-38. For comment on the legal complications arising over tithes, see Constable, pp. 120-125.
89. *Rotuli curiae regis,* I, 3, 66-67.
90. *Curia Regis Rolls,* I, 236, 335; Makower, pp. 421-422.

several women, involving as it did possible prior marriage, was a subject for archiepiscopal decision. Other disputes in which the questions at issue brought them into the archbishop's jurisdiction involved the nullification of a marriage within the prohibited degrees of relationship, restoration of conjugal rights, and advice to a priest about handling a question of breach of promise to marry.[91]

To be sure, the question of illegitimacy as a bar to inheritance was only one of a number of questions that were automatically ecclesiastical cases to be referred to church courts when the question of jurisdiction was raised during the proceedings in a royal court. The institution of a man presented to a church was another such question, yet one closely related to the exclusive competence of royal courts in disputes about advowson.[92] However, the records from Archbishop Hubert's tenure are fragmentary and by no means complete in regard to the kinds of cases he must have heard. Another type of interaction with secular courts occurred when William Burdun and his wife Agnes sought a judgment in 1203 on their claim to some land. The archbishop sent letters patent to the royal court that they were both excommunicate, thus ending the suit and leaving the couple to seek absolution from the archbishop.[93] Supporting documents in a similar case include a letter from the archdeacon of Derby and Hubert's clerk, Godfrey de Insula, reporting the execution of the archbishop's mandate concerning Aliz Clement, a nun who had left her convent. After trying unsuccessfully to persuade her to return to the convent, they finally had excommunicated her and her accomplices, and this excommunication remained a bar to her attempt to appear in a royal court in 1208.[94]

Other cases were transferred from royal jurisdiction to the court of the archbishop when he made a valid claim that the type of case or the person involved fell under ecclesiastical jurisdiction. An example of such a transfer is a case in which Archbishop Hubert intervened in a royal proceeding to seek his court's jurisdiction for a plea of land between the earl of Leicester and the bishop of Lincoln.[95] King Richard also granted the archbishop custody of all clerks arrested for whatever reason, and the

91. Canterbury, D. and C. Mun., Christ Church Letters, vol. II, #-03 (on verso of front cover), 229, 233, 239, 251, 252. Historical Manuscripts Commission, *Various Collections*, I, 239-240 prints #233, 251.

92. Makower, p. 435. See also G. B. Flahiff, "The Writs of Prohibition to Court Christian in the Thirteenth Century," *Mediaeval Studies*, VI (1944), pp. 274-276.

93. *Curia Regis Rolls*, II, 181.

94. *Ibid.*, V, 185.

95. *Rotuli curiae regis*, II, 183.

justices, sheriffs, constables, ministers, and bailiffs of the king were ordered to surrender such clerks to the archbishop and were prohibited from detaining any clerk when the archbishop requested his custody. This grant was later renewed by King John.[96] These criminous clerks were later tried in ecclesiastical court, but the lenient procedures in most church courts made the handling of such cases something of a scandal throughout the thirteenth century, for which more evidence is available than in the time of Hubert Walter.[97]

In another case that must have concerned him personally Hubert seems to have encountered some difficulty in carrying out the provisions of the last will and testament of William Glanvill, who was probably related to Hubert's mentor, Ranulf Glanvill.[98] Almost inevitably the human side of Hubert Walter's career tends to become submerged in the myriad details of the many responsibilities he bore. Yet the name of Glanvill occurs now and then among the records of his pontificate, suggesting that he continued some sort of connection with descendants and relatives of the man in whose household he got his start. Although Hubert was changed in many ways by the pomp and wealth that he acquired as archbishop, he does not seem to have turned his back on his own more humble origins. Certain names that are mentioned in association with the archbishop, although they do not constitute definite proof, suggest that he kept a close relationship with men who came from East Anglia near his own birthplace. Furthermore, two charters serve to remind us that despite the cares of diocesan and metropolitan service, as well as his labors in royal service, Hubert Walter continued his interest in the house of Premonstratensian canons he had founded at West Dereham early in his career.[99] The boy from the fields of East Anglia and the youth from Glanvill's household were never completely lost in the splendid robes and mitre of the "Primate of all England."[100]

96. Lambeth Palace Library, MS. 1212, pp. 50, 206; *Rotuli chartarum*, I, Pt. 1, 68a.

97. John R. H. Moorman, *Church Life in England in the Thirteenth Century* (Cambridge, 1946), pp. 155 ff.

98. Canterbury, D. and C. Mun., Christ Church Letters, vol. II, #226; Sede Vacante Scrap-book, I, 132, #2.

99. P.R.O., Records of the Duchy of Lancaster, Deeds 27/90; F. M. Stenton, *Documents Illustrative of the Social and Economic History of the Danelaw* (London, 1920), p. 381.

100. Hubert Walter's mitre and parts of his vestments were removed from his tomb when it was opened and now can be seen in the library at Canterbury Cathedral. A description of the opening of the tomb with color reproductions of some of the finds can be found in W. H. St. John Hope, "On the Tomb of an Archbishop Recently Opened in the Cathedral Church of Canterbury," *Vetusta Monumenta* (Society of Antiquaries), VII, Part I (1893).

# 7 KING RICHARD'S JUSTICIAR

To look at Hubert Walter's career as archbishop of Canterbury is to see only one side of the coin, even though his ecclesiastical duties probably represent the least-known side. Contemporaries like St. Hugh of Lincoln and Abbot Samson found it difficult to disentangle the strands of his ecclesiastical and secular authority, and the truth must be that Hubert himself made no consistent separation, preferring to deal with problems and questions of policy in the pragmatic manner of the successful man of affairs. Hubert's position was unique from the moment that King Richard used his influence on the election to Canterbury and then chose Hubert as justiciar in December 1193. When King Richard left England for Normandy in May 1194 to deal with his possessions on the Continent and to take personal command of his war with King Philip Augustus of France, the governing of England was left to the justiciar, who shouldered this burden for four and one-half years until his resignation in July 1198. As it happened, the king never returned from the Continent, yet these years were in no sense an interregnum. Not only was the government conducted in an energetic manner, but numerous administrative improvements were made that provide a link between the period in which Henry II had given his personal attention to innovations in government and the later personal intervention by King John in these matters.

The center of the administrative activities under the authority of the justiciar was the Exchequer, but the work done there was as much judicial as financial in nature. Most of the men who staffed the king's courts had backgrounds similar to that of Hubert Walter. They had training in the common law and yet some acquaintance with canon law, for many of them also presided over ecclesiastical courts in their capacities as bishops or archdeacons. The consequence of this overlapping of personnel has been pointed out by H. G. Richardson:

And under Richard I the king's judges at the exchequer, without apparently even leaving the bench, might in another capacity, hear an ecclesiastical case. It is to our mind inconceivable that, with this identity of personnel, the practice of the common law of England remained unaffected by the procedure of canon law, and therefore of civil law.[1]

1. H. G. Richardson and G. O. Sayles, eds., *Select Cases of Procedure without Writ under Henry III* (Selden Society, LX, London, 1941), pp. lix-lx. Two

The feet of fines, numerous after the middle of 1195, list the judges present and thereby give a clear indication of this personnel. Normally Hubert Walter presided; generally present were Gilbert Glanvill, bishop of Rochester, and Richard fitz Nigel, bishop of London; sometimes present were Godfrey Lucy, bishop of Winchester, and Herbert le Poore, bishop of Salisbury; two archdeacons usually present were Ralph of Hereford and Richard Barre of Richmond; and other clergy sometimes present were Master Henry de Castellion, archdeacon of Canterbury, and William de Ste. Mère Eglise, who was later elected bishop of London. Lay nobles of high rank were "conspicuously absent," and those laymen commonly in attendance were men whose training in royal service would qualify them as professional judges: Geoffrey fitz Peter, William de Warenne, Simon Pateshull, Richard Heriet, Osbert fitz Hervey, and Oger fitz Oger.[2] Whether clergy or laymen, the common bond among these judges was a professionalism born of long training in royal service, reminiscent of the professional atmosphere with which Hubert Walter had been familiar since his apprenticeship in Glanvill's household.

This increased influence of the professional element in government reached its peak during the justiciarship of Hubert Walter, reversing the trend that had seen the barons regularly taking an active part in the government during King Richard's absence on the Third Crusade. The practice (after about 1191) had been to call general meetings of all the leading men of the realm to give their counsel in deciding the more important questions that arose before the justiciars who ruled England for the absent king. Apparently, the purpose was to find a broad basis of consent before undertaking new policies in a period of insecurity and uncertainty.[3] This system continued to be employed while the king was in captivity and after Hubert Walter had returned to England to assume the leadership of the government. Plans for organizing the collection of the ransom were made in such a council, and after he had been appointed justiciar, Hubert called a council to deal with John's rebellion. Only the frequency of such councils and the heavy dependence upon them by the justiciars was new,

---

books that have appeared since this chapter was written should also be consulted: John T. Appleby, *England without Richard 1189-1199* (Ithaca, N. Y., 1965) and Francis West, *The Justiciarship in England 1066-1235* (Cambridge, 1966) which deals with Hubert Walter on pp. 78-96.

2. Frederic W. Maitland, ed., *Three Rolls of the King's Court in the Reign of King Richard the First. A.D. 1194-1195* (P.R.S., XIV, London, 1891), p. xxvii. See also F. J. West, "The *Curia Regis*," pp. 174-176, 180.

3. Wilkinson, pp. 508-509.

for, in legal theory, such councils were in effect especially full meetings of the royal "great council," presided over by the justiciar in place of the king. Essentially these meetings were the same as that over which Richard presided to deal with John and his fellow rebels after he returned to England and the rebellion was put down.

Once Hubert Walter had thoroughly established himself in the justiciarship, reliance upon the barons was dropped. This marks a significant change in the political development of England. No longer do meetings of great councils figure in the narratives of the chroniclers, except for one council held at Oxford in December 1197, and even in this case the justiciar was able to circumvent his opponents.[4] Hubert's method was to place men he could rely on in positions of authority and to accomplish his ends through the masterly use of the regular administrative machinery. Possessing the complete confidence of the king and knowing that the king was no longer cut off from England by distance or imprisonment, the justiciar did not need to seek support among the barons for his policies, and, for the most part, Hubert had the political wisdom to avoid the kind of confrontation that would unite them in opposition to him. Nevertheless, this diminishment of the barons' participation in major decisions, coupled as it was with increasing demands for money and knights to aid Richard's campaigns in France, laid the foundations for baronial discontent that erupted during the reign of King John.

As a practical matter, the justiciar's power was supreme in England as long as the king remained on the Continent. Not only could he preside over a council in the place of the king, but also such a routine matter as the enforcement of an assize provided that it could be done either before the king or the justiciar.[5] Theoretically, it would have been possible to appeal to the king against the decisions of the justiciar, had it not been clear that Hubert Walter strongly discouraged such a move. When Geoffrey, the archbishop of York, attempted to go to the Continent and lay his problems before the king himself, the justiciar issued an order that prevented him from leaving England.[6] At a somewhat later date, Hubert was incensed when he discovered that another man had succeeded in reaching the king with his appeal.[7] Hubert's ecclesiastical position added to his secular power. When the canons of Salisbury sought to ob-

---

4. *Magna vita*, I, xlii-xliv; II, 98-101. This council is discussed more fully below.

5. Roger of Hoveden, IV, 33-34.
6. Gervase of Canterbury, I, 523.
7. Roger of Hoveden, IV, 5.

tain a license from the king to elect a new bishop, the justiciar granted the license on his own authority without seeking the king's approval.[8] Since his position as archbishop of Canterbury gave him ecclesiastical control over the consecration of the bishop, he was thus able to bring both secular and ecclesiastical influence to bear upon such an election if he wished to do so.

King Richard seems to have been content to allow his justiciar to govern as he liked as long as money and knights were forthcoming when needed. The one exception was when the abbot of Caen persuaded the king in 1196 that he was getting only half the revenues due him from England because of fraud by royal officials. Richard sent the abbot to England to make reforms necessary to prevent this loss. The abbot was received by Hubert Walter, who summoned the sheriffs to appear before the abbot and account for their jurisdictions. However, when the abbot died before the accounting was made, the king made no further effort to force the issue.[9] Richard's attitude toward his powerful justiciar is clearly revealed when that same year he refused to allow Hubert to resign his position because there was no one else upon whom he could rely to rule the country; Hubert continued to rule England for two more years.[10]

During his rule as justiciar, Hubert was, of course, in communication with King Richard, and many of his actions were merely the execution of some royal command received in letters from the king.[11] There was also the possibility of consultation with the king if the justiciar wished before he made decisions. Nevertheless, in most cases he acted on his own responsibility in place of the absent king. Writs were issued in his own name with specific instructions for such royal officials as the justices of the bench at Westminster, the sheriff of Devon, and the treasurer.[12] Because, on the one hand, Hubert's correspondence as archbishop was not influenced by the characteristics of royal chancery style, and, on the other hand, his writs as justiciar do not resemble his provincial, diocesan, and personal correspondence, it would seem that the clerical staff for the two positions were distinct. Richardson concluded from his study of this question that

8. Ralph de Diceto, II, 116.
9. William of Newburgh, in Howlett, II, 464-465.
10. Roger of Hoveden, IV, 12-13.
11. *P.R. 6 Ric. I*, p. 190 is an example of actions taken "per breue H. Cant'
archiepiscopi per breue R. de ultra mare."
12. P.R.O., Special Collections 1 (Ancient Correspondence), vol. I, #17, 18; vol. XLVII, #2.

the clerical establishment of the justiciar was provided by chancellor's clerks working at the Exchequer.[13]

Illustrations of the justiciar's position in acting for an absent king are found in several cases from the *curia regis* rolls. When a man called the king to warrant his claim to certain lands on October 10, 1194, he had a royal writ addressed to the archbishop but did not know what the writ contained. The judges postponed settlement of this case, and the record is endorsed "speak with archbishop." Another case was postponed until the coming of the king as ordered by a writ from the archbishop. The justiciar played a decisive part in a third case that was initiated when Adam de Benningefeld and his wife claimed they had been disseised of some land by Robert Malluvel during the rebellion of Count John. Robert had supported Count John, who had given him possession of the land in question, and his land was, therefore, taken into the king's hand when the rebellion was put down. However, as Hugh Bardolf testified, Robert had since given a fine to the king to retain possession, and the sheriff of Nottingham produced royal letters to this effect. At this point, Hubert Walter said that he had heard the king say that he would return seisin of all lands to those who were disseised by Count John and that such people had legal right to the land. The justices decided in favor of Adam and his wife on the ground that what the king ordered verbally had greater weight than what was commanded by letters. Such a decision, based solely on the comments of the justiciar, even in the face of written evidence to the contrary, shows the power and prestige of his office.[14]

Certain kinds of cases heard by the archbishop in his court at Canterbury were very closely connected with the right to present rectors or vicars to churches, and the determination of such a question of advowson by the royal courts obviously touched upon ecclesiastical concerns. This interconnection was compounded when the secular determination of advowsons came before a justiciar who was at the same time archbishop of Canterbury. Not only did this combination of offices give Hubert Walter unparalleled power over such questions that impinged upon both secular and ecclesiastical jurisdiction, but also his position as archbishop enabled him to handle some problems in a special manner. For example, when royal foresters became involved with the monks of Witham in a dispute over customs exacted by the monks for pasture, the archbishop was told

13. *Memoranda Roll 1 John*, p. lxxxiv.    14. *Rotuli curiae regis*, I, 9, 41, 47.

that those customs were incongruous for men professed to religion and might even be considered cruel for secular persons. However, because of Hubert's ecclesiastical position, the prior invited him to stop off on a journey he was making to Glastonbury Abbey and took the opportunity to present the monks' side of the dispute.[15] The archbishop was thus persuaded of the reasonableness of the customs in a way that might not have been possible except for the easy personal communications between the monks and the archbishop. The chronicler Ralph of Coggeshall thought that Hubert restrained and tempered the orders of King Richard when the king oppressed church officials in his need for money.[16] Yet, in spite of the fact that Hubert might use his influence as justiciar for aiding the church, there was an unfortunate contradiction in his position as head of both church and state. This contradictory position is exemplified by a reference to a judicial duel fought before the archbishop and other justices, and even more by his involvement in judgments that might involve death or mutilation.[17]

In September 1194, less than a year after being named as justiciar, Hubert Walter sent out the itinerant justices with instructions that envisioned a broad new program upon which much of his reputation as an administrator has rested. Lady Stenton gives this evaluation of his program:

The eyre of 1194 was a great administrative achievement carried through remarkably quickly. Hubert Walter desired to overhaul the local administration, raise as much money as possible, and satisfy the local demand for justice. He was obliged to postpone the searching inquiry he had planned into the behaviour of local officials, but the organization soon to develop into the Exchequer of the Jews was set up and the office of coroner was established.[18]

The instructions for the eyre have little detail about the procedure for dealing with crown pleas, as if Hubert was able to take for granted the sort of detail that King Henry II had felt it necessary to spell out fully. A general inventory of the feudal and other rights of the king foreshadowed a stricter enforcement of these rights. The fact that inquiries about escheats were to go back to the time when King Richard left for the crusade and that other inquiries were to be made concerning properties of the supporters of Count John indicates a desire to clear away a backlog of unfinished

---

15. Wilmart, p. 225.
16. Ralph of Coggeshall, p. 92.

17. B.M., Additional Charter, 20246.
18. *P.R. 7 Ric. I,* p. xxiii.

business preparatory to a general tightening up of administrative enforcement.[19] No wonder that a postponement of a case involving Croyland Abbey from October 15 to November 2, 1194, had to be made because the justiciar was too busy to hear it on the earlier date. The escheator's accounts on the Pipe Roll show the efficiency of the investigations, including an estimate of how much stock the lands in the king's hands should bear, and it becomes evident from the records that Hubert had to intervene personally by associating himself with the justices to assess tallage.[20]

The twentieth item in the instructions may be said to have instituted the office of coroner if it is remembered that the duties of that office were not new in 1194 but had already been performed by other local officials. The item provides that "three knights and one clerk are to be elected in each county as keepers of crown pleas." The coroner thus established was less eminent than the county justiciar whose office had been suppressed by Henry II when it had become too powerful, yet he was more important than the sergeant of a hundred because the coroner's office was county-wide in scope, elective in nature, and not responsible to the sheriff. A general improvement in efficiency could be anticipated from relieving the sheriff of some burdens and by having an official to concentrate on preserving the details of crown pleas between judicial eyres.[21] Like most of Hubert Walter's administrative changes, the office of coroner represents a consolidation of previous responsibilities, not something entirely original, and a step toward greater efficiency as a logical extension of previous developments.

The instructions for the eyre of 1194 also set up administrative machinery designed to introduce a new efficiency in dealing with the wealth of the Jews and to leave little room for neglect, carelessness, or corruptibility on the part of royal officials by which Jews could escape the harsh demands of the king. Records were to be made of all debts, pledges, lands, houses, rents, and possessions of Jews. Some six or seven places were to be established where Jews could make loans in the presence of a panel consisting of two Christians, two Jews, two scribes, and the clerks of two itinerant justices. Such loans were drawn up in the form of a chiro-

---

19. Roger of Hoveden, III, 262-267.
20. *P.R. 7 Ric. I*, pp. xxii-xxiv.
21. R. F. Hunnisett, *The Medieval Coroner* (Cambridge, 1961), pp. 1-3.

Cf. Richardson and Sayles, *The Governance of Mediaeval England*, p. 209, who see little importance in the eyre of 1194 for the office of coroner.

graph, and one part was placed in a chest with three locks. The key to one lock was kept by the two Christians, to the second by the two Jews, and to the third by the clerks of the justices. All three groups on the panel were provided with rolls on which transcripts of the transactions were recorded, and no other transactions or changes, even payments of a loan, could be made later except before the authorized panel or, at least, a majority of the men on the panel. Later Pipe Rolls contain some evidence of these justices of the Jews (as the panel came to be called) at work. Among those named is Joseph Aaron, perhaps a converted Jew and certainly a trusted clerk in the service of Hubert Walter. These Pipe Rolls also indicate that the justiciar raised money by selling privileges to the Jews, usually that of royal assistance in collecting their debts. Other sums in the records suggest that Hubert sometimes adopted even more strong-handed methods in his efforts to extract money from the Jews, but the references are too brief to permit a complete judgment on this point.[22]

In the year following the general eyre the justiciar revised the local machinery for keeping the peace. This new edict in language similar to the Assize of Clarendon of 1166 provided that everyone was obliged to aid in the capture and trial of malefactors. Knights were assigned in all counties to receive a general oath from all males over fifteen years of age that they would fulfil this obligation, thus beginning the office that was to be known later as justice of the peace. The immediate effect of the measure was that knights were elected in each county and after taking testimony under the procedure of the new edict they arrested many suspected persons and held them for trial. At first there seems also to have been some panic caused by fear of the new regulations.[23] However, the more lasting effects of the edict were to provide the machinery for local knights to receive the oaths and to set the age limit at fifteen. This age limit later was incorporated into the Assize of Arms. Although the edict of 1195 was concerned with keeping the peace, it contained procedures that could also be useful in establishing military obligations. In 1205 a universal levy was called out, for the first time linking the obligation to bear arms with a general oath of fealty.[24]

As justiciar, Hubert Walter bore responsibility for military affairs as

22. *P.R. 6 Ric. I*, p. 141; *P.R. 9 Ric. I*, p. xx; *P.R. 10 Ric. I*, p. xxix, 247; *Memoranda Roll 1 John*, p. 71.
23. Roger of Hoveden, III, 299-300.

24. Michael Powicke, *Military Obligation in Medieval England* (Oxford, 1962), pp. 58-59.

well as for keeping peace within the realm. In practice, this meant first of all the problem of endemic fighting and rebellion in Wales. Henry II had attempted the conquest of Wales on a large scale in the summer of 1165 and failed; because of his involvement in fighting on the Continent he made no further attempt. Clashes along the borders continued to occur similar to those which Glanvill faced as justiciar for Henry II and in which the younger Hubert Walter had been given his first introduction to the situation in this area. King Richard had no time to deal with Wales, and his brother John, sent to the area immediately after Richard's first coronation, was more interested in patching over the trouble in order to return as quickly as possible to England where he had more ambitious plans for his own future. Thus, Hubert Walter as justiciar was faced with a festering problem for which no real solution had been found.

After the years of drift and neglect, the English adopted bolder policies in 1195 as a first indication that Hubert was aware of potential difficulties and would be prepared to deal with them. The accession of Gwenwynwyn to South Powys caused enough trouble so that Hubert had to intervene personally in September 1196.[25] By his own writs he obtained more than £700 to finance the strengthening of English positions in several places and to outfit his own successful expedition that took the castle at Welshpool from Gwenwynwyn by undermining the walls.[26] Within a few months the castle was again in Welsh hands, demonstrating that real settlement would not come so easily. In April 1197 the death of the most powerful Welsh prince, Lord Rhys, and the dispute about the succession plunged Wales into deeper confusion.[27] The justiciar conferred at the border with the designated heir, Gruffydd, and recognized his rights to his father's possessions, but such troubled waters gave Gwenwynwyn a chance to intervene in support of another claimant and his own long-range plan for the independence of Wales. His attack on the English stronghold of Painscastle in July 1198 precipitated another English expedition to Wales. However, before the expedition got under way Hubert Walter had resigned the justiciarship, and his successor, Geoffrey fitz Peter, led the English forces to a decisive triumph on August 13.[28]

There seems to be little doubt that Gerald of Wales was confused when

25. Lloyd, II, 579-580, 583.
26. *The Chancellor's Roll for the Eighth Year of the Reign of King Richard the First*, ed. Doris M. Stenton (P.R.S., XLV, London, 1930), p. xxiv.
27. Roger of Hoveden, IV, 21.
28. Lloyd, II, 584, 586; *P.R. 10 Ric. I*, pp. xxxj-xxxij.

he referred to Archbishop Hubert as the leader of the English army on this occasion, and he is himself inconsistent on the point. But his criticism of an archbishop serving as a military leader still applies to Hubert Walter, even though the specific charges are in error. In a letter to the archbishop, Gerald wrote these mocking words of congratulation:

Blessed be God who has "taught your hands to war and your fingers to fight." Blessed be God who by the hand of His annointed has given you such a glorious victory over your enemies. And blessed be His Holy Name who was ordained that this great realm should be ruled by law and pacified by arms through the unwearied labour of His Pontiff and Primate, strong both in spiritual and worldly warfare, fighting with either sword, and by his marvellous skill moulding himself to meet the vicissitudes of these times.[29]

Writing to the pope about a year and a half after the battle, he complained that the archbishop was blocking his own promotion and charged that he was using his power of excommunication against all Welshmen who opposed the English. He also charged that when the archbishop was informed of the English victory in which three thousand Welsh were killed he ordered the *Te Deum laudamus* sung "like a good shepherd giving thanks to God that on that day he had sent down to Hell the souls of so many of his sheep. . . . So on that occasion he made an evil use of both the swords committed to him and to speak the truth it was an evil thing that he should at that time have had both swords at once in his grasp."[30] Hubert Walter's final involvement in the Welsh situation came when he and Geoffrey fitz Peter negotiated the treaty of July 11, 1201, by which the new Welsh leader, Llywelyn the Great, swore fealty to King John.[31]

The second principal military problem with which Hubert as justiciar had to deal was supplying knights and money needed by King Richard for his fighting on the Continent. On April 15, 1196, for example, the king wrote the justiciar to issue a general summons for the knight service of England in preparation for war with the king of France and to place all royal castles in safe hands. Anyone refusing to obey the summons was to be sent to the king, who would speak to him personally.[32] As time went on, the customary knight service and even the money payments to avoid

29. Giraldus Cambrensis, I, 96 (English translation, p. 131).
30. *Ibid.*, III, 25-26 (Butler, p. 181).
31. Lloyd, II, 615.
32. Printed in Ralph de Diceto, II, lxxx.

service were shown to be inadequate to the new demands for long-time service on the Continent and the almost continuous warfare in which the king was engaged.

The justiciar's attempt to deal with this problem at a council held at Oxford in December 1197 brought the dispute between the king's representatives and his ecclesiastical tenants-in-chief to the point of crisis. As presiding officer at the council, the justiciar presented the king's demand for a force of three hundred knights for one year's service overseas. He and the bishop of London were ready to agree to this demand; but Hugh, the bishop of Lincoln, when asked his opinion, spoke in opposition, voicing the feelings of most of the bishops, who were afraid to speak out openly. He said that he would not agree to an action that would add to the burden of the church under his care and further maintained, mistakenly it would seem, that the church at Lincoln was not bound to military service outside England. The archbishop, his lips trembling in anger at this opposition, turned to Herbert, bishop of Salisbury, only to find him in agreement with Bishop Hugh. According to one account, Hubert, enraged by this response, dissolved the council and informed the king of the failure and of those responsible. More likely Hubert was an astute enough politician to recognize that Bishop Hugh spoke for a majority of bishops, and not wishing to push them into taking a firm stand in opposition, he covered up the failure of the council by a show of anger and thus both avoided a complete stalemate and also shifted the blame to others. The king ordered seized the personal possessions of the two bishops who had spoken against his demand, but no one dared touch the possessions of Bishop Hugh, according to his biographer.[33] The possessions of the bishop of Salisbury were seized, and he crossed in February 1198 to seek the king's favor, returning in June. Bishop Hugh crossed to the king in August, but no agreement seems to have been reached. After abandoning his original plan, the justiciar demanded one-tenth of the knight service, which would have produced about the three hundred knights originally sought but without the obligation for a full year's service. Twelve monastic tenants were allowed to compound for money payments in lieu of producing even this amount of knight service.[34] The whole episode is important mostly for its negative effect. The failure to establish a long-term army and to solve the problem of overseas service contributed to difficulties that reappear

33. Roger of Hoveden, IV, 40; *Magna vita*, I, xlii-xliv; II, 98-101.

34. *P.R. 10 Ric. I*, pp. xix-xxi, xxiv.

in Magna Carta and under Henry III. An understanding of the dispute also helps to explain the lack of co-operation by the tenants-in-chief in the years immediately prior to the loss of Normandy.[35]

Hubert Walter's task of raising money for King Richard was by no means ended when enough of the ransom was raised to allow the king to be released from captivity. Finance remained a continual problem as long as he was justiciar. The Pipe Roll that reflects his first months in office lists four types of fines: those arranged earlier by Walter of Coutances, new fines made by Hubert Walter, those inflicted on men who supported Count John, and payments from military tenants who did not cross to Normandy for service with the king. Though such preoccupation with raising money gave Hubert a reputation for harshness, a chance reference to a transaction handled both by the justiciar and by the king is interesting and might, if this one instance is typical, help Hubert's reputation. Roger Bigod offered the justiciar one hundred marks to obtain trial in the king's court of a dispute with his half brother over their inheritance; later he had to pay seven hundred marks when he directly sought the king's favor in the matter.[36]

Hubert's dealing with William of Yarmouth, who in 1195 collected the tithes on shipping entering ports in Norfolk and Lincolnshire, indicates that the justiciar insisted on careful performance of duties by his subordinates. Two years later Hubert imposed on William a fine of five hundred marks "for having the king's favor and his lands and his goods that were seized into the hand of the king. . . ." Although the nature of William's fault is not given, it is worth noting that the justiciar assessed this large fine in spite of the fact that several names among the pledges for William are those of men closely associated with Hubert Walter, most notably Henry Castellion, archdeacon of Canterbury; Geoffrey de Bocland, a member of Hubert's *familia*; Thomas de Ardene, a friend of Ranulf Glanvill; and others whose surnames may indicate relationship with men of the *familia*. Another indication of relationship between the two men is that William later gave a church in his patronage to Hubert's monastic foundation at West Dereham.[37]

One of the expedients for raising money hit upon by the king was

35. *Magna vita*, p. xlv.
36. *Memoranda Roll 1 John*, pp. xxvj, xxxj.
37. *P.R. 7 Ric. I*, p. 79; *P.R. 8 Ric. I*, p. 278; *P.R. 9 Ric. I*, pp. xviij, 233-234, 247-248; B.M., Additional MS. 46353, f. 290 v.

the granting of licenses to hold tournaments. The church had long opposed tournaments. That opposition was reformulated at the Third Lateran Council in 1179 and reiterated for the duration of calamities in the Holy Land by Pope Celestine III in 1193.[38] Nevertheless, King Richard wrote to Archbishop Hubert authorizing tournaments at five specified places in England and establishing a schedule of fees for participants: twenty marks for earls, ten marks for barons, four marks for landholding knights, and two marks for landless knights.[39] Although the king named William, earl of Salisbury, to administer the new policy, the justiciar made his brother Theobald the collector of these fees. The sums were paid directly to the king rather than being accounted for at the Exchequer.[40] Hubert's influence was also used to help his brother when he became one of the itinerant justices and to secure delay for some court cases in which he was involved.[41]

In at least one instance the new regulations about tournaments caused trouble. In spite of a royal license Abbot Samson forbade a tournament to be held near St. Edmund's, but he had little success in his prohibition. Later after a return bout, some eighty young men came to the town of St. Edmund's seeking lodging. The abbot ordered the gates barred and the young men shut in, presumably thinking to punish them for participating in a tournament against his prohibition. Next day when they promised not to leave without his permission, they all were invited to eat with him, but after Abbot Samson had retired they persisted in dancing and drinking, completely ignoring him when he ordered them to desist. Finally, they broke down the gates of the town and forced their way out. However, the abbot had the last say when he excommunicated the whole group on the advice of Archbishop Hubert.[42] How Hubert reconciled his role as justiciar in licensing tournaments through his brother with his ecclesiastical support for the abbot in his prohibition of tournaments is impossible to say.

As another facet of his responsibility as justiciar, Hubert Walter took over the exploitation of the tin mines in Devon and Cornwall. The changes made during his justiciarship laid the foundation for the stannary administration of the later Middle Ages. The actual administration of the mines

38. Benedict of Peterborough, I, 226; Rymer, I, Pt. 1, p. 56; William of Newburgh, in Howlett, II, 422-423.

39. Lambeth Palace Library, Codex 8, f. 158; Rymer, I, Pt. 1, 65.

40. Roger of Hoveden, III, 268; *P.R. 10 Ric. I*, p. xxx.

41. *Rotuli curiae regis*, I, 89.

42. Jocelin of Brakelond, pp. 55-56.

was entrusted to William de Wrotham. His report to the justiciar in 1198, which is the first full record of the mines, shows that he had already made some administrative changes. These prepared the way for more important changes soon to follow. With the aid of juries assembled from the miners themselves he rectified the weights used in the official measurement of tin blocks. He also imposed a tax on tin, appointed other administrative officials, and established a code that brought all tin production under view of royal officials. The annual output of the mines was increased under his administration, and the king obtained more revenue from tin than from all the remaining sources of revenue in Cornwall.[43]

Although he was overburdened with the necessity of raising money, the outstanding quality of Hubert Walter's justiciarship was his passion for regularizing and improving the administrative machinery of the royal government. Another example of this aspect of his work as justiciar was his Assize of Measures, issued in November 1196. Its principal provision was that all measures used throughout England were thereafter to be of a standard size or weight. In each city, borough, vill, and county, four to six men were to be chosen to enforce the assize and insure that all buying and selling would be done by these standard measures. Anyone who confessed or was convicted of breaking the assize was to be imprisoned and his property seized into the king's hands; he could not be freed except by direct order of the king or the justiciar. As part of the implementation of the measure, the justiciar directed the citizens of London to make standard measures—gallons, iron rods, beams, and weights—and to send these to all the counties of England. Payments were also made from the treasury for those making similar measures at Winchester and Portsmouth. Two years later the nineteenth article in the instructions for the itinerant justices was to inquire whether the Assize of Measures was being enforced.[44] The forest eyre of 1198, which Hubert Walter also carried out, adds to the impression of his industry, but unlike most of his administrative actions it attempts no innovation or improvement. The instructions

43. George R. Lewis, *The Stannaries* (Harvard Economic Studies, III, Cambridge, Mass., 1924), pp. 34-36, 38, 233, 235.

44. Roger of Hoveden, IV, 33-34, 62, 172; *P.R. 9 Ric. I*, pp. xxj-xxij where the correct date for the assize is established. An incidental reference to measurement of land by the "iron ell of John, King of England" shows that enforcement of standard measurements was continuing in the next reign. However, such a reference also implies that the particular unit of measurement was not universally used, or no specification as to the unit employed would have been needed. P.R.O., Exchequer, The Treasury of the Receipt, E. 42/54.

for this eyre even retain the cruel punishment of mutilation by removing the eyes and testicles of men convicted of forest offenses.[45]

In 1198 the justiciar called upon his experience in raising the ransom for King Richard to initiate a general reassessment of taxes. This carucage for all of England was based upon a unit of land and amounted to a revival of the old Danegeld under another name. The administrative machinery consisted of a clerk and a knight to work in each county with the sheriff and knights elected there. Sworn testimony was then taken concerning the amount of land in each knight's holdings in the county, and copies of the testimony were to be given to the clerk, the knight, the sheriff, and the bailiff who represented the knight whose lands had been enumerated. The tax, which at first amounted to two shillings on each carucate of land and was later raised to three, was to be paid to the sheriff, who would account for it at the Exchequer. Sergeants, exempted from this procedure, made money compositions with the king. Although all the returns of knights made in connection with this carucage have disappeared, the transcripts for sergeants are extant for nineteen counties.[46] Other evidence for the carrying out of this taxation may be found in the payments for carucage that appear at the beginning of John's reign, in the Pipe Roll for the next year, but the sums there appear to be compositions, since they are given in round figures, and not the results of the strict inquiry that Hubert Walter had initiated.[47] Certainly there had been some difficulties in assessing the carucage; the clergy had at first refused to pay but had then been made willing to do so when the king withdrew the protection of the law from them.[48]

Turning from such administrative detail, it should be emphasized that the essential function of the justiciar was to rule England during the absence of the king. Hubert Walter had been doing this for three consecutive years when King Richard summoned him to Normandy in 1197. He left England on June 17 and remained with the king some four and one-half months that summer and autumn, employed chiefly as a diplomatic representative. Even then, English affairs were not completely laid aside, for he received some fines at Les Andelys from business pertaining to English lands.[49]

45. Roger of Hoveden, IV, 63.
46. Ibid., pp. 46-47; The Book of Fees Commonly Called Testa de Nevill (London, 1920-31), I, 1-2, 4-13.
47. P.R. 1 John, p. xix.
48. Roger of Hoveden, IV, 66.
49. P.R. 9 Ric. I, pp. 114, 219.

Hubert's involvement in diplomacy was not a new departure for him. He had shown his ability in this sphere when he negotiated with Saladin during the Third Crusade, when Richard was being held captive by the German emperor after the crusade, when he dealt with Welsh princes, and when he attempted to negotiate a marriage and settlement of land for Richard's daughter in 1195.[50] Now in September 1197 he was asked to mediate at a meeting between King Richard and his inveterate enemy, Philip Augustus of France. One is tempted to speculate that Hubert may have enjoyed friendly relations with the French king during the crusade, but there may be other reasons why Richard brought him to the meeting. In any event, an agreement for a truce lasting one year was reached by the two kings.[51] Two months later Hubert arranged a treaty between King Richard and Baldwin, count of Flanders, thus making a successful diplomatic coup, for both the king of England and the king of France had been making overtures to the count for more than two years.[52] The archbishop had also used his influence with Richard to obtain milder treatment for the bishop of Beauvais, cousin of the French king, who had been captured while fighting as a knight against the English, and to help in arranging an agreement between the king and the archbishop of Rouen, from whom the king had taken L'Ile d'Andely for the construction of his new castle on the Seine.[53] Thus, for the first time since 1194 the outlook on the Continent seemed to promise peace, at least for a time, and King Richard began making preparations for a return to England. But the justiciar returned alone to resume the burden of governing England, and Richard was never able to leave his post on the Continent.

On the whole, Hubert Walter's term as justiciar was successful and constructive, and he made several improvements in the machinery of government that were of more than transitory importance. Although his position as archbishop of Canterbury at times worked for easier relations in dispatching the business of the justiciar, that position was also the cause of the principal scandal that occurred during his justiciarship. Considerable unrest had developed in the city of London by March 1196 over the heavy financial demands made by the king, and the poorer citizens raised their usual charge that the wealthier men had used their control

50. Roger of Hoveden, III, 308.
51. Gervase of Canterbury, I, 544; Roger of Hoveden, IV, 61.
52. Ralph de Diceto, II, 158; *P.R. 9 Ric. 1*, xxij-xxiij.
53. Ralph de Diceto, II, 157-158; F. M. Powicke, *The Loss of Normandy (1189-1204)* (Manchester, 1913), pp. 172 ff.

of the political machinery in the city to shift the burden of royal taxes to the poor. The discontent was brought to a fever pitch by the efforts of demagogues who harangued the mobs that flocked into the streets.

The most effective of the orators was William fitz Osbert, also known as "William with the beard," who two years earlier had appeared in royal court with charges of treason against his own brother and some of the magnates of London.[54] Now he organized groups of the poor against the rich, began collecting tools for breaking into houses, and warned in an apocalyptic tone that the second coming of Christ was at hand, when the people would be divided and the faithful would be chosen to obtain a reward denied the proud oppressors of this world. Such sentiments provoked a riot near St. Paul's, and when the authorities intervened, William and a few companions barricaded themselves in the tower of St. Mary-le-Bow Church. Hubert Walter as justiciar called a meeting of persons of authority who happened to be in London—several justices, bishops, and abbots—and sought advice on what to do to prevent possible damage and bloodshed. The consensus was that the ringleader would have to be punished. Twice the justiciar sent men to summon William to leave the church and stand trial for his part in the riot, but both efforts failed. In both public and private meetings Hubert obtained undertakings from the citizens that they would be loyal to the king and would preserve the peace, and these pledges were secured by hostages given over to the justiciar. Armed men patrolled the streets to enforce the peace. The whole proceedings reached a climax when the tower of the church was set on fire. Although nobody seemed quite sure how the fire began, it probably was set on orders from the justiciar and then got out of control. In any event, the fire forced William and his fellows into the waiting hands of the justiciar's men. William's supporters among the Londoners made no attempt to aid him because they feared for the safety of the hostages they had given to the justiciar. Brought to the justiciar himself at the Tower of London for trial by the *curia regis,* William and nine others were found guilty and dragged to the gallows at Tyburn. Afterward, Hubert quickly punished a priest who spread rumors that miracles had been produced by the body of William and suppressed all attempts to hail him as a martyr.[55]

When the king heard about the way his justiciar had handled the disturbances in London, he sent him a special letter of commendation for his efforts in restoring peace.[56] Nevertheless, the incident gave Hubert Walter's enemies the opportunity to charge that he had ordered the burning of a church belonging to the monks of Christ Church, Canterbury, as well as providing a particularly vivid example of the archbishop ordering a judgment of blood in contradiction to the canons of the church. More than once Hubert Walter urged the king to allow him to resign as justiciar, and if the chronicler Roger of Howden has not muddled his dates, as he frequently did, he made a strong request to be relieved in 1196. One special point he made was that he had raised 1,100,000 marks over the two years in which he had been justiciar.[57] His health may also have begun to show the strain of his many responsibilities, for he was too ill even to celebrate mass on Christmas of that year.[58] Still he changed his mind about continuing in the office and, in fact, remained another two years until he was finally relieved on July 11, 1198.

The circumstances of Hubert Walter's removal in 1198 are not entirely clear. Roger of Howden wrote that the monks of Christ Church complained to Pope Innocent III about the archbishop's involvement in secular affairs such as judgments of blood, specifically using the Fitz Osbert incident. The pope then wrote King Richard, warning him that for the good of his soul he should not retain a bishop or priest in secular administration, and the king obeyed by deposing Hubert Walter from the justiciarship.[59] The difficulty in accepting this explanation is that Roger of Howden is the only contemporary chronicler to give this account and his connections were in the north where the archbishop of Canterbury had a number of enemies. Neither of the two sources closest to the monks of Christ Church, Gervase of Canterbury and the *Epistolae Cantuarienses,* gives this story, even though in 1198 the controversy between the monks and the archbishop over Lambeth Chapel was at its height and the monks

---

1198 of an archdeacon ordering fire to smoke monks out of a disputed church is mentioned in Roger of Hoveden, IV, 69.

56. Ralph de Diceto, II, lxxix.
57. Roger of Hoveden, IV, 12-13.
58. Ralph de Diceto, II, 150.
59. *Ibid.*, IV, 47-48. For recent comment, see Z. N. Brooke, *The English Church and the Papacy: From the Con-* *quest to the Reign of John* (Cambridge, 1931), p. 221, who accepts Howden's account; Cheney, *From Becket to Langton*, pp. 25-26, and Austin L. Poole, *From Domesday Book to Magna Carta 1087-1216* (Oxford, 1955), pp. 222-223, who accepts the account with reservation; and Doris M. Stenton, ed., *P.R. 10 Ric. I*, p. xxxiij, and West, *Justiciarship*, p. 96, who reject the account.

were using against him all the charges they could find. There is no confirmation among the papal records, though they are not complete for this period, and no examples of similar intervention by Pope Innocent III. It may also be relevant that there seems to have been no papal objection when Hubert became King John's chancellor the following year. In view of the silence in the written sources at Canterbury, King Richard's letter accepting the justiciar's resignation should be taken at face value. The reasons given there for the change—burden of work and ill health—are quite sufficient to explain the resignation of a man who had borne the heavy responsibilities of ruling England for four and one-half years and had only continued to fill the office with reluctance for at least two years.[60]

With his resignation as justiciar, Hubert Walter might be expected to have had more time for his position as archbishop, but instead he crossed to Normandy on the king's orders during the last week of September. There he went again to negotiate with King Philip Augustus by specific orders of the French king and with King Richard's approval. This time, however, Hubert failed to arrange a peace between the warring kings because all negotiations broke down when Richard remained adamant in his insistence that any agreement would have to include his ally, the count of Flanders.[61] In spite of the breakdown of negotiations, the archbishop was still on the Continent when King Richard's unexpected death on April 6, 1199, abruptly changed the entire political situation and thrust Hubert Walter into the whirlpool of political passions that swirled about the question of succession to the empty throne.

60. Lambeth Palace Library, MS. 1212, p. 38; printed from a B.M. MS. in Rymer, vol. I, pt. 1, p. 71.

61. Gervase of Canterbury, I, 574; Roger of Hoveden, IV, 61.

# 8 THE POPE'S AGENT

During nearly the entire time that Hubert Walter served as King Richard's justiciar, he was also papal legate for all England. Appointed by Pope Celestine III on March 18, 1195, he served until his commission expired with the pope's death in January 1198.[1] Although the legatine commission

1. The pope's commission is given in Ralph de Diceto, II, 125-126, and in Stubbs, *Epistolae Cantuarienses,* pp. 368-369. Hubert's profession to the pope as legate is found in Lambeth Palace Library, Wharton 580, p. 261.

itself was not unusual for an archbishop of Canterbury in the twelfth century, that authority had been restricted to the province of Canterbury since the time of St. Thomas.[2] Hubert's commission as legate differed from that of his predecessors by extending beyond the province. As legate he was, of course, brought into direct contact with Rome, but in the normal course of events as archbishop of Canterbury he already had the responsibility for executing papal mandates within his province and had taken a place in the hierarchical chain of command within the church. For example, while Hubert was still only archbishop-elect and before he had received the pallium from Rome, the pope ordered him to have the body of St. Thomas removed from its resting place in the crypt of Canterbury and to construct a shrine more fitting the eminence of the martyred archbishop. Furthermore, on receiving the pallium, he made his profession to the pope in terms that involved complete submission to papal authority.[3] Both his role as papal legate and his participation in a number of celebrated ecclesiastical controversies of the day called for the highest order of statesmanship and a considerable degree of political knowledge and influence.

One of his first actions under his authority as papal legate was to conduct a visitation in the province of York. With the archbishop of York on the Continent trying to repair his differences with King Richard, and with the redoubtable bishop of Durham, Hugh du Puiset, recently dead, the church in the north was in need of leadership and supervision. As Hubert himself explained, the church there was set in distant parts and was most needful of visitation; acting on the premise that the graver the infirmity the quicker the need for a cure, he decided first to turn northward.[4] Before going himself to York, he sent Peter, prior of Binham in Norfolk, and Master Gervase of his own household with letters from the pope and from himself to the canons and officials of the archbishop of York announcing his intended visitation. The clergy at York, carefully guarding the dignity of their own archbishop, agreed to receive him as legate, not as archbishop or primate.[5]

2. Helene Tillmann, *Die päpstlichen Legaten in England bis zur Beendigung der Legation Gualas (1218)* (Bonn, 1926), pp. 34, 146.

3. Stubbs, *Epistolae Cantuarienses*, pp. 367-368. The place of the English church as an organic part of the church at large was the thesis established by Z. N. Brooke, *The English Church and the Papacy,* concisely stated in his own words on pp. 99, 113.

4. Stubbs, *Epistolae Cantuarienses*, p. 370; William of Newburgh, in Howlett, II, 442. See Lady Stenton's comment in *P.R. 7 Ric. I*, p. xxviii.

5. Roger of Hoveden, III, 293.

On June 11, 1195, Hubert Walter arrived in York and was received with all the honor due him as papal legate. It would be interesting to know his thoughts as he once again found himself in surroundings he had known formerly as dean of York or to know whether he thought about how he had once been passed over for archbishop of the place where now he arrived commissioned with greater authority. On the following day, with characteristic industry, he presided over the assizes of crown pleas as justiciar and over ecclesiastical cases as papal legate.[6] Later, during his visitation of St. Mary's Abbey, with the complaints of the monks ringing in his ears, he deposed Abbot Robert, who had not even been able to appear before his monks because of his debility and illness.[7] Of more general significance was the council Hubert held on June 14 and 15 in the church of St. Peter. However, even though the council was convened by legatine authority, its purpose was to restore order in the northern province, not to promulgate rules for general application throughout England. Many of the canons of the council dealt with defects in the manner of administering the sacraments and prescribed remedies for abuses; others provided instructions appropriate to the proper functioning of the church in York.[8] Little more is known of Hubert's legatine visitation in the north except that the clergy of York were willing to report to the pope later that the legate had carried out his visitation with mildness and that they had no complaints on the subject.[9] In fact, there was little time for the legate to linger about his ecclesiastical business in the north, for he was needed in London where pressing royal business awaited his attention. Before returning, he visited Durham, where he appointed three abbots to continue the visitation in churches in that area, which he had not had time to visit personally.[10]

One of the difficulties he encountered as papal legate was that some monasteries jealous of their independence and exemption from supervision by secular clergy were not willing to receive him. In July or August of 1195 Archbishop Hubert wrote the monks of St. Augustine's, Canterbury, citing his favorable reception at York and announcing his plans to visit

6. *Ibid.*, III, 294.

7. *Ibid.*; Ralph de Diceto, II, 151; Gervase of Canterbury, I, 529.

8. Roger of Hoveden, III, 294-297; C. R. Cheney, "The Earliest English Diocesan Statutes," *The English Histori-* *cal Review*, vol. 294 (1960), 12-13; Cheney, *From Becket to Langton*, pp. 35, 142.

9. Ralph de Diceto, II, 148.

10. Gervase of Canterbury, I, 529.

their monastery on September 8.[11] The reaction of the monks is shown by the chronicler of that abbey, who writes that Archbishop Hubert has begun to persecute the monastery, partly owing to the pride he has in his secular power and partly because he has become legate. The chronicler further charges that Hubert has obtained the legatine authority at the instigation of the monks of Christ Church, the great rivals of St. Augustine's, or has been seduced by them because he is a layman who is illiterate and ignorant of the law.[12] Mistaken as he undoubtedly was in suspecting the monks of Christ Church of being influential in obtaining the legatine commission, the chronicler might well have questioned the legal grounds for the proposed visitation. Pope Celestine himself upheld the exemption of St. Augustine's from the ordinary legatine powers of Archbishop Hubert with the finding that that abbey was responsible only to the pope himself.[13]

Even within the province of Canterbury Hubert sometimes proceeded on the basis of his authority as papal legate. On one such occasion, obviously unsure of his authority in relation to St. Edmund's Abbey, he sent two clerks with sealed letters to ask whether Abbot Samson and the monks would receive him as legate and with verbal instructions to set forth his plans more fully if they refused. Not wishing to offend such a prominent royal official and their spiritual father, the monks decided to receive him but to resist the exercise of his legatine powers on the grounds of exemption, meanwhile appealing to the pope. As it happened, the archbishop was delayed by other business and a papal reply was received before the announced visitation to East Anglia was begun. The pope's decision that the monastery was exempt from all visitation except by a legate *a latere* included the firm statement that Archbishop Hubert was not to visit St. Edmund's.

When he reached Colchester on his itinerary through East Anglia, Hubert sent a messenger secretly to the abbot to tell him that he had heard that letters had been received from the pope and to ask him to send them. Apparently Hubert wanted to avoid the embarrassment of a public rebuff, for he bypassed the abbey completely, perhaps thinking that he might be refused entrance if he persisted. Later, early in 1199, the archbishop and Abbot Samson met on the highway between Waltham and London, and the archbishop complained that the abbot had refused to

---

11. Stubbs, *Epistolae Cantuarienses*, p. 371.

12. Thorne, p. 132.

13. *Ibid.,* pp. 132-133; P.R.O., Exchequer, Miscellaneous Books I/27, fos. 68-68 v.

meet him as the king's justiciar. The abbot objected that Hubert had traveled as legate, not as justiciar, and continued to argue until the archbishop broke off the conversation. Hubert ended with the indignant statement that they need not continue such a discussion, for he knew that Abbot Samson was a good logician and a better clerk than he. However, this temporary rift between friends was forgotten when Samson and other abbots wrote the pope on behalf of the archbishop to counter the rumor that Hubert had oppressed the churches during his legatine visitations and had made a profit of 30,000 marks.[14]

Although the principle of exemption was naturally a serious matter for a monastery, the whole incident seems to have been taken too seriously by the monastic chronicler. Hubert Walter and Abbot Samson were clearly close friends; the abbot even looked upon Hubert as almost one of his own because he was born on land adjoining that of St. Edmund's. Year in and year out the two men worked together on ecclesiastical business and counseled with each other when faced with problems. Although it seems to have escaped the chronicler, the very tone of their dispute is that of two men who understood each other well and who respected each other for upholding the authority of their respective offices as duty demanded. Nor should one conclude that as legate Hubert was accustomed to act independently of the pope's wishes. When he found that new pensions had been established in churches in violation of canon law and that old pensions had been increased by use of threats, he asked papal advice and was authorized to revoke and reduce such pensions.[15] The general approval of the pope must have been similar to his letter of June 9, 1197, in which he confirmed the blessing of abbots, institutions to vacant churches, and other ordinations done in churches throughout England by Archbishop Hubert acting on his authority as papal legate.[16]

Whether or not Hubert was papal legate, he was certain to be drawn into papal service simply because of his office as archbishop. After his legatine authority had lapsed, he continued to serve frequently as judge delegate for Pope Innocent III. Cases that were appealed to Rome from the church courts in England were often referred to such representatives of the pope in England for final settlement with general instructions as to procedure but with the details left to be determined by the judges delegate. Because of his position, Archbishop Hubert was often chosen as one of

14. Jocelin of Brakelond, pp. 82-85; Holtzmann, III, 571-572.

15. Holtzmann, II, 480.

16. *Ibid.*, II, 479.

these representatives. A contemporary idea of the qualifications for such a judge delegate can be found in Jocelin of Brakelond's comments on Abbot Samson's appointment by the pope. Jocelin writes that Samson is unfitted by knowledge or experience, although he is learned in the liberal arts and Scripture and was once a schoolmaster. In deciding his cases, however, he has the help of two clerks skilled in law. He has also studied the decrees in Gratian and subsequent papal pronouncements to such an extent that with some experience he has come to be regarded as a wise judge. In addition he has had some experience in secular courts. The under-sheriff Osbert fitz Hervey said of him, "This Abbot is a fine disputer: if he goes on as he has begun, he will blind us all, every one." And so, in addition to serving as a papal judge delegate, he was made a justice in eyre.[17] An example of Abbot Samson as a papal judge delegate can be seen in the letter sent to Hubert by the bishop of Norwich, Abbot Samson, and the prior of St. Edmund's notifying the archbishop that they have been appointed delegates in a certain case.[18] Abbot Samson, like Archbishop Hubert, probably had little professional competence in canon law, but he too could call upon the expert knowledge of several members of his *familia* to supply this deficiency in his own qualifications.

The most thoroughly documented case from this period illustrating the process of papal appeals is the Christ Church case, in which both Archbishop Hubert and Abbot Samson became involved in different ways. However, since the persons interested in the case included men of such high position—an archbishop, a king, and some cardinals—this was obviously not a typical case, and the final decision was much delayed by the tortuous political maneuvering on all sides. There was, in fact, nothing that could be called "normal procedure" in cases involving the use of judges delegate in the early thirteenth century (as is shown by the *Decretales* of Pope Gregory IX), but this case illustrates the general process in some detail.[19] A bare outline of the appeal as it was handled by Pope Innocent III would begin with his first mandate prohibiting construction of the chapel, which he issued on the basis of representations by the monks alone and against which the archbishop appealed on June 1, 1198. It was some months before representatives of all parties were as-

17. Jocelin of Brakelond, pp. 33-34.
18. Canterbury, D. and C. Mun., Sede Vacante Scrap-book, I, 133, #4.
19. B. G. Barraclough, Review of Kutt- ner, *Repetorium der Kanonistik, The English Historical Review*, 53 (1938), p. 494.

sembled in Rome and the pope himself had returned from a journey outside the city. Finally, the appeal was heard on October 21 and 22, and a judgment was drawn up on November 6 and dispatched to England on November 20.

Papal delegates first appear in the case at this point, for the pope appointed the bishops of Lincoln and Ely and the abbot of St. Edmund's to execute the mandate within thirty days of its receipt. The archbishop accepted this mandate but asked the pope for a new license to build a new church. On May 19, 1199, the pope appointed the same three delegates to reopen the case and decide whether to grant the new request, outlining in some detail the points into which they were to inquire before making their judgment. The first hearing was set by the judges for September 30, but the monks failed to appear, and since other investigation took some time, the hearing was not resumed until January 26, 1200. Then the monks were so displeased with the decision of the judges that they used their influence to persuade the pope to rescind his commission to the judges delegate on May 21 and recall the case for hearing at Rome. As it happened, the archbishop suggested a compromise arrangement with the former judges as arbiters; this compromise was adopted and the arbiters gave their award on November 6. Both parties accepted this award and signified their agreement to the pope, who concluded the case by ratifying the settlement on June 30, 1201, approximately three years after the archbishop had formally made his appeal to Rome.[20]

In a dispute with some similar points at issue, Hubert's friend and suffragan, Gilbert, bishop of Rochester, became involved with the monks of his chapter even before Hubert reopened the Christ Church case. Gilbert's monks brought definite action only after the Canterbury case had been settled, however. Trouble had been brewing since 1191 and had became more intense with the bishop's founding of a hospital at Strood the following year, an action that received the confirmation of the archbishop.[21] The monks were not disturbed by the exemption of the inmates of the new hospital from the jurisdiction of archdeacons and deans, of course, but they did contest the bishop's right to some of the churches with which he endowed the new foundation. They complained to the bishop himself about his actions, and possibly to the archbishop, finally lodging a formal appeal to Rome against him in 1203.

20. Stubbs, *Epistolae Cantuarienses*, 512, 517.
pp. 407, 459, 468-469, 490-492, 496-497,    21. Moule, p. 18; Thorpe, I, 392-393.

The pope appointed Archbishop Hubert, the bishops of London and of Chichester, the prior of Christ Church, and the archbishop's clerk, Master Simon of Southwell, to hear the case.[22] The monks presented a lengthy brief to the judges which opened with the phrase "Concerning the lake of our miseries and oppressions . . ." and which summarized the history of their church, with each bishop listed as either a friend or despoiler of the monks. Gilbert was noted as a bishop "Who despoiled us of all the presentations of churches that became vacant in his time because he gave them where he wished without consulting us." [23] As usual, the differences were settled by both sides withdrawing their appeals and submitting to arbitration. In this case, as in the Christ Church case, the judges delegate (including Archbishop Hubert) were accepted as the arbiters. A summary description of the settlement is that it increased the episcopal authority over the monks in every respect.[24] But papal approval of the settlement came only after the archbishop's death, and Archbishop Hubert's letter citing the papal approval is a somewhat clumsy forgery, probably emanating from an outbreak of contention between a later bishop and the monks.[25]

In most cases the relationship between the archbishop and the pope placed the archbishop in the position of enforcing papal mandates. Pope Celestine III ordered the archbishop-legate to compel the archdeacon and deans to desist from forcing the canons of Waltham to pay money as penance and to substitute more fitting penalities.[26] Pope Innocent III commissioned the archbishop along with the bishops of London and Ely to stop the clergy who were setting up chapels in Northampton in defiance of the privilege held by the monks of St. Andrew that they might possess all the churches in that town.[27] Similar papal letters to Archbishop Hubert dealt with restoring a church to a man dispossessed by William Brewer,

22. Moule, p. 20; Canterbury, D. and C. Mun., Sede Vacante Scrap-book, III, p. 157.

23. Canterbury, D. and C. Mun., Chartae Antiquae, R70a, R70b.

24. Other documents bearing on the case are found in Holtzmann, II, 463-464; Thorpe, I, 52-55, 69-70, 147, 153, 530, 631-632, 634, 639-640, 687-688. Some of those printed by Thorpe have been verified in Rochester, D. and C. Mun. (on deposit at Kent County Ar-chives, Maidstone), Register of Temporalities, fos. 128 v.-131.

25. The charter printed in Thorpe, I, 104-106 should be compared with a charter of Herbert of Salisbury in the manuscript Register of Temporalities, f. 132. Moule gives a full discussion of this forgery in his Appendix IV, pp. 282-291.

26. Holtzmann, I, 626.

27. Cheney and Semple, p. 25.

a trusted intimate of King John; restraining suffragans of Canterbury and their officials from taking money for chrism and services; enforcing ordinances that tithes were to be paid to churches in the parishes where the tithe-payers lived; reforming the monastery at Waltham; inquiring into the dower King John owed Richard's wife, Berengaria; and inducing the king to allow an election to Winchester or compelling the monks and archdeacon of that diocese to make provision for their church.[28] The role of the archbishop might also be to proclaim and reaffirm papal privileges, such as his letter ordering that the papal privilege of exemption from tithes for the Cistercians be enforced throughout the province of Canterbury.[29]

When Pope Innocent III established an income tax on the clergy in 1199, the administration of the tax depended upon the archbishops and bishops of the provinces. The role of Archbishop Hubert is particularly illuminating. On December 27, 1199, a papal order was sent to many provinces for collection of a fortieth of ecclesiastical revenues and rents for one year to raise money for the crusade, but the delay in collection until 1201 may indicate resistance on the part of the bishops. For England the work of the bishops was supplemented by a papal notary, Master Philip, who arrived in England before April 24, 1200, and was still there on June 1, 1206. He probably brought the papal bull authorizing the collection and was in charge of transmitting the funds raised to the pope. The disposal of the money was handled laxly, for Archbishop Stephen Langton received some money from Exeter in 1213 that had been collected more than seven years earlier.[30] Master Philip had also aroused opposition, and the rumor reached the pope that his conduct was bad. As a result, on August 12, 1202, the pope moved to protect his own reputation by ordering Archbishop Hubert to investigate. In his letter, Pope Innocent referred to Hubert as a person in whom he had full confidence, as he must have had to ask him to investigate the conduct of a papal notary. An undated letter from the abbot of Whitby is the only extant reply to the investigation that Hubert launched. It raises some questions of interpretation because

28. Canterbury, D. and C. Mun., Chartae Antiquae, G 187; Holtzmann, II, 482; W. H. Bliss, *Calendar of Entries in the Papal Registers Relating to Great Britain and Ireland* (London, 1893), I, 7-9, 18, 21.

29. B.M., Campbell Charter, XXII. 6; Cotton MS., Nero C. III, f. 192.

30. William E. Lunt, *Financial Relations of the Papacy with England to 1327* (Cambridge, Mass., 1939), pp. 240-242.

Archbishop Hubert was conducting the inquiry beyond his own province into York, even though he no longer had any powers there as legate.[31]

Gerald of Wales throws a distorted light on these proceedings with his own peculiarly egocentric interpretation. He writes that the archbishop suggested the papal tax when he instructed his representative in Rome to propose the tax as a bribe if it appeared the papal decision in the case between the archbishop and Gerald might be going in Gerald's favor:

For the Archbishop, being a man full of worldly foresight and cunning had enjoined upon him that, if he saw that Giraldus had won so much favour with the Court as to make it likely that he would be promoted then and there, he should forthwith suggest to the Pope that he should send an envoy from among his chaplains and the clerks of his Court to seek an aid from the clergy in England, while the Archbishop himself should further the business by setting an example to the rest, making a contribution himself and persuading others to do the same, so that a great sum should be forthcoming to the Pope as a result of their advice.[32]

The historical value of such a comment is small, except that it does serve as an indication that execution of papal orders might easily prove difficult and make the archbishop unpopular, for Gerald must have hoped to make use of some feeling against the archbishop in making his distorted charge. Presumably, Hubert's later role as investigator of abuses by the papal notary would have been more pleasing to the English clergy, but a man with his experience in both ecclesiastical and secular administration would hardly have been much concerned with the question of winning popularity in performing his duties.

In fact, Archbishop Hubert's role in restoring the monks of Coventry in the immediately preceding years had thrust him into a situation between the party of the secular clergy and that of the monks in which he could expect to lose the support of one group or the other. Hugh of Nonant, bishop of Coventry, was the most outspoken critic of the English custom of monastic chapters in the cathedrals and even advised the king to rid all England of monks when King Richard was considering what to do about the quarrel between Archbishop Baldwin and the monks of Christ Church. In 1190 he obtained papal permission to expel the monks and install secular canons at Coventry, and he lost no time in doing so. Four

31. Cheney and Semple, p. 46; Canterbury, D. and C. Mun., Christ Church Letters, II, #1; C. R. Cheney, "Master Philip the Notary and the Fortieth of 1199," *The English Historical Review*, LXIII (1948), pp. 342, 344.

32. Giraldus Cambrensis, III, 178-179 (English translation, p. 191).

years later, the prior on behalf of the monks brought the case into royal court by a writ of *novel disseisin* because it involved the transfer of lands from the monks to the canons. One incident shows the extent to which passions were aroused by this controversy. Prior to the time the monks were expelled the bishop attempted to hold a synod, only to have a quarrel erupt during which some monks wounded the bishop by striking him with a cross from the church. Nevertheless, the archbishop intervened in the royal court to seek his court in the case, with the result that the royal officials postponed decision and apparently did not take the case up again.[33]

The archbishop's own controversy with the monks of Christ Church over Lambeth chapel, in progress when he received the papal commission late in 1197, might have inclined his sympathies to the secular clergy in the Coventry dispute, but the papal mandate left no discretion to the delegates—the archbishop, the bishop of Lincoln, and Abbot Samson of St. Edmund's—whose only choice was to remove the canons and restore the monks.[34] When a hearing was held by the judges at Oxford, they received a letter from the king asking them to postpone the execution of the papal mandate, and the archbishop and bishop of Lincoln were silent "as though they were courting the favour of the clerks. . . ." Abbot Samson spoke up for the monks and at his suggestion they were given simple seisin by a book, but personal institutions were postponed to please the king.[35] The monks were restored by the archbishop on January 18, 1198. However, Pope Innocent III on June 3 reiterated the order of his predecessor, whether because he had not been informed of the previous settlement or to confirm it is not stated.[36]

In spite of the claims of the pope to his *plenitudo potestatis,* the effective execution of his policies depended upon the loyalty of men like Archbishop Hubert. Since the time of the truce that ended the Third Crusade the launching of a new expedition to the Holy Land had been much on the minds of the popes. Pope Celestine wrote Hubert as his legate for England lamenting the state of affairs in Palestine and com-

33. *Rotuli curiae regis*, I, 66-67.

34. Ralph de Diceto, II, 159; Gervase of Canterbury, I, 550; Roger of Hoveden, IV, 35. The contemporary impact can be seen in the dating of an agreement made "on the feast of St. Matthew the Apostle in the year in which the monks of Coventry were restored to their house by the hand of the lord archbishop of Canterbury": B.M., Harley Charter, 84. D. 14.

35. Jocelin of Brakelond, p. 94.

36. Innocent III, *Opera Omnia,* in J. P. Migne, ed., *Patrologiae . . . series latina* (Paris, 1855), vol. 214, cols. 208-209; H. E. Butler's comments in his notes to Jocelin of Brakelond, pp. 155-156.

manding him to urge the king and nation to send men for the defense of the Holy Land.[37] What response such an appeal brought in the heart of a former crusader can only be conjectured, but Hubert did write the officials at York in January 1197 outlining the papal request and ordering a search in all the parish churches for persons who had made a vow and had since laid aside their plans to go on a crusade. He further ordered that such persons were to resume the cross before Easter or be excluded from communion.[38] Later, in 1201, in response to an appeal from Pope Innocent III he ordered his suffragans to compel men having taken vows as crusaders to take up the cross again.[39] Gerald of Wales saw political implications in such actions, for he expected his case against the archbishop, then on appeal before the pope, to be decided in favor of the archbishop since the pope was depending upon him to promote a crusade and could not afford to alienate him with an adverse decision.[40] In furtherance of other policies Pope Innocent was similarly dependent on the co-operation of the archbishop. In one instance he warned Hubert not to receive King Sverri of Norway, whom the pope had excommunicated for having forced a bishop to crown him against a papal prohibition and for continuing his opposition to papal policy. The archbishop was also forbidden to buy dogs, birds, or any other goods from the king, or to receive such as gifts as long as the king remained excommunicate.[41]

Archbishop Hubert played the principal role in the process of canonization of two English saints under the strict procedure newly introduced by Pope Innocent III. A papal notary advised the English prelates interested in promoting the cause of Gilbert of Sempringham to investigate thoroughly before submitting it to Rome, and he committed this work to the abbots of the province. The archbishop then joined in the supplication to the pope, circulated a dossier to influential bishops and abbots reporting the miracles of Gilbert, and even influenced the king and some barons to write in support of this cause. The pope replied asking for more specific inquiry from witnesses to miracles, rather than testimonials, and commissioned the archbishop, the bishop of Ely, and the abbots of Peterborough and Wardon to carry out the inquiry. On September 26, 1201, these com-

---

37. Ralph de Diceto, II, 132-135.
38. Roger of Hoveden, III, 317-318.
39. *Ibid.*, IV, 173; Innocent III in Migne, vol. 216, col. 1261.
40. Cheney, *From Becket to Langton*, p. 73.

41. Canterbury, D. and C. Mun., Christ Church Letters, II, 14a, and printed in Historical Manuscripts Commission, *Report on Manuscripts in Various Collections*, I, 219; Roger of Hoveden, III, 270-271.

missioners journeyed to Sempringham where for four days they held an inquest and had the unusual experience of witnessing a new miracle while they
were on the spot. On January 30, 1202, the pope issued the bull of canonization, which followed closely the wording of the report received from Hubert
and his colleagues. At the same time the task of translating the body of
Gilbert to a place selected by the master of the Gilbertine order was given
to the archbishop. This translation of the newly recognized saint took
place on October 13, and the archbishop set an indulgence relaxing forty
days of penance for those who prayed at the tomb of the new saint.[42]
The previous month, together with the bishop of Ely and the abbots of
St. Edmund's and Woburn, he had already visited Worcester on papal
orders to investigate miracles alleged to have taken place at the tomb
of Wulfstan. Once again the investigators found evidence of miracles and
left "praising, impressed by the glory of many healings and the testimony
concerning these." Their favorable report was approved by the pope, who
issued the bull of canonization for St. Wulfstan on April 21, 1203.[43]

During the period from 1195 to 1198 when Archbishop Hubert's *acta*
bear his title as papal legate, his position as the pope's agent in England
was perfectly explicit, but a closer examination of the records shows that he
had already been considered by the pope as such an agent before the
legatine commission was granted and that he continued in this relationship after the expiration of his commission at the death of Pope Celestine
III. Moreover, Hubert's actions as papal agent were both in the regularly
defined position as a judge delegate in the ecclesiastical court system of
the Roman church and in a much looser responsibility of executing *ad hoc*
commands of various sorts from the pope. Not only is there no evidence that
he resisted the will of the pope, but there is every indication that he performed his role loyally and conscientiously. Fortunately, no great controversy developed between the popes and King Richard or King John
before Hubert's death in 1205 so that his potentially conflicting loyalties
as papal agent and royal official never caused him to have to choose
between serving God and man.

---

42. Raymonde Foreville, ed., *Un procès de canonisation à l'aube du XIIIe siècle (1201-2): Le livre de saint Gilbert de Sempringham* (Paris, 1943), *passim*; Cheney and Semple, pp. 26-31.

43. Annals of Worcester in Henry R. Luard, ed., *Annales monastici* (R.S., London, 1869), IV, 391-392; William of Malmesbury, *Vita Wulfstani*, ed. Reginald R. Darlington (Camden Society, 3rd. ser., vol. 40, London, 1928), pp. xlvii-xlviii, 149.

# 9 KING JOHN'S CHANCELLOR

Hubert Walter was archbishop of Canterbury for twelve years, but at almost no time was he able to devote himself exclusively to this position, mainly because of the demands of his important offices as King Richard's justiciar and King John's chancellor. The exceptional months when he was archbishop only came at the beginning and the end of Richard's reign when his appointment as justiciar began about seven months after his election to Canterbury in 1193, and when he was relieved of that office on July 11, 1198, some ten months before Richard's death and his appointment as chancellor by the new king. Even so, both these periods were also filled with royal business, the months of 1193 being occupied with raising the king's ransom, and the last months of Richard's reign marked by the archbishop's involvement in diplomatic negotiations. Richard's unexpected death in the prime of life as the result of a chance wound by the bolt from a crossbow brought to the forefront the question of succession to the throne in a practical as well as a legal sense. The archbishop had once again to engage in pacifying the discontent that arose in England at the king's death, as he had at the beginning of his pontificate when King Richard was in captivity and Count John's followers rebelled to disturb the peace of the land.

The poet who sang of the deeds of William Marshal told a colorful story of the succession of King John, but more sober records of the period contradict his account. According to the poet's story, King Richard realized that the wound he had received might prove mortal and sent a confidential messenger with special orders to give the news only to William Marshal and Archbishop Hubert. When those two loyal servants of the king met and discussed the question of the succession, Hubert argued for the king's nephew, Arthur, because there must be a quick succession, and the marshal, pointing out that Arthur should be rejected because he was under the influence of bad counselors, put the case for John. Finally, Hubert was convinced by William's argument that the laws governing descent of land would be in favor of John (an amusing reversal of positions when one considers the backgrounds of the two men and, especially, Hubert's long practical experience in legal administration), but he predicted that the marshal would repent of his choice.[1] In fact, both men as early as 1197 had witnessed charters of Count John that implied that John was Richard's heir, and thus they had been committed to this course long before the supposed discussion.[2]

Yet the poet was correct in thinking that the support of these two men was important to John's accession. They were sent ahead to England to deal with disturbances that had broken out there. Joining with the justiciar, Geoffrey fitz Peter, they held a meeting at Northampton where the earls whose loyalty might be doubted were summoned to appear. These earls were then assured that John would deal with them justly. Such a commitment coming from these three men was readily accepted by the earls as though given by the new king himself, and they were willing to swear fealty to John on that basis. The one exception was King William of Scotland who demanded the return of Northumberland and Cumberland. However, John's spokesmen would not permit the Scottish king's messengers to be sent to John overseas and told him that he must await John's coming to England before his demands could be discussed. On May 25, 1199, John landed at Shoreham and proceeded to London where the archbishop of Canterbury and a number of bishops came to meet him. Although the bishop of Durham made a perfunctory appeal against a coronation in the absence of the archbishop of York, John was crowned immediately by Archbishop Hubert in the church of St. Peter at Westminster in the midst of pomp and ceremony appropriate to the occasion.[3] For the second time in his career, Hubert Walter had successfully played an important role in restoring peace to an England threatened with disturbances against the king.

The same day that John was crowned, May 27, he chose Hubert Walter to be his chancellor. There seems to have been no objection to this appointment from the pope or the monks of Christ Church, who might have been expected to raise difficulties if the story that Hubert had been forced out of the justiciarship by papal pressure were true. Roger

---

1. *L'Histoire de Guillaume le Maréchal*, II, 60, 62-64. See also Sidney Painter, *William Marshal* (Baltimore, 1933), pp. 118-120.

2. Landon, p. 122; Richardson and Sayles, *The Governance of Mediaeval England*, p. 141.

3. Roger of Hoveden, IV, 88-90; Ralph of Coggeshall, pp. 98-100; *P.R. 1 John*, p. xiii. The speech Archbishop Hubert was said to have made on elective monarchy at the coronation of King John, now agreed to be a fiction, rests on the account by Roger of Wendover. For the best text, see this passage in Matthew Paris, *Chronica majora*, ed. Henry R. Luard (R.S., London, 1872-1883), II, 454-455.

of Howden, the only chronicler who shows concern about clergy serving in positions of secular authority, recorded the sarcasm with which one royal official greeted the new appointment: when Hubert was glorying in the power of his new office and boasted of his familiarity with the king, Hugh Bardolf answered him, "Lord, if I may be allowed to comment, certainly if you would consider the strength of your name and the dignity of your office, you would not take upon yourself this yoke of servitude, for we have never heard nor seen an archbishop become a chancellor, but we have seen a chancellor become an archbishop."[4] The implied rebuke that Hubert should have lived up to the example of St. Thomas Becket, who resigned the chancellorship when he was elected archbishop, telling the king that the two positions were not compatible, was lost on the new chancellor whose whole career had been based upon the combination of ecclesiastical and secular offices.

One of the principal questions about Hubert's chancellorship is whether he was responsible for the practice of chancery enrolment that produced the series of records so valuable for the operation of government and for the historian. The direct evidence for attributing this practice to him is slight, but there is none pointing to anyone else. Three weeks after Hubert became chancellor the system of enrolling charters and writs on a method similar to that used in the king's court and the Exchequer was already established. Earlier, on June 7, 1199, King John had renounced the exorbitant fees that had been charged for documents under the great seal during Richard's reign, and "at the urging of our chancellor, our venerable father, Hubert, archbishop of Canterbury" had fixed a schedule of fees based on those charged in the time of Henry II. The chancellor's portion of fees under the revised schedule was one mark of gold or ten of silver for a new charter, one mark of silver for a confirmation with no additions, and two shillings for a letter of simple protection. Anyone disobeying this schedule would incur the wrath of God and the king, and all the bishops who laid hands on the king at his consecration would join the archbishop in a sentence of excommunication.[5]

The two parts to the question would seem to be the relation, if any, of the regulation of fees for use of the great seal to the practice of enrolling documents, and, secondly, whose was the initiative for the establishment of this practice. The argument that a practice so laborious as copying com-

4. Roger of Hoveden, IV, 90-91.     5. Rymer, I, Pt. 1, 75-76.

plete charters into the charter rolls was undertaken to provide a record for collecting fees is not convincing.[6] A short note containing the main points of a charter could easily have accomplished that purpose, and such a note could have been produced according to set form following an almost purely mechanical procedure which would require very little training of the clerk doing the work. The purpose for establishing the charter rolls, and, for that matter, the other chancery enrolments, must be sought in their usefulness to the men within the royal administration. The present author's guess would be that the charter rolls from the beginning were useful for the same reason they were useful later in the thirteenth century— as a record to which royal justices could refer in lieu of original charters that had been lost.[7] If the rolls were also useful in the collection of fees, so much the better; they were probably also used as formularies and in other ways which we might not be able to guess. The relation between the practice of chancery enrolment and King John's schedule of fees would seem to be purely coincidental, both being produced under the impetus of a new reign and a new chancellor actively seeking solutions to the problems of the department.

The question regarding the person responsible for the innovation usually is answered with the name of Hubert Walter, but some writers have pointed to the king himself.[8] Certainly there must have been co-operation between the two men for any such reform. Circumstantial evidence would suggest that Hubert provided the initiative for the practice of enrolment, just as the king asserted he did for the new fees, but in the absence of more direct evidence there can be no definitive answer. Hubert had had experience with Exchequer procedure where enrolments had long been kept, so it would not be surprising if he introduced similar practices in other departments. He had shown himself an innovator with the earliest final concord containing a third part to be kept as a Treasury record. This came in 1195 from a case in which he presided as justiciar and which concerned his brother Theobald as one of the parties.[9] The Curia Regis

6. See the development of this argument by H. G. Richardson in his introduction to *Memoranda Roll 1 John*, p. xliij.

7. This use is shown in *Placita de Quo Warranto* (Rec. Comm., London, 1818), p. 121a.

8. F. M. Powicke, in *Cambridge Medieval History* VI, 220-221; Reginald L. Poole, *The Exchequer in the Twelfth Century* (Oxford, 1912), p. 186; Chrimes, p. 76; *P.R. 6 John*, p. xxxvij; W. L. Warren, *King John* (New York, 1961), p. 126.

9. *Feet of Fines of the Reign of Henry II. and of the First Seven Years of the Reign of Richard I.*, p. 21.

Rolls also begin in the year when Hubert presided for an absentee king. From his chancellorship there are the Fine Rolls, the Charter Rolls, *Originalia* Rolls, Close Rolls, and Patent Rolls. In regard to ecclesiastical documents, an unusual number of his original *acta* as archbishop of Canterbury survive, but this might be only by chance were it not that copies of his *acta* are also exceptionally frequent in monastic cartularies. The impression given by the coincidence of Hubert's tenure in several offices with the production and preservation of administrative records for these offices is therefore suggestive. To be sure, there is some evidence of enrolments before Hubert became chancellor, but it is quite in keeping with his career as a whole that he should have introduced to the Chancery the practice of producing and systematically preserving these records, and this conclusion is consistent with the only direct evidence available. Most likely, Hubert regularized procedures that had appeared somewhat casually in the nature of experiments before his tenure. This conclusion may detract from the originality usually attributed to Hubert Walter, but it points to his ability to comprehend the real value of the systematic keeping of records, and his influence to institute procedures that outlasted his lifetime and guaranteed that the practice of enrolments would become a permanent part of the administrative procedures followed at the Chancery.

The relation between Hubert Walter as chancellor and Geoffrey fitz Peter, his successor as justiciar, could easily have produced jealousies that would have wrecked the orderly administration of government, but there is no hint of conflict between the two men even when they worked in areas where their efforts overlapped. H. G. Richardson in his edition of John's first Memoranda Roll made this comment:

Although the justiciar was ruler of the kingdom in the king's absence, and there is no doubt that Geoffrey fitz Peter exercised the authority reposed in him, great influence and a large measure of authority were enjoyed also by Hubert Walter. Exactly how the two men co-operated—for there seems to be no suspicion of rivalry—it is hard to say, and the many references on the Memoranda roll to Hubert Walter do not serve to elucidate the problem.[10]

The most striking entry Richardson found was when Hubert Walter and the other barons of the Exchequer, with no mention of the justiciar, ordered all imprisoned Jews brought to court at the Jews' own expense.

10. *Memoranda Roll 1 John*, p. lxxxix.

Presumably, Hubert was presiding at this occasion. It is true that traditionally the chancellor had a seat at the Exchequer beside the justiciar, but this had not been occupied for many years. There is other evidence to find him participating in judicial proceedings with Geoffrey fitz Peter. Cases concerning weights and measures were postponed in the Memoranda Roll until Hubert could be present; a question whether a sheriff should pay an increment to the farm for his county was deferred to the chancellor and the justiciar; and Hubert collected fines both by himself and jointly with the justiciar.[11] The two jointly pledged for a convention made before them and several royal justices in 1203, and the convention contained the curious agreement that if one of the parties should wish to go back on the agreement then he agreed that the archbishop "might distrain him by means of ecclesiastical justice."[12] The degree of co-operation between the two highest officials was lauded by a contemporary who commented on the vicissitudes of King John's fortunes and added: "Meanwhile, through the grace of God, England under the leadership of Archbishop Hubert of Canterbury and Geoffrey fitz Peter rejoiced in peace and tranquility."[13]

The explanation for this degree of co-operation between the justiciar and the chancellor probably is that they knew each other well and were friends of long standing. Both these men and King John himself had known each other in their youth in the household of Ranulf Glanvill when Glanvill served as Prince John's guardian and the other two were members of the household. Geoffrey also worked with Hubert Walter when the latter was justiciar, for one of the few surviving writs by Hubert as justiciar has Geoffrey as a witness. Lady Stenton pointed to the significance: "It is interesting to see the future Justiciar witnessing this writ and so well established as second in office that 'G. fil. P.' is all the clerk writes."[14] After Geoffrey became justiciar, the co-operation continued, and when Hubert became chancellor was resumed rather than broken, with such good effect as to justify Gervase of Canterbury's complimentary remarks. It is tempting to think that King John, too, carried with him some influence of his early experience in Glanvill's household as demonstrated in the unusual interest he took in the details of administration and in law. "An examination of the king's activities as a judge during the years

---

11. *Ibid.*, lxxxix-xc, 9, 10, 19, 24, 65; *Cartae Antiquae Rolls*, p. 81; *Rotuli de oblatis et finibus*, pp. 2-3.

12. *Curia Regis Rolls*, III, 6.

13. Gervase of Canterbury, II, 95.

Confirmation of this view is provided by the entries in the pipe roll according to the editor of *P.R. 4 John*, p. xvj.

14. Doris M. Stenton, *Pleas before the King*, pp. 350-351.

before 1209 reveals neither oppression nor indifference. What it suggests is a hardworking king, well served by able judges and their clerks, trying to keep peace with an ever increasing volume of litigation and to ease as far as possible the difficulties of litigants and jurors required to attend a moving court."[15]

The office of chancellor had risen considerably in status since the days of Thomas Becket, and Becket had been most influential in making that office great. Before his time the chancellor had so little official dignity that his usual preferment was an archdeaconry, but King Richard's chancellor from 1189 to 1197, William Longchamp, had remained chancellor after he became bishop of Ely.[16] Of course, as Hugh Bardolf noted, there was no precedent for combining the office with that of archbishop of Canterbury. Many of the routine duties of the office had to be delegated to subordinates when the chancellor had such ecclesiastical responsibilities, and the unofficial use of "vicechancellor" foreshadowed the day when that official would be the actual working head of the department. However, under Hubert Walter there was a subtle change in that the former practice of delegating the powers of the chancellor was not followed. When senior clerks were responsible for issuing a charter, they were not stated to be exercising the power of the chancellor. The great seal always technically remained in Hubert Walter's keeping, except for a period of about a week in 1201 when the king took it into his own hand during a dispute with his chancellor. This slight technical change suggests that Hubert Walter was keeping stricter control over Chancery administration than that exercised by his immediate predecessors. Of course, many charters had to be issued by clerks, and the men who most frequently deputized for Hubert as chancellor were his clerk, Simon, archdeacon of Wells, and John de Gray, later elected bishop of Norwich.[17]

At times the king was in arrears in money he owed the chancellor, and on another occasion he ordered a loan of £100 made to the chancellor, indicating a harmonious relation in this most sensitive area.[18] In fact, several other references show that the king found his chancellor the kind of a man he could trust to speak for him in various sorts of business.

15. Doris M. Stenton, "King John and the Courts of Justice," *Proceedings of the British Academy*, 44 (1958), p. 115.

16. T. F. Tout, *Chapters in the Administrative History of Mediaeval England* (Manchester, 1920-33), I, 133-134.

17. *Ibid.*, p. 134; *Rotuli chartarum*, I, Pt. 1, xxxi; Sidney Painter, *The Reign of King John* (Baltimore, 1949), pp. 63, 79.

18. *Rotuli litterarum clausarum*, I, 6a, 17b.

These examples include an order to the treasurer and chamberlains to take three thousand marks from the Treasury at Winchester and deliver it to London to be paid out as the chancellor should direct through his letters patent; a note to the reeve of Bruges to do what the chancellor should tell him about royal business; notification to the men of the Cinque Ports to send twelve men from each port to meet with the chancellor and the sheriff of Kent who were being sent on the king's business; a similar notification that the chancellor and justiciar were being sent to the men of the Cinque Ports; and a mandate for the prior and convent of St. Swithin to meet with Hubert to "hear our will."[19] With Hubert Walter holding the office, the chancellorship became more important than its name would indicate, and the king did not hesitate to call upon the judgment and experience of this faithful official in assigning him various tasks in government. His position in the church could also be useful. Though the evidence is rather insubstantial, King John seems to have exacted a tax of one-seventh of movable property in 1203 on the grounds that his barons had deserted him in Normandy. The justiciar, Geoffrey fitz Peter, was appointed to collect from the lay barons and Archbishop Hubert to collect from the clergy.[20]

The diplomatic experience that Hubert Walter had gained during the reign of King Richard proved to be of direct value when he was again employed in diplomatic moves by King John. In 1201 he and the justiciar led a group being sent west to Salisbury with full powers to deal with a dispute between the king and the Welsh prince, Llywelyn.[21] The pattern remained essentially the same on the Continent, too. The following year, after spending five months with the king who continued to wage the struggle with the king of France that both his brother and father before him had fought, Archbishop Hubert and the bishop of Ely were sent back to England to report on relations with France with the assurance that they spoke with the same authority as the king himself.[22]

During the king's visit to England in 1203 and lasting into 1204, the French king was making gains, and John sent Hubert Walter, William Marshal, and the earl of Leicester to try to arrange a peace. They met with no success. Still John decided upon one more try and secretly sent

---

19. *Ibid.*, I, 6b; *Rotuli litterarum patentium*, pp. 33b, 38b, 43b, 48b.
20. *P.R. 6 John*, p. xl; Mitchell, p. 16.
21. *Rotuli chartarum*, I, Pt. 1, 103b-104a.
22. *Rotuli litterarum patentium*, p. 10b; *P.R. 8 John*, pp. 155-156.

the marshal and Hugh of Wells to open further discussion with Philip Augustus. The marshal's biographer wrote that when Hubert Walter heard of these secret overtures, he became furious that the king had not sought his advice. He sent Ralph de Ardene to visit the count of Boulogne and tell Philip through him that the two envoys had no authority to make peace, thus effectively undercutting their efforts. Furthermore, Ralph arrived in England before the envoys and reported they had acted badly and that William Marshal had done homage and sworn allegiance to the King of France against John. It pleased Hubert Walter greatly that William Marshal was now out of the king's favor, because he had been jealous of his influence.[23] Although other writers do not confirm the second part of this story and the marshal's biographer suffered from a bad case of hero worship, Hubert Walter's employment of Ralph de Ardene, Glanvill's son-in-law, as his agent sounds like an authentic touch.

The combination of the chancellor's office with the ecclesiastical dignity of the archbishop of Canterbury made it most probable that Hubert Walter would be one of the most powerful men in England, and his own reputation and personality insured that position. His manner of living was as lavish as that practiced by Henry II's chancellor, Thomas Becket, before Thomas was elected archbishop. In 1203 Hubert invited King John and many other great men of the realm to spend the Christmas feast with him and entertained them extravagantly. The conversation that a contemporary imagined to have taken place between King John and the archbishop when the king was taking his leave after enjoying three days of such hospitality was as follows:

The king said, "My Lord Archbishop, do you know why I have stayed here so long?" The archbishop replied, "Why except to do me honor?" "By God's teeth!," said the king, "Things are quite otherwise. You are so generous, so worthy, and such a lavish spender that no one could rival you. You yourself want to have the most magnificent court in England, but, thank God, I have so treated you that you will never be able to give help nor will you have anything to eat." And when the archbishop heard these words, it grieved him greatly, so he answered the king, "How do you think that you have destroyed me? You haven't. I am not so easy to destroy. Since you have said this, tell me where you will be at Easter." "What business is that of yours?," asked the king. "By St. Julien!," replied

23. *L'Histoire de Guillaume le Maré-chal*, II, 98-99, 101, 103-105, 107, translated and paraphrased by Jessie Crosland, *William the Marshal* (London, 1962), pp. 89-91. The embassy and its failure (with no reason given) is confirmed by Ralph of Coggeshall, pp. 144-145.

the archbishop, "You will not be able to hide it from me. Do you know why I asked? For the reason that I would like to be there where you will be, and if the town is not large enough that my people and yours can lodge within, I will stay outside. And I will undertake to hold a finer court than you and in the court I will spend more than you, give more clothes, make more new knights, and do more good works than you. And at Pentecost I will do the same thing if I am alive then, and still Hubert Walter will have something to eat."[24]

Comments by other chroniclers in reference to festive occasions the two previous years indicate that Hubert's rivalry with the king in the splendor of his court was not entirely idle gossip, and the Pipe Roll provides confirmation that the king was entertained at Christmas in 1203.[25]

Such a spectacular mode of living must have appealed to the son of a poor East Anglian knight who had achieved notable success in royal service, but Hubert Walter also was capable of using the influence of his office as chancellor for more practical gains. Earlier he had used his influence with King Richard in favor of his elder brother, Theobald, and it is not surprising that Theobald continued to benefit from his brother's success during the reign of John. It might seem that Theobald would have had less need of this influence after John became king, for he had long been in John's service, accompanying him to Ireland as a young man, laying the basis there for the Irish house he founded, and enjoying the office of John's butler for Ireland. Yet his surrender of one of John's

24. *Histoire des ducs de Normandie et des rois d'Angleterre*, ed. Francisque Michel (Paris, 1840), pp. 105-106.

25. F. Liebermann, *Ungedruckte Anglo-Normannische Geschichtsquellen* (Strassburg, 1879), pp. 139-140, 143; *P.R. 6 John*, p. xxxiv; Roger of Wendover, *Chronica sive flores historiarum*, ed. H. O. Coxe (The English Historical Society, London, 1841-44), III, 165-166. The English ballad known as "King John and the Abbot (or Bishop) of Canterbury" pictures the king as becoming angry over the lavish household of the abbot (or bishop) in a vein that parallels the quarrel between John and Archbishop Hubert. See John W. Hales and F. J. Furnivall, *Bishop Percy's Folio Manuscript* (London, 1867), I, 508. Unfortunately, the oldest manuscript of this ballad dates from about 1650 and the various motifs in the ballad are found very widely, especially the theme of a test by the king asking various questions. The motivations attributed to the king or emperor in asking these questions fit much less easily into any category of classification, but in this part of the ballad which parallels history a number of other versions also assign a similar motivation. See Walter Anderson, *Kaiser und Abt. Die Geschichte eines Schwanks* (Folklore Fellows Communications, No. 42, Helsinki, 1923), pp. 16, 243-244. The nature of the evidence, although it does not rule out the possibility that the ballad preserves a fragment of authentic historical detail, allows no real proof that this is the case and parallelisms in other versions of the story warn against such an assumption in the absence of concrete evidence.

castles to his brother, the justiciar, in the rebellion of 1193-1194, and his close identification with King Richard in the subsequent years may have led to some estrangement between John and Theobald. In any event, one of the fines recorded in 1199 shows the two brothers working closely together in building up the lands of the elder.[26] Although Richard had removed Theobald as sheriff of Lancaster in 1198, John restored him to this office at the beginning of his reign, and within a year complaints began to mount against him for arbitrary disseisins of land. Other land grants also show John was at first favorably inclined toward Theobald. Yet even his brother's influence was unable to protect Theobald in 1200 from being deprived of nearly all the lands that made up his Amounderness estate, probably as a result of charges of unjust actions as sheriff being made against him. Quite possibly the mediation of Hubert lay behind the king's decision to restore the estates to Theobald; certainly they were restored within two years after they had been taken from him.[27]

At the time of Hubert Walter's death, it was felt that he had held a restraining influence over the king, and there is no better example of this than his use of influence in favor of the Cistercian order in the year 1200. When King John attempted to force the abbots to make him a grant of money, they replied that they could not do so without the consent of the General Chapter of the order and thereby incurred the king's wrath. As a means of intimidation, the king issued a mandate to his sheriffs to refuse the Cistercians justice throughout the land. The abbots then appealed to Hubert Walter, archbishop of Canterbury, to intercede for them. When the archbishop reproached the king for his cruelty against an order noted for practicing an austere and meritorious life, John revoked his mandate to the sheriffs, but his anger remained unpacified. Wise in the ways of practical politics, Hubert pledged the king one thousand marks on behalf of the Cistercians on condition that John confirm all their charters that Richard had confirmed, a move that would give the king the money he sought and yet not infringe upon the Cistercian immunity from royal taxation.

Upon his return to England from the Continent, the king continued to apply pressure to the Cistercians by ordering that all animals belonging

26. *Rotuli de oblatis et finibus*, p. 30.

27. Roger of Hoveden, IV, 153; *Rotuli de oblatis et finibus*, p. 123, and other refs. under Theobald's name; Farrer, *Chartulary of Cockersand Abbey*, p. 263 n. Gervase of Canterbury, II, 410; *Victoria History of Lancaster,* II, 191 n; Jolliffe, pp. 65-68; Painter, *William Marshal*, p. 80.

to them must be removed from royal forests. At the same time, the archbishop continued to attempt a reconciliation by a preliminary session with the abbots to plan for a meeting between them and the king himself. During the debate over payment of the amount the archbishop had pledged for them, the abbot of Meaux, a former notary and close associate of the archbishop, produced a letter from the General Chapter urging the English abbots not to agree to any payments that might abridge their exemptions and tempt other rulers to try similar pressures. The communication thanked the archbishop for his efforts on behalf of the order, but when the session broke up with a decision not to pay the king and a request that the archbishop present their case to the king, Hubert's task became even more difficult. When he attempted to take the case before the king on November 23, the king refused to hear it, but on Sunday three days later Hubert's intercession was successful in getting the king to agree to meet with the abbots.

When the abbots had assembled before the king, John ordered the archbishop to address them and announce that he had relaxed his anger against them. A general reconciliation followed with the king vowing to build a house for Cistercians and promising to become a patron of the order.[28] In a letter informing the pope of King John's intentions, the archbishop reported that the king had confessed to him and that he had imposed the duty of sending one hundred knights for a year to the Holy Land and of building a house for the Cistercians. Of the first promise, there is no evidence of compliance, but the Cistercian house of Beaulieu in Hampshire was the ultimate result of this particular settlement. It should be said that, unfortunately, John's later attitude toward the Cistercian order was not always consistent with his promise to act as a patron toward them.[29]

The thrust of Hubert Walter's influence over King John seems to have been in the direction of moderating some of the proposed actions of the king, and the chancellor's long experience in royal government was in itself a stabilizing influence in the first part of John's reign. An example of the role as mediator often taken by Hubert concerns an incident in 1202. In fighting on the Continent the king had captured a number of persons only to have one, Savaric de Mauléon, escape after getting his guards drunk. When the king faced the former prisoner over the walls of Corfe

28. Ralph of Coggeshall, pp. 102-109; *Annales de Margan*, in Luard, I, 25.

29. Cheney and Semple, p. 38 and note.

castle in which the escapee had managed to make his stand, John was preparing to institute a siege, but Hubert Walter, that "very valliant clerk, famous for largesse and feudal courtesy," was able to negotiate an agreement between the two hotheaded antagonists that gained the services of Savaric for the king.[30] Payments to the Exchequer and cases before the *curia regis* were also postponed until the advice of the archbishop was obtained.[31] When after the loss of Normandy the king faced implacable opposition from his nobles to an expedition he planned to lead to Poitou in 1205, it was Hubert Walter and William Marshal who persuaded him to abandon his plans, probably avoiding for the time being outright rebellion on the part of some of the nobles.[32] Those who blamed the archbishop for accepting the chancellorship might have done well to remember that his acquired influence with the king could be exercised for the benefit of the church. For example, when the bailiffs of the English king despoiled a Cistercian abbey in La Rochelle, the archbishop of Bourges in his appearance before King John appealed to Archbishop Hubert to help him make the case for restitution. Nor was he disappointed in his appeal, for a second letter later sought the archbishop's continued help in the case.[33]

The evidence for Hubert's financial dealings during his chancellorship shows him in a much less favorable light, for there was good reason for his reputation as a man given to arbitrary disseisins and a penchant for collecting profitable wardships. Instances in which Hubert went surety for several men imply a deeper involvement on his part in various business deals of which there is no full evidence.[34] There is, of course, no balance sheet for the income of the chancellorship, but the income collected during the period of vacancy after Hubert Walter's death while the office was in the king's hand was recorded. The figure for the period covered approximately one-fifth of a year, and multiplication by five would give about £436 for a full year.[35] Whether these eleven weeks during the summer and early autumn of 1205 represent normal income from the office cannot be determined, but the figure of £436, if accurate within even a very wide range of error, would at least indicate that the ex-

30. *Histoire des ducs de Normandie*, p. 101.

31. *Rotuli litterarum clausarum*, I, 30a; *Curia Regis Rolls*, I, 417.

32. Ralph of Coggeshall, p. 152; *L'Histoire de Guillaume le Maréchal*, II, 113.

33. Canterbury, D. and C. Mun., Christ Church Letters, II, #2, 3.

34. *Rotuli de oblatis et finibus*, pp. 205, 242; *Memoranda Roll 1 John*, p. 7.

35. *Rotuli litterarum patentium*, p. 70a.

tremely large sums Hubert Walter was able to pay to obtain wardship of various minor heirs in the king's hands could not have been derived from the profits of his office as chancellor. Possibly earlier, but certainly from the reign of King Richard, Hubert was actively involved in obtaining wardships over heirs to feudal properties from which he could profit until the heirs came of age.[36] As careful of his own business affairs as he was of those of his archbishopric, he obtained confirmation of the wardships he held both from King Richard and others shortly after the accession of King John.[37]

Both the advantage of Hubert's offices and the profits to be made from wardships are shown in a story from St. Edmund's. When one of the men holding lands from the abbey died, Abbot Samson might reasonably have received three hundred marks (£200) for the wardship of the heir, an only daughter. But since the girl's grandfather had taken her away secretly and the abbot could only have gotten possession of her with the help of the archbishop, he was willing to grant the wardship to the archbishop for £100. The latter then granted the wardship to Thomas de Burgh, brother of the king's chamberlain, for five hundred marks, thus reaping an easy profit of some £233. When trouble over some of the manors later resulted between the abbey and Thomas de Burgh, the archbishop was completely clear of any responsibility in the matter.[38] In other cases Hubert followed a similar policy of selling off the wardships he obtained, although one example transferring an heir to Roger de Basingham, a member of his own household, may have been concerned more with providing for Roger than with making a profit for the archbishop. Hubert's tenacity in the matter of wardships was illustrated in 1201 when he conceded some land and its heir to Philip de Burnham only after the dispute between them had been tried in royal court.[39]

The archbishop's wardship over Ralph de Clare produced considerable controversy both during Hubert's last years and immediately after his death. One potential source of trouble was avoided when the widow of Roger de Clare, who had since remarried, conceded to the archbishop and his ward the knight service that belonged to her by right of dower as

---

36. *Curia Regis Rolls*, VII, 123; Lambeth Palace Library, MS. 1212, p. 37; *P.R. 10 Ric. I*, p. 33.

37. *Rotuli chartarum*, I, Pt. 1, 24b, 68b.

38. Jocelin of Brakelond, p. 123.

39. Lambeth Palace Library, MS. 1212, p. 91; *P.R. 7 John*, pp. 33, 239; *Curia Regis Rolls*, I, 264, 375, 418.

widow of Roger.[40] However, the archbishop and his ward were involved in considerable litigation over other lands, including the case in which the archbishop was consulted as an authority on law whether his ward could legally implead a man in royal court while he was still a minor. Shortly after the archbishop's death, the earl of Warenne was granted custody of this heir, but Walter de Abernum contested the boy's right to some lands, claiming that he had been unjustly disseised of these by the late archbishop when the heir was in the archbishop's custody.[41]

A much greater amount of money was involved when Hubert Walter successfully purchased the wardship of Robert, the heir of William de Stuteville who had been a colleague of Ranulf Glanvill as sheriff of York under Henry II, for a fine of four thousand marks (£2,666 13s. 4d.), paying five hundred directly to the Treasury and another five hundred to William Brewer as a loan from the king. The remainder was to be paid in instalments of five hundred marks twice yearly at the meetings of the Exchequer with the careful stipulation that whatever might happen to Robert, the archbishop or the person to whom he might assign the wardship should hold it for at least four years or long enough to recoup his expenditure.[42] During the approximately one-half year that the fief was in the hands of the king before Hubert purchased the wardship, the income to the Exchequer amounted to £986 10s. 11d. and some small sums.[43] Not surprisingly, the archbishop having agreed to such a sizable payment seems to have ordered an inquiry into the operation of some of the lands to test the efficiency of the bailiff, but the details are obscured by the extensive damage to the document in which the results were reported to the archbishop.[44] When the heir to the Stuteville fief died about a year after Hubert's death, his brother, Nicolas de Stuteville offered the tremendous fine of ten thousand marks (£6,666 13s. 4d.) for having the lands his brother had held. The income from these lands during the year they had been in the king's hands after the death of

---

40. Lambeth Palace Library, MS. 1212, p. 99.

41. *Curia Regis Rolls*, I, 279; II, 22; IV, 13, 15, 110; *Rotuli litterarum clausarum*, I, 42b.

42. *P.R. 6 John*, pp. xlviij, 191-192; *Rotuli litterarum patentium*, p. 30a; *Rotuli chartarum*, I, pt. 1, 108a; *Rotuli litterarum clausarum*, I, 4a, 16a, 94; *Rotuli de liberate*, p. 48.

43. *P.R. 5 John*, pp. xv, 222-224.

44. Canterbury, D. and C. Mun., Christ Church Letters, vol. II, #-04 (inside front cover). This seems to be the purport of the document, but I am by no means certain that I have interpreted it correctly.

Archbishop Hubert was £1,306 7s. 9½d.[45] With either this figure or the earlier amount for about one-half year, Archbishop Hubert's shrewd business sense is demonstrated by his payment for the wardship of an amount that would be recovered in about two years, a guaranteed continuance in holding the wardship until he had recovered his investment, and the possibility of even greater profits if he could improve the efficiency with which the lands were administered or hold the wardship for a longer time.

Because of the almost complete disappearance of private records from Hubert Walter's time, nothing is known of any wardships that he may have purchased from feudal lords, although the terms by which King John confirmed Hubert in his wardships from the time of Richard and the story concerning St. Edmund's show that he did hold such wardships. References to scutage owed by the archbishop from lands in his custody, such as the thirty-eight marks he owed from the fiefs of nineteen knights in the honor of the countess of Brittany in 1200, are sufficient to confirm the impression that his collection of wardships was considerable.[46] In accordance with the exemption from scutage for barons of the Exchequer, he did not actually pay the scutages, which were first listed to his account and then marked quit by order of the king.[47] Random entries of payments for custody of wards, such as five hundred marks for the heir of Simon of Odell, six hundred marks for custody of Gilbert, son of Gilbert Hausard, and two hundred marks for the heir of Robert de Amundevill, or references to certain lands being in the custody of the archbishop, are further evidence of his involvement in a widespread traffic in wardships adding up to a total value that only a very wealthy man could finance.[48] Of those wardships known from royal records, Archbishop Hubert during the reign of King John held custody of fiefs that totaled seventy knights' fees.[49] Earlier under King Richard his accumulation of wardships had been on a more modest scale, but it should be remembered that he had been interested in this source of income at least as early in his career as when he was bishop of Salisbury.[50] When Hubert died, a number of men rushed

45. *Rotuli chartarum*, I, Pt. 1, 166a; *P.R. 7 John*, pp. 38-40, 59.

46. *P.R. 2 John*, p. 91.

47. *Memoranda Roll 1 John*, p. 48; *P.R. 1 John*, p. 211; *P.R. 2 John*, p. 209; *P.R. 3 John*, p. 255; *P.R. 4 John*, p. 214; *P.R. 5 John*, p. 25. Exemption for barons of the Exchequer is outlined in Richard fitz Neal, *Dialogus de Scac-* cario (London, 1950), p. 52.

48. *Memoranda Roll 1 John*, p. 86; *Chancellor's Roll*, pp. 159, 171, 172, 261; *P.R. 2 John*, p. 130; *Rotuli de liberate*, p. 28.

49. Painter, *Reign of King John*, p. 163.

50. See above p. 29.

to make fines with the king to regain properties, with charges that Hubert had put one fief in seisin of his ward unjustly, that without judicial authorization he had given his brother Theobald some land belonging to a ward, that two properties taken into the king's hand along with posses-sions of Hubert had only been mortgaged to him, and that other lands had fallen into royal hands by a similar chance without giving any reason why Hubert had had them in his holding when he died.[51] Such references as these reveal something of the source of that wealth that allowed the chancellor to live so sumptuously, and throw into glaring relief the mercenary side of Hubert Walter's character that may not have earned him obloquy at the court of either King Richard or King John but that seems incongruous with his position as archbishop of Canterbury.

In the last years of his life, the archbishop, like many of the great men of his day, bethought himself of a means by which he might atone for the sins that troubled his conscience. As early as 1203 he petitioned the Cistercian order to allow him to found an abbey on his own, which would have been in addition to the influence he had exercised on King John to get him to found Beaulieu.[52] Whether his dealings in wardships would have been considered by Hubert as part of the sins for which he sought to atone is problematical, and foundation of a religious house would have been a normal action of the noble class, whose other actions in distributing largesse and creating knights Hubert had sought to imitate. In any event, he had already acquired considerable property with which he intended to endow an abbey at Wolverhampton, but these intentions were cut short by his death, and the abbey was never founded.[53] Only the house of Premonstratensian canons established by him early in life remained to commemorate his name as its founder.

The death of Hubert Walter on July 13, 1205, in some ways marked the end of an era, for his experience in government provided a personal link from the reign of Henry II to that of John. The story first given currency by Roger of Wendover that King John rejoiced at the death of Hubert Walter saying, "Now for the first time I am king of England!" is demonstrably false, even though repeated by most writers who have since

51. *Rotuli de oblatis et finibus*, pp. 334-335, 337, 354, 371, 441.

52. Joseph M. Canivez, ed., *Statuta capitulorum generalium ordinis Cisterciensis* (Louvain, 1933), I, 285, 303.

53. Lambeth Palace Library, MS. 1212, pp. 19-20, 21; *P.R. 6 John*, pp. xxxix, 209; *P.R. 7 John*, p. 156; *Rotuli chartarum*, I, 135b, 152b, 153a, 154a; *Rotuli litterarum clausarum*, I, 34b.

had the occasion to refer to his death.[54] Nevertheless, the truth of the matter seems to have been that with Hubert Walter as chancellor and Geoffrey fitz Peter as justiciar there was a wealth of governmental experience that provided a restraining influence on the king not equalled in the years after Hubert's death. Time after time Hubert had demonstrated that he had a fine sense of politics as the art of the possible that led him to use his influence with the king in the role of a mediator and conciliator and prevented potentially explosive incidents from erupting. Although he left his successors an office where the routine of administration was well-established and where the preservation of various series of records was a part of that routine, none could have the influence he had had over the king. And none combined the secular and ecclesiastical authority that his being both chancellor and archbishop concentrated in the hands of one man, and that man one who never shrank from using his authority.

54. Roger of Wendover, in Matthew Paris, *Historia Anglorum*, ed. Frederic Madden (R.S., London, 1866-69), II, 104; V. H. Galbraith, *Roger Wendover and Matthew Paris* (Glasgow, 1944), p. 18.

# 10 "BY HIS INDUSTRY HE PROSPERED BOTH CHURCH AND KINGDOM"

The supreme irony of Hubert Walter's life is that most people who recognize his name remember this extremely active and industrious man mainly in connection with his death and the ensuing crisis over the election to Canterbury. His contributions to the governing of England during a career that covered at least twenty years of royal service and formed a personal link between the innovations of King Henry II and the more fully developed administration of King John have all been overshadowed by the drama triggered by his death. Attention shifts to the stormy pontificate of Stephen Langton and the struggle between King John and Pope Innocent III, and then becomes fixed hypnotically upon Magna Carta. In general, even historians have treated Hubert Walter in this way, somewhat as do hundreds of tourists who visit Canterbury Cathedral where they stand gazing upon the splendidly decorated tomb of Edward, the Black Prince, never noticing the plain, rather crude sarcophagus at their backs against the wall in which repose the mortal remains of Archbishop Hubert. Of course, his career has been given more attention by those scholars interested in administrative history, with some of them even proclaiming him one of the greatest medieval administrators; other scholars dealing with the history of the church in England during the twelfth century use him as an example of an ecclesiastic engaged primarily in secular business with no trace of spiritual vocation.[1] Such partial views of his career surely distort our understanding of his life almost as much as the more usual neglect that includes his name only in a footnote to explain why there was a disputed election to Canterbury in 1205.

It was typical of Hubert Walter that death should find him actively engaged in the business of his province, in spite of the fact that he had had some warning of its approach and had made his final peace with the monks of Christ Church before leaving Canterbury. When his fatal illness came, he had just met the monks of Rochester near Boxley and reconciled them with their bishop. Turning aside from his path, he lay ill four days at the archiepiscopal manor of Teynham where he died on July 13, 1205. Although his physicians used heroic measures to curb the ulcers that appeared on his lower back and the accompanying high fever, nothing seemed to have much effect. On the third day of the fever Master Gilbert del Egle, who was attending the the archbishop, admonished him to make his confession. He then confessed to the prior of St. Gregory's, the tiny archiepiscopal foundation in Canterbury; to Master Aaron, confessor of Christ Church monastery; and to Master Firminus, who had been a secretary of St. Thomas Becket. The archbishop's answer to further urging that he should make his last will and testament was that he had done so seven years earlier while he was in full possession of his faculties, and since that time he had followed the practice of making an annual inventory of his goods and jewels for the purpose of any necessary revisions to his will.

The archbishop chose to postpone receiving extreme unction until the following day when the arrival of Bishop Gilbert Glanvill of Rochester was expected, in order that his lifelong friend could administer the sacrament,

1. The quotation that forms the chapter title is from an account of the exile of the monks from Canterbury during the struggle between John and Innocent III over the election to Canterbury. B.M., Add. MS. 38,686, f. 4. Examples of the views cited are V. H. Galbraith, *Studies in the Public Records* (London, 1948), p. 126; A. L. Poole, p. 369; Knowles, *The Monastic Order in England*, pp. 326, 334. The most judicious evaluation of his ecclesiastical role is Cheney, *From Becket to Langton*, p. 41.

and then postponed it again when he seemed to be rallying. Toward vespers he joined in the services, even standing with assistance as he gave the benediction three times "in a voice full of elation and with a beautiful expression on his face." During the night he fell into a coma and died sometime the next day without regaining consciousness.[2] That contemporaries felt his death an event of some importance is emphasized by such things as the dating clause of an agreement "made at Ripon on the octave of St. Martin [November 18] next after the death of Archbishop Hubert of Canterbury," and another document recording a payment with the indication of date being merely that it was made at the Exchequer on Easter after the death of the archbishop.[3] The tomb ascribed to Hubert Walter along the south wall of the cathedral was opened in 1893, and the items found at that time make the identification probable.[4] Undecayed parts of the crozier are now displayed near the tomb, and the mitre and portions of the vestments and clothing found in the tomb are kept in the cathedral library.

The religious atmosphere that surrounded the last days of Hubert Walter as he lay near death was suitable for a man who was archbishop of Canterbury and who had risen through various church offices throughout his adult life. Nor when his life is viewed as a whole is it entirely a matter of his finally making a "deathbed confession," for there is evidence of a religious sincerity about the man that is often too heavily discounted by those writers who see something cynical about an ecclesiastic being as worldly successful in royal service as Hubert was. Of course, the founding of monasteries and gifts to such institutions was part of the accepted ethic of the feudal class, an ethic that Hubert Walter attempted to emulate in other ways, but his gifts scattered over the years reflect something of a sustained interest in such things. When dean of York he founded the Premonstratensian abbey at West Dereham, and as archbishop and

2. Ralph of Coggeshall, pp. 156-159. A briefer account is given by Gervase of Canterbury, II, 413. Coggeshall explained that he gave a full account of the archbishop's last illness because some people had asserted he had died intestate. See Howell, pp. 46-47. The practice established for England by King Henry II was that the testament of a bishop would be followed only if made rationally before the period of his last illness. In the case of a bishop dying unexpectedly, his personal property should be distributed for the good of his soul.

3. Brown, II, 85-86; *A Descriptive Catalogue of Ancient Deeds in the Public Record Office* (London, 1890-1915), I, 136, #A1197.

4. Hope, "On the Tomb of an Archbishop Recently Opened."

justiciar he did not forget the canons there. His plans for establishing a new Cistercian house at Wolverhampton were frustrated by his death.

As bishop of Salisbury, Hubert gave the revenues of two churches to the hospital of St. Lawrence in Reading for use of the poor, and the revenues of another church to the abbey there for the maintenance of thirteen poor men daily in the hospital.[5] Similarly, when he was archbishop, he gave certain revenues to the hospital of St. Thomas of Eastbridge in Canterbury.[6] An inventory taken at Salisbury in 1222 contains reference to another type of gift when it lists silken cloths given for use on the high altar of the cathedral by King Richard and Bishop Hubert, with the likely presumption being that the bishop had influenced the king in making his gift to the cathedral.[7] It is hardly possible to get a complete picture of such gifts when the evidence depends upon such things as the chance survival of an inventory. However, another of Hubert's gifts is known even more incidentally: the monastic chronicler, in relating how Abbot Samson removed the body of St. Edmund to a new shrine in 1198, mentions that the old coffin was wrapped in a linen cloth and then in a costly new silken cloth that the archbishop had given the monastic church that same year.[8] Gervase of Canterbury made a detailed and lengthy list of the jewels, vestments, books, and other personal items that the archbishop bequeathed to the monks of Christ Church with the provision that the monks would spend three hundred marks a year for the good of his soul.[9] When he came to Canterbury after the archbishop's death, King John heard of Hubert's gift, asked to see the furnishings of his chapel, marveled at the wealth these represented, and ordered them taken away to be given to the bishop of Winchester.[10] The delivery of these furnishings from London to Winchester was made at the cost of twenty-five shillings to the king and considerable ill-feeling toward him by the monks.[11]

Such charitable gifts tell little about the man who made them in any but an outward and formal sense, but a more revealing insight into the religious interests of Archbishop Hubert was given by his actions during a visit to the Carthusian house at Witham. He was then justiciar and came to the priory because of a dispute over pasturage rights held by

5. B.M., Egerton MS. 3031, fos. 71-71 v.; Jones and Macray, p. 46.

6. Cyprian Bunce, *A Register of Loans and Charitable Donations to the Poor of Canterbury* (MS catalogue and index in Canterbury Cathedral Library dated 1798), I, 525.

7. Jones, II, lxxxii.

8. Jocelin of Brakelond, p. 115.

9. Gervase of Canterbury, II, 413-414.

10. *Ibid.*, II, 98, 414.

11. *P.R. 7 John*, p. 121.

the monks. Naturally, they were anxious to please him and received him with all respect, but they had not anticipated his request to talk with one of their number named Adam of Dryburgh. The archbishop had heard some of his clerks talking of this unusual man of learning and piety who had resigned as abbot of a Premonstratensian house to become a simple monk at Witham. To be sure, Adam was hardly the type of man to appeal to a worldly archbishop, but he was a close friend of St. Hugh of Lincoln. During St. Hugh's annual retreat to the monastery, he and Adam often discussed the shortcomings of their present age while each pointed out to the other how far he personally fell short of the ideal in his calling.[12] Before the archbishop had an opportunity to meet this exemplary monk, he attended mass and was so shocked at the simplicity of the vestments worn by the celebrant that he immediately ordered one of his own chasubles given for use in the service at the altar. After mass the monks conducted the archbishop to another part of the monastery where he heard Master Adam preach in a manner that greatly impressed him and his clerks. In fact, Hubert was so moved that he accompanied Adam to his cell, laid aside his outer garments, confessed to the monk, and submitted himself to being whipped as part of the disciplinary penance. Such was the influence of this monk on Hubert Walter that afterward when the prior of Witham was traveling on business, the archbishop asked the prior to join him at table and to have his horse stabled with that of the archbishop. On another occasion, when the archbishop was crossing the Channel on royal business and the prior was on his way to the general chapter of the Carthusians, the archbishop invited the prior to join him on his ship where they sat together discussing religious questions during the crossing.[13]

That Hubert Walter had some purely religious interests would hardly be guessed from most books that refer to him, but the estimates of his character by his own contemporaries are hardly more helpful. Clearly his liberality was exceptional even for a great official, but not everyone put the same value upon that trait. To feudal eyes he must have appeared a "moult vaillans clers et moult larges et moult courtois," and even the Cistercian abbots gave him a good reference on that score when in 1198 they praised his continual gifts to the poor.[14] But to the Cistercian chronicler, Ralph of Coggeshall, such immense expenses led to his greatest fault

12. *Magna vita*, II, 52-54.
13. Wilmart, pp. 224-228.
14. *Histoire des ducs de Normandie*,

p. 101; Stubbs, *Epistolae Cantuariensis*, p. 424.

of collecting lands, rents, money, and offices until the end of his life to pay for his expenses. In the chronicler's opinion, none of Hubert's predecessors and no prince or contemporary king compared with the archbishop in his pomp, his affluent table, or the crowd of clerks, knights, and noble clients that surrounded him. He was also unrivaled for his gifts and for the sumptuous buildings that he constructed. In consequence, the income of the archbishopric was insufficient without the royal chancellorship, and both together still had to be supplemented by the traffic in wardships in which the archbishop engaged.[15] In spite of their differing interpretations, one thing on which all sources agree is that Hubert Walter's style of living was unusually lavish even for an archbishop.

This particular trait of character reflects the outlook of a self-made man. His family background placed him in the lower ranks of the feudal class, which was typical of the men who entered royal service under the Angevins. Richard de Lucy and Ranulf Glanvill, his predecessors as justiciar, and Geoffrey fitz Peter, his successor, were all men of similar background.[16] It was from such beginnings that Geoffrey fitz Peter rose to become earl of Essex, and Hubert Walter became archbishop of Canterbury, with lands in his control rivaling those of an earl. His position also gave him the opportunity to amass personal wealth. Along with his rise in social position and wealth, Hubert adopted the outlook of the nobility and attempted to rival even the king in the lavishness of his court.

There also seems to be a consensus among those who knew him that he was openhanded in his hospitality with no trace of stinginess. In spite of the high positions he held, he remained accessible to those in humbler circumstances and was especially friendly with monks. He would invite them to make their beds in his own chamber, even sharing the straw from his bed with them, so that he was taken as an example for all priests in their relationship with monks.[17] Such comments from more than one monastic chronicler confirm the conclusion reached about his long and sometimes bitter quarrel with the monks of Christ Church: it was the result of his extreme tenacity in attempting to carry out the wishes of his

15. Ralph of Coggeshall, pp. 160-161. Other writers who emphasize Hubert's sumptuousness are Gervase of Canterbury, II, 410-411, and Giraldus Cambrensis, I, 427. The last two lines of a four-line Latin poem about Hubert added to a thirteenth century manuscript are "Kent, feast your pastor with your prayers, he who was accustomed to feast kings, princes, and the needy." Corpus Christi College Library, Cambridge, MS. #236, f. 71.

16. West, *Justiciarship*, pp. 37-38, 54, 98.

17. Ralph of Coggeshall, pp. 159-160. See also Gervase of Canterbury, II, 411.

friend and predecessor, Archbishop Baldwin, and not of personal animosity toward the monks or even because he shared the adverse opinion of monks in general held by several contemporary bishops.

As his executors attempted to close accounts, fragmentary references to the archbishop's business affairs bear out the opinions of his critics about his financial involvement. King John, who had confirmed Hubert's will on two occasions, not only diverted his chapel furnishings but also took an active interest in the temporalities of Canterbury that came into his hands during the vacancy.[18] The executors of the will were James Savage and Master Elias of Dereham, two members of the archbishop's household, and the king placed William of Wrotham, who had once administered tin mines when Hubert Walter was justiciar, and Reginald of Cornhill as royal custodians for the see.[19] Royal mandates ordering payment of debts that Archbishop Hubert owed the king and claims entered in the Pipe Rolls for debts amounting to £913 1s. indicate that King John was pressing to collect all that he could from the executors. Most of the listed debts, going back as far as 1196, resulted from money Hubert had collected as King Richard's justiciar which had not been completely accounted for at the Exchequer by the time of his death. King John's own custodians later reported they had taken an income of almost £5,170 from the see of Canterbury for the period from June 24, 1205, to May 30, 1207.[20] After Hubert's death, there was also some litigation to determine whether he had seisin of certain lands when he died, to free lands taken into the king's hands along with the lands belonging to Canterbury because they had been in the custody of the archbishop at his death, and to protest alleged disseisins made by the late archbishop.[21]

Even these tangled remnants from his financial affairs and the difficulties they posed for his executors point to the chief characteristic of the man. Whatever else Hubert Walter may have been, he was industrious. This was as true in his trading in wardships as a means of building up his personal wealth as it was in his official capacities. Though they some-

18. Lambeth Palace Library, Carte Miscellane, XI, 11; MS. 1212, pp. 43-44. John's charter was printed in Rymer, I, Pt. 1, 78.

19. *Rotuli litterarum clausarum*, I, 61a; *P.R. 8 John*, pp. 54-55.

20. *Rotuli litterarum patentium*, p. 61a; *P.R. 6 John*, pp. 217, 219; *P.R. 7 John*, p. 116; *P.R. 8 John*, pp. 54-55. Other references to payments and financial adjustments resulting from Hubert Walter's death are *Rotuli litterarum clausarum*, I, 42a-b, 43a, 57b, 66a.

21. *P.R. 8 John*, pp. 141, 219; *P.R. 9 John*, p. 36; *P.R. 10 John*, p. 100; *Rotuli litterarum clausarum*, I, 69b; *Rotuli de oblatis et finibus*, pp. 301, 318; *Curia Regis Rolls*, VI, 139, 271.

times questioned his motives, even his enemies admitted this quality. It is clear from a study of his career that he applied himself with equal energy to his ecclesiastical positions and to his royal offices, from laboring as Glanvill's clerk to governing England for King Richard. Just as no other official had wielded the authority that Hubert Walter had as justiciar and archbishop of Canterbury, so none of his predecessors in either office had borne the burden that such a combination entailed, and his acceptance of the chancellorship meant that he continued to bear extremely heavy responsibilities to the end of his life.

One thing that must have helped him in this regard was that there was a certain continuity in several of the problems that he faced. For example, even during his apprenticeship as Glanvill's clerk he was introduced to the unrest on the Welsh frontier and the whole question of Wales with which he later dealt energetically from 1195 to 1198 as King Richard's justiciar and again as King John's chancellor. His involvement with the Christ Church case as archbishop came after considerable experience gained as a participant in royal attempts to mediate the dispute both while he was dean of York and while he was bishop of Salisbury. Similarly, years of experience in dealing with the problems which came before a royal justice preceded the famous regulations for the eyre of 1194 that he issued as justiciar. Of course, there were also many unexpected problems, but a gradual introduction to at least some problems helped to make it possible for him to deal with the total burden of his responsibilities.

For men of his time the major importance of Hubert Walter's career was that it provided an element of stability and continuity in government. In fact, at two crucial moments he was one of the leaders in saving England from rebellion and potential rebellion—when he put down John's rebellion against the captive King Richard and when he supported John as Richard's successor. Not only did Hubert Walter govern England in the absence of King Richard, but his experience and counsel were necessary to the good government that characterized the early years of King John's reign when there was co-operation among the justiciar, the chancellor, and the king, all three having received their earliest administrative training with Glanvill. Hubert's influence with both Richard and John had the effect of restraining them from impulsive actions to which each was inclined. As an archbishop as well as royal official, Hubert was especially able to serve as a kind of protector and advocate for the church. Although there might

be some objection to his rhetorical style, the statement by Gerald of
Wales that Hubert Walter was the "bridle to the prince and an obstacle
to tyranny" is not far wrong.[22]

What Archbishop Hubert did for the church is not easy to decide.
Clearly he was no theologian, no great preacher, nor even an example of
piety. The major theme of his pontificate seems to have been an orderly and
efficient administration. He restored and increased the property of the
church, he was active in administering ecclesiastical justice, and he selected
and patronized a group of educated men who made up his household.
Characteristically, he seems to have been active in visitations at a time
when regular visitation was yet unknown. Although not the author of
important legislation for the church, the canons of his council at Westminster had some later influence in giving order to the synodal legislation
of the next generation. No dramatic confrontation with the king marked
his career as it did that of St. Thomas Becket before him and Stephen
Langton after, but Archbishop Hubert's good relations with the kings he
served were not purchased at the expense of the church, and, in fact,
the church benefited in practical (if not spiritual) ways from the influence
he exercised at the royal court. His relations with successive popes, whom
he served conscientiously both as papal legate and by virtue of his position
as archbishop, were cordial. In his short biography of Archbishop Hubert,
Gervase of Canterbury thought it worthy of notice that Pope Innocent III
particularly reposed great confidence in the archbishop and granted him
special privileges.[23]

In the long view of history, the final estimate of Hubert Walter's importance will continue to rest upon his contributions as an administrator.
His greatness was that, in carrying on the routine of government, he had
the foresight to help create an administrative structure suitable to the
expanding activities of royal government, that he instituted the records
necessary to provide precedents and patterns for administrative decisions,
and that he helped train men who would carry on the job. In many ways
he was not original, and better methods of administration and record-
keeping were also being developed in the papacy and other governments,
but Hubert Walter was outstanding in England. His long career ties together administrative improvements from King Henry II to King John and
serves as a link between developments in church and state. The singular

22. Giraldus Cambrensis, I, 427.    23. Gervase of Canterbury, II, 412.

inventiveness in administrative experiment between 1193 and 1205, often noticed by historians, was in great part due to the efforts of this man, who put his varied experience to work in whatever task he was called to undertake. The significance of this continuity in administrative personnel and tradition can best be demonstrated by contrast with the arbitrary government of King John after the continuity began to be broken—to some degree by his personal intervention in the details of government after the loss of Normandy in 1204, to an increasing extent after the death of Hubert Walter in 1205, and reaching a height in the excesses of his final years after the death of Geoffrey fitz Peter in 1213.

To the historian who tries to understand the governing of England during this period, the career of Hubert Walter is important beyond his contributions as an individual, for his central position makes him something of a key to the system as a whole. Many of the men engaged in the administrative work of both church and kingdom were accustomed to working together because they had been close associates in various positions, in some cases even for a period of many years. Like Hubert Walter, some of them learned their jobs by training in the household of important officials, but by the time Hubert had formed his own household, men with formal training in the universities were more prominent. Such men became attached to the royal household or that of some great ecclesiastic, and in the case of Archbishop Hubert there was an overlapping and confusion of royal and archiepiscopal clerks who served him. It was among these men that definite administrative traditions and practices were established.

The process of administration cannot be understood apart from the men who created and maintained it, and the attempt to discover something about the relationships of these men needs to be made, even though the nature of the surviving sources precludes any revolutionary success in such an investigation. J. E. A. Jolliffe in emphasizing the personal element in the rule of the Angevin kings has provided a necessary corrective to the overly theoretical and artificial approach found in most constitutional and administrative histories dealing with twelfth-century England.[24] Yet, to consider only the personal influence of the king is too limited, for there was also the personal factor of his administrative agents, and this factor was of supreme importance during most of Hubert Walter's career be-

24. See his *Angevin Kingship*.

cause of the absence from England of both King Richard and King John. Similarities of training and background made the administrative personnel a significant element in the governing of England, and these men were also tied together by years of personal experience in co-operating on the business of both church and state. After Hubert Walter became justiciar, the names of the itinerant justices reveal such personal connections between many of the justices and the justiciar. With the justiciar being allowed a free hand in England, the successes and failures of these men working together had more immediate impact on the governing of England than the whims of an absentee king. On the whole, the emerging professional approach to government which they represent, and of which Hubert Walter is a prime illustration, served as a moderating influence upon the king. Not only Hubert Walter's personal influence but also the inherent inertia of the regular procedures that the administrators employed—in contrast to the arbitrariness of *ad hoc* personal decisions by the king—worked for moderation.

Certainly, neither Hubert nor his colleagues attempted to block royal power on the basis of any constitutional theory. In fact, after he became justiciar, Hubert broke with the practice of dependence upon the Great Council and its common consent for any major decisions that had been developing during Richard's absence on the crusade. Nevertheless, the adoption of regularized procedures had the effect of moderating arbitrary royal power, until King John returned permanently to England after the loss of Normandy and made himself a master of the administrative machinery. It is probably significant that Jolliffe found most of his examples of arbitrary actions of the Angevins either under Henry II or during the later years of King John. The foundations were being laid as early as the time of Hubert Walter for the power struggle that developed in the mid-thirteenth century over whether the king or his barons would control the machinery of government that Hubert and his colleagues had helped to create. In the meantime, the justiciarship of Hubert Walter and the partnership of his successor, Geoffrey fitz Peter, and the chancellor provided an interlude during which the administrative innovations of King Henry II were perfected.

Most historians writing of this period of English history discuss the development of the common law as an outgrowth of the legal experiments of King Henry II. The later twelfth century was also a period in which there was significant development in canon law, especially during the pontificates of Alexander III (1159-1181) and Innocent III (1198-1216), and England had an important part in that development. That the same men were busy implementing both kinds of laws in England has not so often been noticed. Not only were Archbishop Hubert and a number of bishops engaged as royal justices in building the common law while presiding over ecclesiastical courts, but the archbishop's household also shows that the coincidence of personnel went much deeper. Men like Henry de Castellion, archdeacon of Canterbury, Master Godfrey de Insula, and Master Simon of Scales administered ecclesiastical justice and royal justice alike, and other men like Geoffrey de Bocland and Ranulf, treasurer of Salisbury, served the king as royal justices and witnessed the *acta* of the archbishop. Even when the same men did not directly participate in both ecclesiastical and royal courts, they associated with men working with both types of law in the households of the archbishop or bishops engaged in royal service and must have influenced each other's work.

Hubert's career also provides an indication that able men who rose to prominent positions might do so as the result of demonstrated ability and not as a matter of mere whim or favoritism on the part of a powerful ruler. It is true that he owed his first positions at the Exchequer and as dean of York to the influence of Ranulf Glanvill, but he had won the confidence of both Glanvill and the king while in the former's household. There he was brought into close association with the men who served the royal court, and he had become familiar with the administration of justice and with specific problems, such as Wales and the Christ Church case, with which he himself had to deal later. As dean of York, he had experience in managing the diocese during a vacancy at the death of the archbishop. His nomination to the bishopric of Salisbury came because his prestige and authority at York made him an obstacle to King Richard's plan of satisfying his illegitimate half-brother with the archbishopric. During the Third Crusade, Hubert Walter showed courage as well as diplomatic and administrative ability. In fact, the king himself explicitly recognized that he was nominating Hubert for the archbishopric of Canterbury because of the favorable opinion he had formed of him during the crusade. The appointment as justiciar was made for similar reasons, strengthened by the energetic manner in which Hubert had also set out to raise the king's ransom. By the time King John chose him as chancellor, he had become the most experienced and reliable administrator in England, a man possessed with something of the authority of an elder statesman.

The fact that Hubert Walter held high positions in the royal government while he was archbishop caused some very real problems, but the apparent violation of canon law seems to have mattered little in England where such dual office-holding was not uncommon. It is true that, on occasion, there was some question of divided loyalties between the obedience owed a justiciar and that owed an archbishop. However, the handling of the incident in London involving William fitz Osbert was the only really scandalous conflict of responsibilities. Yet most historians dismiss Hubert's work as archbishop with some such evaluation as the following: "He may also be criticized for neglect of his position as head of the church in England. The monks of Canterbury complained to the pope that he was too much engaged in secular business to give proper attention to the affairs of the church."[25] When one considers that the monks were embroiled with the archbishop in a bitter dispute over his proposed chapel at Lambeth, they would hardly seem ideal witnesses on such a point. Of course, there are general statements against the involvement of bishops in secular business, and specific statements about Hubert are found in the writings of Gerald of Wales and Ralph of Coggeshall.[26] Against these charges there is the evidence from such of his archiepiscopal records as survive. As discussed in previous chapters, these show him engaged in nearly the full range of duties expected in the twelfth century of an archbishop as diocesan, metropolitan, and papal legate. Such activity seems sufficient to disprove the charges of neglect. More important than this conclusion in regard to Hubert Walter as archbishop is that one does not unthinkingly fall into the view that holding offices in both church and state necessarily meant neglect of the ecclesiastical office.

Except for the importance of his offices, Hubert was typical of a period in which both prelates and kings managed to support the learned clerks so necessary to their administrations by providing them with ecclesiastical benefices. The easy interchange between royal service and ecclesiastical position tells us much about government in the later twelfth century. We need to remember that our understanding of that period can be obscured all too easily by the way in which the historian tends to approach the

25. Poole, p. 443.
26. Giraldus Cambrensis, I, 427; Ralph of Coggeshall, pp. 160-161.

period, either through his interest in administrative history or in church history, rarely showing equal interest in both. Historians have discussed the influence of canon law upon English law based upon this overlapping of offices, but the matter of influence was not a one-way street. Trained administrators like Hubert Walter brought efficiency to the offices they filled in the church, and their experience in secular jurisdiction was valuable in their ecclesiastical administration and the execution of ecclesiastical law as interpreted by their own courts in England or decisions being made by the pope in Rome. Of course, the overlapping of offices in church and state could mean a neglect of ecclesiastical duties, but it could also mean that the church benefited from having spokesmen at the center of royal government. Examples have been given where Hubert Walter used his positions as justiciar and as chancellor for the benefit of the church.

For Hubert, such a combination of offices meant that he was more than ever dependent upon the ability of the men who made up his household. He had carefully chosen these men, and some of the same men who managed the bishopric of Salisbury during his absence on the Third Crusade helped to provide the efficiency of his archiepiscopal household or served as his representatives in ecclesiastical courts. One of them, Master Simon of Scales, was with him even longer, for he had been a fellow witness to one of Glanvill's charters. Viewed in this broader perspective, Hubert Walter's accomplishments are seen as the result of a system that rested upon the loyalty and ability of an administrative class serving church and king with distinction, and he himself stands out as the finest example of that class.

# BIBLIOGRAPHY

## I. Sources

### A. *Manuscript*

British Museum. London.

Additional Charters 7620; 10,643; 15,238; 19,611; 20,246; 33,596.
Additional Manuscripts 38,686; 46,353 (Abbey Leger of Dereham).
Campbell Charters XXII.6.
Cotton Charters V.75.
Cotton Manuscripts: Claudius A.VI (Cartulary, Boxgrove); Claudius D.XIII (Register, Binham); Galba E.II (Register, St. Benet of Holm); Julius D.II (Register, St. Augustine's, Canterbury); Nero C.III (misc. charters); Titus C.VIII (Register, Wymondham); Vespasian A.XXII (Register, Rochester, fragmentary); Vespasian C.XIV (misc. modern copies of charters); Vespasian E.XIV (Register, Leiston); Vespasian E.XXIII (Cartulary, Durford); Vitellius A.XI (Cartulary, Bradenstoke).
Egerton Manuscripts 3031 (Cartulary, Reading).
Harley Charters 43.G.25; 43.I.18; 83.C.27; 83.C.28; 84.C.42; 84.D.14.
Harley Manuscripts 391 (Register, Waltham); 662 (Cartulary, Little Dunmow); 2110.
Stowe Charters 509.

Cambridge.

Corpus Christi College Library. Manuscript #236.
University Library. Manuscripts Ee.V.31 (Register of Prior Henry de Eastry); LL.#15 (Cartulary, St. Gregory's, Canterbury).

Canterbury, Dean and Chapter Muniments.

Bunce, Cyprian. A Register of Loans and Charitable Donations to the Poor of Canterbury. Also of the Documents of Certain Hospitals. 2 vols. 1798. A handwritten catalogue and index with copies of some manuscripts no longer extant.
Chartae Antiquae A5, A43, A191, C28, C30, C71(V), C105, C106, C137, C175, C1305, D111, E190, F85, G187, H102, H103, L129a, L130, L131, L132, L133, L134, L135, L136, L137, L138, L376, M263, M264, P46, P50, R70a-b, S231, S269, S302, S303, S352, Z134, Z144-145, Z186, Z202.
Christ Church Letters, Vol. II.
Eastry Correspondence, Group III #25; Group VI #1.
Ecclesiastical Suits #1.
Register A.

Register B.
Sede Vacante Scrap-book, 3 vols.

Ely, Dean and Chapter Muniments.
Papal Legates, #81.

Exeter, Dean and Chapter Muniments.
Cartulary #3672.
MS. #810-813.

Lambeth Palace Library, London.
Carew MS. 613.
Cartae Miscellane V, 97, 102, 111; XI, 11, 12, 15, 16, 17, 18, 21, 22, 32, 45.
Codices Manuscripti Lambethani 8.
Codices Manuscripti Whartoniani 580 (copies of manuscripts by Henry Wharton in 1688).
Lambeth Manuscripts 241 (Cartulary, Dover Priory), 1212.
Register Warham.

Kent County Archives, Maidstone.
Cartulary of Leeds Priory. Location number U120 Q13.

Norwich, Dean and Chapter Muniments.
Original archbishops' charters. Temporary #953.
Register I.
Register IV.

Oxford University, Bodleian Library.
MS. Charters: Essex a.2 #32; Northants a.I #2; Oxon a.3 #147.

Peterborough, Dean and Chapter Muniments.
MS. 1.

Public Record Office, London.
Chancery, Ancient Deeds C.146/3242, 9717, 10365.
Chancery, Masters' Exhibits C115/A1-2, A4, A6 (Cartularies, Llanthony Priory).
Exchequer, Augmentation Office. Ancient Deeds E326/8941, 11830, 11842, 11843; Miscellaneous Books E315/31, 35, 45, 61 (Cartulary, Pershore Abbey).
Exchequer, King's Remembrancer. Ancient Deeds E210/3242, 11282; Miscellaneous Books E164/27 (Cartulary, St. Augustine's, Canterbury), 29 (Cartulary, Langdon Abbey).
Exchequer, The Treasury of the Receipt E40/13750, 13751, 13993, 14000, 14127, 15418; E42/54.
Lancaster, Records of the Duchy. Cartae Miscellaneae D.L. 36/I/16, 203; Deeds D.L.25/8, 3394 #3; D.L.27/4, 51, 52, 90.

Special Collections 1 (Ancient Correspondence), vols. 1 and 47. SC1/1, 47.

Rochester, Dean and Chapter Muniments. On deposit at the Kent County Archives, Maidstone.

Registrum Temporalium. No modern foliation. Citations are to numbers in black ink in the register itself.

Title Deeds DRc T53/9, 10 (Rochester numbers B1309, 1311); T60/1-3 (Rochester numbers B307a-c).

Salisbury, Dean and Chapter Muniments.

Charters Box E.5.

Liber Evidentiarum C(ii.3).

Wells, Dean and Chapter Muniments.

Liber Albus I-II.

Windsor, St. George's Chapel, Dean and Canons Muniments.

Arundel White Book, or The White Leiger Book.

Manuscript XI.G.11 #4, 7; XI.G.39.

### B. *Printed*

Ambroise. *L'Estoire de la guerre sainte*, ed. Gaston Paris. (Collection de documents inédits sur l'histoire de France.) Paris, 1897. Translated by M. J. Hubert, *The Crusade of Richard Lion-Heart*. New York, 1941.

Behâ ed-Dîn. *The Life of Saladin*. London, 1897. Original and French translation in *Récueil des historiens des croisades, Historiens orientaux*, vol. III.

Benedict of Peterborough. *Gesta regis Henrici Secundi*, ed. William Stubbs. (Rolls Series.) 2 vols. London, 1867.

Bliss, W. H. *Calendar of Entries in the Papal Registers Relating to Great Britain and Ireland*. Vol. I only. London, 1893.

*The Book of Fees Commonly Called Testa de Nevill*. 3 vols. The Deputy Keeper of the Records. London, 1920-1931.

Brown, W., ed. *Cartularium prioratus de Gyseburne*. (Surtees Society, 86, 89.) 2 vols. Durham, 1889-1894.

*Calendar of the Charter Rolls*. 6 vols. The Deputy Keeper of the Records. London, 1903-1927.

Canivez, Joseph M. *Statuta capitulorum generalium ordinis Cisterciensis*. Vol. I only. Louvain, 1933.

*The Cartae Antiquae Rolls* (1-20), ed. L. Landon and J. C. Davies. (Pipe Roll Society, 55, 71.) 2 vols. London, 1939-1960.

*The Chancellor's Roll for the Eighth Year of the Reign of King Richard the First*, ed. Doris M. Stenton. (Pipe Roll Society, 45.) London, 1930.

Cheney, C. R., and W. H. Semple. *Selected Letters of Pope Innocent III Concerning England (1198-1216).* London, 1953.

Chibnall, Marjorie. *Select Documents of the English Lands of the Abbey of Bec.* (Camden Society, 3rd ser., 73.) London, 1951.

*Chronicon abbatiae de Evesham,* ed. William D. Macray. (Rolls Series.) London, 1863.

*Curia Regis Rolls of the Reigns of Richard I. and John.* 13 vols. *The Deputy Keeper of the Records.* London, 1922-.

Davies, J. Conway, ed. *Episcopal Acts and Cognate Documents Relating to Welsh Dioceses 1066-1272.* (Historical Society of the Church in Wales.) Vol. I only. n.p., 1946.

Denholm-Young, N. *Cartulary of the Medieval Archives of Christ Church.* (Oxford Historical Society, 92.) Oxford, 1931.

*A Descriptive Catalogue of Ancient Deeds in the Public Record Office.* 6 vols. The Deputy Keeper of the Records. London, 1890-1915.

Dugdale, William. *Monasticon Anglicanum.* 6 vols. in 8. London, 1830.

Fantosme, Jordan. See Richard Howlett, *Chronicles.* Vol. III.

Farrer, William, ed. *The Chartulary of Cockersand Abbey of the Premonstratensian Order.* (Chetham Society, new series, 38-40, 43, 56-57, 64.) 7 parts in 3 vols. Manchester, 1898-1909.

———. *The Lancashire Pipe Rolls.* Liverpool, 1902.

*Feet of Fines for the County of Lincoln for the Reign of King John 1199-1216,* ed. Margaret S. Walker. (Pipe Roll Society, new series, 29.) London, 1954.

*Feet of Fines of the Reign of Henry II. and of the First Seven Years of the Reign of Richard I* (Pipe Roll Society, 17.) London, 1894.

fitz Neal [Nigel], Richard. *Dialogus de Scaccario,* trans. Charles Johnson. London, 1950.

Flahiff, G. B. *"Deus Non Vult.* A Critic of the Third Crusade," *Mediaeval Studies* (Toronto), IX (1947), 162-88.

Foreville, Raymonde, ed. *Un procès de canonisation à l'aube du XIIIᵉ siècle (1201-2): Le livre de saint Gilbert de Sempringham.* Paris, 1943.

Foster, C. W., ed. *The Registrum Antiquissimum of the Cathedral Church of Lincoln.* Vol. I only. (Lincoln Record Society, 27.) Lincoln, 1931.

Fowler, G. H., and Joyce Godber. *The Cartulary of Bushmead Priory.* (Bedfordshire Historical Record Society, 22.) Aspley Guise, 1945.

Gervase of Canterbury. *Historical Works,* ed. William Stubbs. (Rolls Series.) 2 vols. London, 1879-1880.

Gilbert, J. T. *Historic and Municipal Documents of Ireland. A.D. 1172-1320.* (Rolls Series.) London, 1870.

Giraldus Cambrensis. *Opera,* ed. J. S. Brewer. (Rolls Series.) 8 vols. London, 1861-1891. Selections translated by H. E. Butler, *The Autobiography of Giraldus Cambrensis.* London, 1937.

Glanvill, Ranulf. *Tractatus de legibus et consuetudinibus regni Anglie qui Glanvilla vocatur,* ed. G. D. G. Hall. London, 1965.

Hales, John W. and F. J. Furnivall. *Bishop Percy's Folio Manuscript.* 3 vols. London, 1867.

Hart, W. H. and P. A. Lyons. *Cartularium monasterii de Rameseia.* (Rolls Series.) 3 vols. London, 1884-1893.

*L'Histoire de Guillaume le Maréchal,* ed. Paul Meyer. 3 vols. Paris, 1891-1901. Paraphrased in English by Jessie Crosland, *William the Marshal.* London, 1962.

*Histoire des ducs de Normandie et des rois d'Angleterre,* ed. Francisque Michel. Paris, 1840.

Historical Manuscripts Commission. *Calendar of the Manuscripts of the Dean and Chapter of Wells.* 2 vols. London, 1907-1914.

————. *Fifth Report.* London, 1876.

————. *Report on Manuscripts in Various Collections.* Vol. I (Canterbury) London, 1901. Vol. IV (Exeter). Dublin, 1907.

Holtzmann, Walther. *Papsturkunden in England.* (Abhandlungen der Gesellschaft der Wissenschaften zu Göttingen, Philologisch-Historische Klasse, neue Folge, 25; Dritte Folge, 14-15, 33.) 3 vols. Berlin and Göttingen, 1930-1952.

Howlett, Richard. *Chronicles of the Reigns of Stephen, Henry II., and Richard I.* (Rolls Series.) 3 vols. London, 1884-1886.

Imâdeddîn. *See Recueil des historiens des croisades. Historiens orientaux.* Vol. IV.

Innocent III. *Opera Omnia* in J. P. Migne, *Patrologiae cursus completus* (Series Latina, 214-217.) Paris, 1855.

Jocelin of Brakelond. *Chronicle,* translated by H. E. Butler. London, 1949.

Jones, W. H. Rich. *The Register of S. Osmund.* (Rolls Series.) 2 vols. London, 1883-1884.

————, and W. D. Macray. *Charters and Documents . . . of Salisbury.* (Rolls Series.) London, 1891.

Lancaster, William T. *Abstracts of the Charters and Other Documents Contained in the Chartulary of the Cistercian Abbey of Fountains.* 2 vols. Leeds, 1915.

Leys, Agnes M. *The Sandford Cartulary.* (Oxfordshire Record Society, 19, 22.) 2 vols. Oxford, 1938-1941.

Liebermann, F. *Ungedruckte Anglo-Normannische Geschichtsquellen.* Strassburg, 1879.

Luard, Henry R., ed. *Annales monastici.* Vols. I and IV. (Rolls Series.) London, 1864, 1869.

McNulty, Joseph, ed. *The Chartulary of the Cistercian Abbey of St. Mary of Sallay in Craven.* (Yorkshire Archaeological Society. Record Series, 87, 90.) 2 vols. n.p. 1933-1934.

*Magna vita Sancti Hugonis*, ed. Decima L. Douie and Dom Hugh Farmer. 2 vols. London, 1961-1962.

Maitland, Frederic W., ed. *Three Rolls of the King's Court in the Reign of King Richard the First A.D. 1194-1195*. (Pipe Roll Society, 14.) London, 1891.

Mapes [Map], Walter. *De nugis curialium*, ed. Thomas Wright. (Camden Society, 50.) London, 1850. Translation by M. R. James. (Cymmrodorion Record Series, no. IX.) London, 1923.

Mayer, Hans E., *ed Itinerarium peregrinorum*. (Schriften der Monumenta Germaniae Historica, 18.) Stuttgart, 1962.

*The Memoranda Roll for . . . the First Year of the Reign of King John (1199-1200)*, ed. H. G. Richardson. (Pipe Roll Society, new series 21.) London, 1943.

Paris, Matthew. *Chronica majora*, ed. Henry R. Luard. (Rolls Series.) 7 vols. London, 1872-1883.

———. *Historia Anglorum*, ed. Sir Frederic Madden. (Rolls Series.) 3 vols. London, 1866-1869.

Peter of Blois, "Epistolae," in J. P. Migne, *Patrologiae cursus completus* (Series Latina, 207.) Paris, 1904.

Pipe Rolls. *The Great Roll of the Pipe 31-33 Henry II*, ed. J. H. Round. (Pipe Roll Society, 34, 36-37.) 3 vols. London, 1913-1915.

———. *The Great Roll of the Pipe 2 Richard I—10 John,* ed. Doris M. Stenton. (Pipe Roll Society, new series 1-23.) 17 vols. London, 1925-1947. The editor for *P.R. 7 John* was Sidney Smith and for *P.R. 9 John* was A. Mary Kirkus.

———. *The Great Roll of the Pipe for the First Year of the Reign of King Richard the First A.D. 1189-1190*, ed. Joseph Hunter. London, 1844.

———. *The Great Rolls of the Pipe for the Second, Third, and Fourth Years of the Reign of King Henry the Second*, ed. Joseph Hunter. London, 1844.

*Placita de Quo Warranto*. Record Commission. London, 1818.

Ralph of Coggeshall. *Chronicon Anglicanum*, ed. Joseph Stevenson. (Rolls Series.) London, 1875.

Ralph de Diceto. *Historical Works*, ed. William Stubbs. (Rolls Series.) 2 vols. London, 1876.

Reaver, F. W. *A Cartulary of Buckland Priory in the County of Somerset.* (Somerset Record Society, 25.) n.p. 1909.

*Récueil des historiens des croisades. Historiens orientaux*. 5 vols. Paris, 1872-1906.

*The Red Book of the Exchequer,* ed. Hubert Hall. (Rolls Series.) 3 vols. London, 1896.

Richard of Devizes. See Richard Howlett, *Chronicles*. Vol. III.

Richardson, H. G., and G. O. Sayles. *Select Cases of Procedure without Writ under Henry III.* (Selden Society, 60.) London, 1941.

Roger of Hoveden. *Chronica,* ed. William Stubbs. (Rolls Series.) 4 vols. London, 1868-1871.

Roger of Wendover. *Chronica sive flores historiarum,* ed. H. O. Coxe. 5 vols. London, 1841-1844.

*Rotuli chartarum,* ed. Thomas D. Hardy. Vol. I, part 1 only. Record Commission. London, 1837.

*Rotuli curiae regis,* ed. Sir Francis Palgrave. 2 vols. Record Commission. London, 1835.

*Rotuli de liberate ac de misis et praestitis, regnante Johanne,* ed. Thomas D. Hardy. Record Commission. London, 1844.

*Rotuli de oblatis et finibus . . . tempore regis Johannis,* ed. Thomas D. Hardy. Record Commission. London, 1835.

*Rotuli litterarum clausarum,* ed. Thomas D. Hardy. Vol. 1 only. Record Commission. London, 1833.

*Rotuli litterarum patentium,* ed. Thomas D. Hardy. Record Commission. London, 1835.

Round, J. H. *Calendar of Documents Preserved in France Illustrative of the History of Great Britain and Ireland.* Vol. 1 only. London, 1899.

Rymer, Thomas. *Foedera.* Vol. I, part 1. Record Commission. London, 1816.

Salter, H. E. *Newington Longville Charters.* (Oxfordshire Record Series, 3.) Oxford, 1921.

Salzman, L. F. *et al. The Chartulary of the Priory of St. Pancras of Lewes.* (Sussex Record Society, 38, 40, supp. vol. for 1943.) 3 vols. n.p. 1932-1943.

Savage, H. E. *The Great Register of Lichfield Cathedral.* (The William Salt Archaeological Society, 1924.) Kendal, 1926.

Stenton, Doris M. *The Earliest Lincolnshire Assize Rolls A.D. 1202-1209.* (Lincoln Record Society, 22.) Lincoln, 1926.

———. *Pleas before the King or His Justices 1198-1202.* (Selden Society, 67-68.) 2 vols. London, 1952-1953.

Stenton, F. M. *Facsimiles of Early Charters from Northamptonshire Collections.* Lincoln and London, 1930.

———. *Documents Illustrative of the Social and Economic History of the Danelaw.* London, 1920.

Stubbs, William. *Chronicles and Memorials of the Reign of Richard I.* (Rolls Series.) 2 vols. London, 1864-1865.

———. *Epistolae Cantuarienses.* See *Chronicles.* Vol. II.

———. *Itinerarium peregrinorum et gesta Regis Ricardi.* See *Chronicles.* Vol. I.

Thorne, William. *Chronicle of St. Augustine's Abbey Canterbury*, translated by A. H. Davis. Oxford, 1934.

Thorpe, John. *Registrum Roffense*. 2 vols. London, 1769.

Vacarius. *The Liber Pauperum of Vacarius*, ed. F. de Zulueta. (Selden Society, 44.) London, 1927.

Van Caenegem, R. C. *Royal Writs in England from the Conquest to Glanvill*. (Selden Society, 77.) London, 1959.

West, J. R. *The Register of the Abbey of St. Benet of Holme*. (Norfolk Record Society, 2.) London, 1932.

William of Malmesbury. *Vita Wulfstani*, ed. Reginald R. Darlington. (Camden Society, 3rd series, 40.) London, 1928.

William of Newburgh. See Richard Howlett, *Chronicles*. Vol. I.

Wilkins, David, ed. *Concilia Magnae Britanniae et Hiberniae*. 4 vols. London, 1737.

Wilmart, André. "Maitre Adam chanoine Prémontré devenu Chartreux à Witham," *Analecta Praemonstratensia*, IX (1933), 209-232.

Woodcock, Audrey M., ed., *Cartulary of the Priory of St. Gregory, Canterbury*. (Camden Society, 3rd series, 88.) London, 1956.


## II. Selected Secondary Works


Adler, Michael. "The Jews of Canterbury," *Jewish Historical Society Transactions*, VII (1911), 19-96.

Allaria, A. "English Scholars at Bologna during the Middle Ages," *The Dublin Review*, CXII (1893), 66-83.

Anderson, Walter. *Kaiser und Abt. Die Geschichte eines Schwanks*. (Folklore Fellows Communications, no. 42.) Helsinki, 1923.

Appleby, John T. *England without Richard 1189-1199*. Ithaca, N. Y., 1965.

Barlow, Frank. "Roger of Howden," *The English Historical Review*, LXV (1950), 352-360.

Barnes, Rosemary G. "Lambeth Ms. 1212 and the White Book of Canterbury," *Bulletin of the Institute of Historical Research*, XXXII (1959), 56-62.

Barraclough, B. G. Review of Kuttner, *Repetorium der Kanonistik, The English Historical Review*, 53 (1938), 492-495.

Blomefield, Francis. *An Essay Towards a Topographical History of the County of Norfolk*. 11 vols. London, 1805-1810.

Bovee, Dorothy. "A Comparison of the Original Sources of the Third Crusade." Unpublished Master's thesis, University of Minnesota, 1930.

Brentano, Robert. *York Metropolitan Jurisdiction and Papal Judges Delegate (1279-1296)*. Berkeley and Los Angeles, 1959.

Brooke, C. N. L. "Episcopal Charters for Wix Priory" in Patricia Barnes and C. F. Slade, eds. *A Medieval Miscellany for Doris Mary Stenton.* (Pipe Roll Society, new series, 36.) London, 1962.

Brooke, Z. N. *The English Church and the Papacy: From the Conquest to the Reign of John.* Cambridge, 1931.

Cazel, F. A., Jr. "Norman and Wessex Charters of the Roumare Family" in Patricia Barnes and C. F. Slade, eds. *A Medieval Miscellany for Doris Mary Stenton.* (Pipe Roll Society, new series, 36.) London, 1962.

Cheney, C. R. "The Earliest English Diocesan Statutes," *The English Historical Review,* 294 (1960), 1-29.

———. *English Bishops' Chanceries 1100-1250.* Manchester, 1950.

———. *English Synodalia of the Thirteenth Century.* Oxford, 1941.

———. *From Becket to Langton: English Church Government 1170-1213.* Manchester, 1956.

———. "Master Philip the Notary and the Fortieth of 1199," *The English Historical Review,* 63 (1948), 342-350.

———. "Legislation of the Medieval English Church," *The English Historical Review,* 50 (1935), 193-224, 385-417.

Chew, Helena M. *The English Ecclesiastical Tenants-in-chief and Knight Service.* London, 1932.

Chrimes, S. B. *An Introduction to the Administrative History of Mediaeval England.* Oxford, 1952.

Churchill, Irene J. *Canterbury Administration: The Administrative Machinery of the Archbishopric of Canterbury Illustrated from the Original Records.* 2 vols. London, 1933.

Clay, Sir Charles T. *York Minster Fasti.* Vol. I only. (The Yorkshire Archaeological Society, Record Series, 123.) n.p. 1958.

Colvin, H. M. *The White Canons in England.* Oxford, 1951.

Constable, Giles. *Monastic Tithes from the Origins to the Twelfth Century.* Cambridge, 1964.

Davis, G. R. C. *Medieval Cartularies of Great Britain. A Short Catalogue.* London, 1958.

*Dictionary of National Biography.* 22 vols. London, 1921-22. Articles on "Theobald Butler" by J. H. Round, "Ranulf de Glanville" by F. W. Maitland, and "Hubert Walter" by Kate Norgate.

Du Boulay, F. R. H. *The Lordship of Canterbury.* London, 1966.

Duggan, Charles. *Twelfth-century Decretal Collections and Their Importance in English History.* (University of London Historical Studies, 12.) London, 1963.

Edwards, J. G. "The *Itinerarium Regis Ricardi* and the *Estoire de la Guerre Sainte*" in J. G. Edwards *et al.* (eds.). *Historical Essays in Honour of James Tait,* pp. 59-77. Manchester, 1933.

Edwards, Kathleen. *The English Secular Cathedrals in the Middle Ages.* Manchester, 1949.

Emden, Alfred B. *A Biographical Register of the University of Oxford to A.D. 1500.* 3 vols. Oxford, 1957-1959.

Eyton, R. W. *Court, Household, and Itinerary of King Henry II.* London, 1888.

Farrer, William. *Honors and Knights' Fees.* 3 vols. London, 1923-1925.

Flahiff, G. B. "The Writs of Prohibition to Court Christian in the Thirteenth Century," *Mediaeval Studies* (Toronto), VI (1944), 261-313.

Foreville, Raymonde. *L'Église et la royauté en Angleterre sous Henri II Plantagenet (1154-1189).* Paris, 1943.

Foss, Edward. *The Judges of England.* 9 vols. London, 1848.

Fournier, Paul. *Les officialités au Moyen Age.* Paris, 1880.

Galbraith, V. H. *Roger Wendover and Matthew Paris.* Glasgow, 1944.

————. *Studies in the Public Records.* London, 1948.

Gibb, H. A. R. "The Arabic Sources for the Life of Saladin," *Speculum,* XXV (1950), 58-72.

Glanville-Richards, W. U. S. *Records of the Anglo-Norman House of Glanville.* London, 1882.

Gray, J. W. "The Ius Praesentandi in England from the Constitutions of Clarendon to Bracton," *The English Historical Review,* 67 (1952), 481-509.

Hope, W. H. St. John. "On the Tomb of an Archbishop Recently Opened in the Cathedral Church of Canterbury." *Vetusta Monumenta* (Society of Antiquaries), VII, part I (1893).

Howell, Margaret. *Regalian Right in Medieval England.* London, 1962.

Hunnisett, R. F. *The Medieval Coroner.* Cambridge, 1961.

Hunt, R. W. "English Learning in the Late Twelfth Century," *Transactions of the Royal Historical Society,* 4th series, XIX (1936), 19-42.

John, Eric. "The Litigation of an Exempt House, St. Augustine's, Canterbury, 1182-1237," *Bulletin of the John Rylands Library,* 39 (1956-57), 390-415.

Jolliffe, J. E. A. *Angevin Kingship.* New York, 1955.

Knowles, Dom David. *The Monastic Order in England.* Cambridge, 1940.

Kuttner, Stephen, and Eleanor Rathbone. "Anglo-Norman Canonists of the Twelfth Century," *Traditio,* VII (1949-51), 279-358.

Landon, Lionel. *The Itinerary of King Richard I.* (Pipe Roll Society, 51.) London, 1935.

Le Neve, John. *Fasti Ecclesiae Anglicanae.* London, 1716.

Lewis, George R. *The Stannaries.* (Harvard Economic Studies, III.) Cambridge, Mass., 1924.

Lloyd, Sir John E. *A History of Wales.* 3rd ed. 2 vols. London, 1954.

Lunt, William E. *Financial Relations of the Papacy with England to 1327.* Cambridge, Mass., 1939.

Madox, Thomas. *The History and Antiquities of the Exchequer.* London, 1711.

Major, Kathleen. "Episcopal Acta in Mediaeval Capitular Archives," *Bulletin of the Institute of Historical Research,* IX (1931-1932), 145-153.

————. "The 'Familia' of Archbishop Stephen Langton," *The English Historical Review,* 48 (1933), 529-553.

Makower, F. *The Constitutional History and Constitution of the Church of England.* London, 1895.

Mitchell, Sydney K. *Taxation in Medieval England.* New Haven, 1951.

Moorman, John R. H. *Church Life in England in the Thirteenth Century.* Cambridge, 1946.

Moule, John. "Gilbert Glanvill, Bishop of Rochester, 1185-1214 and the Relationship of the See of Rochester to Canterbury to 1238." Unpublished Master's thesis, University of Manchester, 1954.

Norgate, Kate. *England under the Angevin Kings.* 2 vols. London, 1887.

Orpen, G. H. *Ireland under the Normans 1169-1216.* 2 vols. Oxford, 1911.

Painter, Sidney. *The Reign of King John.* Baltimore, 1949.

————. *William Marshal.* Baltimore, 1933.

Pollock, Sir Frederick and Frederic William Maitland. *The History of English Law before the Time of Edward I.* 2nd ed. 2 vols. Cambridge, 1923.

Poole, Austin L. *From Domesday Book to Magna Carta 1087-1216.* 2nd ed. Oxford, 1955.

Poole, Reginald L. *The Exchequer in the Twelfth Century.* Oxford, 1912.

Powicke, F. M. *The Christian Life in the Middle Ages and Other Essays.* Oxford, 1935.

————. "England: Richard I and John" in *The Cambridge Medieval History.* Vol. VI. Cambridge, 1929.

————. *The Loss of Normandy (1189-1204).* Manchester, 1913.

————, and E. B. Fryde. *Handbook of British Chronology.* 2nd ed. London, 1961.

Powicke, Michael. *Military Obligation in Medieval England.* Oxford, 1962.

Powley, Edward. *The House of de la Pomerai.* London, 1944.

Richardson, H. G. "Glanville Continued," *The Law Quarterly Review,* LIV (1938), 381-399.

————. "The Oxford Law School under John," *The Law Quarterly Review,* LVII (1941), 319-338.

————, and G. O. Sayles. *The Governance of Mediaeval England from the Conquest to Magna Carta.* Edinburgh, 1963.

Robinson, J. Armitage. "Peter of Blois," in *Somerset Historical Essays.* London, 1921.

Runciman, Steven. *A History of the Crusades.* 3 vols. Cambridge, 1951-1954.

Russell, Josiah C. "The Many-Sided Career of Master Elias of Dereham," *Speculum*, V (1930), 378-387.

Saltman, Avrom. *Theobald Archbishop of Canterbury*. London, 1956.

Sanders, I. J. *English Baronies*. Oxford, 1960.

Scammell, G. V. *Hugh du Puiset Bishop of Durham*. Cambridge, 1956.

Setton, Kenneth M. *A History of the Crusades*. 2 vols. printed. Philadelphia, 1955-.

Sherwood, Leslie. "The Cartulary of Leeds Priory," *Archaeologica Cantiana* (Ashford, Kent), LXIV (1952), 24-34.

Southern, R. W. "A Note on the Text of 'Glanville,'" *The English Historical Review*, 65 (1950), 81-89.

Stenton, Doris M. "King John and the Courts of Justice," *Proceedings of the British Academy*, 44 (1958), 103-128.

———. "Roger of Howden and 'Benedict,'" *The English Historical Review*, 68 (1953), 574-582.

Stenton, F. M. "Acta Episcoporum," *Cambridge Historical Journal*, III (1929), 1-14.

Stubbs, William. *Registrum Sacrum Anglicanum*. Oxford, 1897.

Thompson, A. Hamilton. "Master Elias of Dereham and the King's Works," *The Archaeological Journal* (London), 97 (1940), 1-35.

Thompson, E. Margaret. "A Fragment of a Witham Charterhouse Chronicle . . . ," *Bulletin of the John Rylands Library*, XVI (1932), 482-506.

Thompson, James W. *The Literacy of the Laity in the Middle Ages*. (University of California Publications in Education, 9.) Berkeley, 1939.

Tillmann, Helene. *Die päpstlichen Legaten in England bis zur Beendigung der Legation Gualas (1218)*. Bonn, 1926.

Tout, T. F. *Chapters in the Administrative History of Mediaeval England*. 6 vols. Manchester, 1920-1933.

Trombelli, G. G. *Memorie istoriche concernenti le due canoniche di S. Maria di Reno, e di S. Salvatore insieme unite*. Bologna, 1752.

Vaughan, Richard. *Matthew Paris*. Cambridge, 1958.

*The Victoria History of the County of Lancaster*. 8 vols. London, 1906-1914.

Warren, W. L. *King John*. New York, 1961.

West, Francis J. "The *Curia Regis* in the Late Twelfth and Early Thirteenth Centuries," *Historical Studies: Australia and New Zealand*, 6 (1954), 173-185.

———. *The Justiciarship in England 1066-1232*. Cambridge, 1966.

Wilkinson, Bertie. "The Government of England during the Absence of Richard I on the Third Crusade," *Bulletin of the John Rylands Library*, 28 (1944), 485-509.

Woodcock, Brian L. *Medieval Ecclesiastical Courts in the Diocese of Canterbury*. London, 1952.

# INDEX